# Secretary of Praise

# Secretary of Praise

## The Poetic Vocation
## of George Herbert

Diana Benet

**University of Missouri Press**
Columbia, 1984

# For Peter

Copyright © 1984 by
The Curators of the University of Missouri
University of Missouri Press, Columbia, Missouri 65211
Printed and bound in the United States of America

Library of Congress Cataloging in Publication Data

Benet, Diana.
    Secretary of praise.

    Includes index.
    1. Herbert, George, 1593–1633.   2. Herbert, George,
1593–1633. Temple.   3. Charity in literature.   4. Grace
(Theology) in literature.   5. Poets, English—Early
modern, 1500–1700—Biography.   I. Title.
PR3508.B4     1983     821'.3     83–1080
ISBN 0–8262–0408–2

# Acknowledgments

I am pleased to have the opportunity to thank publicly the scholars and friends who have given me assistance and encouragement. Frank Kastor and later C. A. Patrides guided me through the theological complexities underlying seventeenth-century literature, Herbert's poetry in particular. In my mind as well as in reality, J. Max Patrick continually asked me challenging questions and did his best to make me a rigorous reader and writer. James W. Tuttleton read an earlier version of the manuscript, gave advice, and suggested the title. My most substantial debts are to Anthony Low and Amy M. Charles, whose scholarship and generosity with their counsel, time, and knowledge are "a Mark to aim at." These are teachers, colleagues, and friends "whom nothing can procure . . . [to] share, not mend the ill"; sometimes, however, I have resisted amendment. What errors remain are mine.

Finally, I am deeply grateful to my husband for his devoted support of all my work.

D. B.
New York
September 1983

# Contents

# 1

# The Poet and His Religion

George Herbert's piety and "sincerity" have appealed to many readers from his day to ours. Frequently anthologized poems like "Vertue," "Love" (III), and "Jordan" (II) reinforce the image of Izaak Walton's saintly Herbert: he is the devout priest of the Church of England who suffers, prays, writes, and occasionally assumes a listening attitude as he waits for God to "supply the want" in his poem. This last detail is not the invention of an overzealous hagiographer. Part of Herbert's attraction is his occasional and enigmatic claim that God dictates or otherwise participates in his writing.

Familiarity with a basic Christian concept at once dispels the strangeness of the poet's claim and reveals the depth of his art. Using Rosalie Colie's explanation of how grace operates in several poems in *The Temple*, we can see Herbert's ostensible eccentricity or pious quaintness as his demonstration of a Christian tenet concerning God's relation to his creatures. Here, for example, is a stanza in which God participates with Herbert in composition:

> Whereas if th'heart be moved,
> Although the verse be somewhat scant,
> God doth supplie the want.
> As when th'heart sayes (sighing to be approved)
> *O, could I love!* and stops: God writeth, *Loved.*
> ("A true Hymne," 16–20)[1]

Without recourse to theology, we may read these lines as the poet's religious idea of inspiration. The poem's want of a rhyming end is supplied with the word *loved* by the power of

---

1. See Rosalie Colie's chapter on Herbert in *Paradoxia Epidemica: The Renaissance Tradition of Paradox*, pp. 190–215. Quotations from the poems and prose are taken from *The Works of George Herbert*, ed. F. E. Hutchinson (1941; reprint, Oxford: Clarendon Press, 1972). Hereafter cited as *Works*.

inspiration this poet calls "God." But this explanation is not satisfactory. The heart that says *"O, could I love"* is answered with *"Loved."* The answer responds not merely to the poet's need for an appropriate final rhyme; "Loved" challenges the assumption that we can equate Herbert's God with inspiration. The word makes an impact instantaneously because it responds not to the heart's spoken request but (as the all-knowing God might do) to its unspoken need, the need "to be approved."

The attribution of the last word in the poem to God, then, is more than an unusual way of giving God credit for the poet's inspiration and artistry. The lines take on a meaning truer to Herbert's religious sensibility when we understand that he is expressing his belief in grace, his conviction that God acts spontaneously and lovingly to help man in his endeavors and to satisfy his innermost need. As Colie comments, "Grace solves the problems of art, as it does the problems of life."[2]

The purpose of this study is to elucidate Herbert's poetry by reference to grace and charity as two of the major themes of *The Temple*. These doctrines lay the foundation for an understanding of Herbert's poetic vocation, his typical didactic strategies, the dramatic and emotional situation on which his book builds, and his spiritual autobiography—a poetic sequence that is a comprehensive exposition of the empirical reality, as Herbert saw it, of grace and charity. Because this sequence has a direct relevance to Herbert's life, it is as vital for the reader to be familiar with the facts known of the poet's life as it is for him to understand the underlying doctrinal bases of the poetry. This introductory biographical and theological summary is followed in subsequent chapters by analyses of Herbert's typical heuristic methods in poems that lead to a deeper awareness of the world of grace and charity as *The Temple* depicts it. Finally, having indicated the assumptions, conditions, possibilities, and difficulties of this world, we shall turn to the

2. Colie, *Paradoxia Epidemica*, p. 204. Colie and William H. Halewood have treated grace in the context of the author's role as a poet engaged in writing sacred poetry; I propose to treat the broader, more universal realm of the Christian speaker's experience in the context of grace and charity. See Halewood's chapter on Herbert in *The Poetry of Grace: Reformation Themes and Structures in 17th-Century Poetry*.

detailed drama of its preeminent inhabitant making his arduous way to the priesthood.

\*        \*        \*

Most poets are safe from the kind of canonization sometimes accorded to George Herbert. Donne's love poetry and Milton's political pamphlets prevent their being suspected of sainthood or of living far removed from the world of passion and action. All of Herbert's poetry reveals a mind concentrated on God and the devout life; his best poetry gives the impression of being so personal that it seems reasonable for the reader to assume a total congruity between his life and his work. Certainly, the priesthood is in harmony with the personality we discern behind *The Temple.* But because Herbert did not become a priest until he was thirty-seven, his delay must arouse curiosity. Unfortunately, what is known with certainty about the poet's choice of vocation cannot yield indisputable answers.

George Herbert, born 3 April 1593 in Montgomery, East Wales, was the seventh in a family that eventually numbered ten children. Richard Herbert's was a prominent Welsh family, and his wife, Magdalene Newport Herbert, was a daughter of Sir Richard Newport, "reputed to be the largest landowner in Shropshire."[3] When Richard died in 1596 his widow took her children to live first with her mother at Eyton, and later at Oxford. In 1601, Mrs. Herbert, reputedly a woman of beauty, wit, and piety, moved the family to London. There she developed her friendship with John Donne, who preached her memorial sermon twenty-six years later. Probably in 1604, George Herbert became a day student in Westminster School. In February 1609, Magdalene Herbert married Sir John Danvers, a stepfather Herbert liked and respected, to judge from his letters to Danvers. In December of that same year, Herbert matriculated from Trinity College, Cambridge. The following month, on New Year's Day 1610, the young poet sent his mother the two sonnets that express perplexity about the

3. *Works,* p. xxii. In the following pages, I am greatly indebted to the work of F. E. Hutchinson, Joseph H. Summers (*George Herbert: His Religion and Art*), and Amy M. Charles (*A Life of George Herbert,* hereafter cited as *A Life*). Charles's very useful chronology deserves special mention.

preeminence of love verses at the expense of sacred poetry (*Works*, p. 206).

Although Herbert's health was poor (and remained so), his career at Cambridge progressed well. He received the B.A. degree on 17 February 1613, the M.A. on 15 March 1616. When he was named major fellow of Trinity College, the acceptance of this election committed him to take deacon's orders within seven years or to resign the fellowship. There followed for Herbert other academic appointments: in October 1617, he became *sublector quartae classis* at Trinity; in June 1618, *praelector* in rhetoric in the university; in October 1619, he was appointed deputy for the university orator; and finally, in January 1620, he was elected university orator. Among the young Herbert's friends and patrons were John Donne, Lancelot Andrewes, Sir Francis Bacon, Sir Francis Nethersole, the Duke of Lennox, the Marquis of Hamilton, and King James. During 1623, the year that Herbert should have taken orders to comply with the terms of his fellowship, he delivered a speech to James on 12 March 1623 and another to Prince Charles on 8 October, a few days after the prince's return from Spain. In November 1623, he was elected to Parliament as member for Montgomery borough and served during the session from 19 February 1624 to 29 May 1624. On 11 June 1624, Herbert was granted a leave of six months from Cambridge.

His activities and acquaintances during the Cambridge years have contributed to the general conclusion that Herbert was "the kind of man likely to do well in the great world of his day, and recognized as such." On the basis of Izaak Walton's biography, it has been generally accepted also that "Herbert naturally aspired toward . . . position" and had "great expectations" of important preferment from his influential friends.[4] These suppositions may explain why he was not ordained in March 1623. Ordination would not commit him beyond the diaconate, but deacons could not hold civil employment. Although the exact date of Herbert's ordination is not known, it was sometime between 3 November 1624 and 5

4. Helen C. White, *The Metaphysical Poets: A Study in Religious Experience*, p. 146; C. A. Patrides, "A Crown of Praise: The Poetry of Herbert," in *The English Poems of George Herbert*, p. 7.

July 1626. The latter date is on the document that records his installation as canon of Lincoln Cathedral and as prebendary of Leighton Ecclesia and that refers to him as a deacon. On 3 November 1624, the archbishop of Canterbury granted Bishop John Williams permission to ordain Herbert at any time, without waiting the requisite year after the young man's declaration of intention. Herbert's request for such a dispensation makes it likely that he was ordained soon after it was granted.[5]

Herbert's whereabouts from June 1624 to December 1625 are uncertain, but when James I died in March 1625, Herbert did not deliver the oration for Cambridge University. It is possible that he spent some time in Kent with an unnamed relative or with a friend, as Izaak Walton suggested.[6] By 21 December 1625, he was at Sir John Danvers's home in Chelsea, his visit coinciding at least in part with John Donne's. Beginning the following spring (1626), for about a year he was at his brother Henry's house at Woodford, Essex, perhaps recuperating from illness. That summer, he was installed canon of Lincoln Cathedral and prebendary of Leighton Ecclesia. Some days later, on 13 July 1626, he delivered his last-known official speech at the installation of the Duke of Buckingham as chancellor of Cambridge University. Herbert was back in Chelsea in May 1627, and in June his mother died. During the next two months, he must have resigned the oratorship, because a new orator was named on 29 January 1628.

For some time during 1628 and early 1629, Herbert lived in Wiltshire at Dauntesey House with the Earl of Danby, Sir John Danvers's brother. Danby was a cousin of Jane Danvers, who became Herbert's wife on 5 March 1629. Nothing is known of the couple's previous acquaintance, but Izaak Walton's story that she fell "in love with Mr. Herbert unseen" and married him after a three-day courtship is fanciful and improbable (*Lives*, p. 279). After their marriage, the Herberts lived at Baynton House with Jane's widowed mother. It was more than a

---

5. Amy M. Charles first published the information about the dispensation dated 3 November 1624 permitting Bishop Williams to ordain Herbert at any time in "George Herbert, Deacon."

6. Izaak Walton, *The Lives of Dr. John Donne, Sir Henry Wotton, Richard Hooker, George Herbert, and Dr. Robert Sanderson* (hereafter cited as *Lives*).

year later, on 16 April 1630, that the Crown presented Herbert
to the living of Bemerton in Wiltshire. He accepted the gift and
on 26 April was instituted as rector and inducted at St.
Andrew's Church, Bemerton. Almost five months later, on 19
September 1630, he was ordained priest. After a period of
illness, George Herbert died in Bemerton on 1 March 1633.

*      *      *

The most tantalizing gaps in the verifiable information are
related to Herbert's priesthood. Izaak Walton's biography of
the poet-priest has long been discredited and is now super-
seded by Amy M. Charles's. But his attempt to fill in the
missing pieces of information, although it was largely pious
fabrication, deserves our attention for two reasons: his *Life*
shaped readers' perceptions of Herbert for three centuries; and
its present status is a reminder that, in the absence of definitive
evidence, statements about Herbert's early plans or hopes for
his eventual vocation and about his delayed ordination are
only theories. As we shall see, the information available is
clearly ambiguous.

Walton, who did not know Herbert, published his *Life* in
1670, almost forty years after the poet's death. David Novarr
has shown that Walton gathered information from Nicholas
Ferrar's "The Printers to the Readers" (1633), from Barnabas
Oley's "A Prefatory View of the Life of Mr. Geo. Herbert"
(printed with *The Country Parson* in 1652), from the poet's
letters, and from Arthur Woodnoth. Novarr details Walton's
indebtedness to the preface to *The Temple*,[7] where Ferrar mentions Herbert's outstanding merits and "that knowledge
which the Kings Court had taken" of his friend. Then Ferrar
adds:

> Quitting both his deserts and all the opportunities that he had
> for worldly preferment, he betook himself to the Sanctuarie and
> Temple of God, choosing rather to serve at Gods Altar, then to
> seek the honour of State-employments. As for those inward
> enforcements to this course (for outward there was none) *which
> many of these ensuing verses bear witnesse of,* they detract not from

7. See David Novarr, *The Making of Walton's Lives,* pp. 326–28.

the freedome, but adde to the honour of this resolution in him. [emphasis added]

It was almost inevitable, then, that Walton should read Herbert's poems on the subject of vocation as pure self-revelation. But, in fact, among other questionable practices, he chose only a few of them as biographical source material.

Though Walton's Herbert was always pious, worldly ambition is said to have overtaken him at Cambridge. The university orator hoped "that as his predecessors, so he might in time attain the place of a Secretary of State, he being at that time very high in the King's favour . . . This, and the love of a Court-conversation, mixed with a laudable ambition to be something more than he was, drew him often from Cambridge, to attend the King wheresoever the Court was" (*Lives*, p. 270). But Walton asserts that after the deaths of the Duke of Lennox in 1624 and the Marquis of Hamilton and King James in 1625, Herbert's influential friends were gone, and with them his hopes for an eminent career. He visited an unnamed friend in Kent to decide his future course. (Ignoring the seventeenth-century meaning of *friend*, Walton does not acknowledge that the visit might have been to a relative.) "In this time of retirement, he had many conflicts with himself," states Walton, "whether he should return to the painted pleasures of a Court-life or betake himself to a study of Divinity, and enter into Sacred Orders" (*Lives*, p. 272). One of the considerations that must have entered into these conflicts was the low esteem in which the ministry was held for men of good family and high connections. Nevertheless, according to Walton, Herbert conquered ambition and emulated Christ's example of humility when he was ordained deacon about 1626. Four years later, when the living of Bemerton was offered to him, he experienced another hesitation. But this time, Walton suggests, "the apprehension of the last great account, that he was to make for the cure of so many souls" made him fast, pray, and consider for a month (*Lives*, p. 280).[8]

8. Charles shows that Walton is in error either about Herbert's month-long hesitation or about the identity of the cousin who recommended him to the King (*A Life*, pp. 145–46).

Novarr demonstrates that Walton's *Life of Herbert* "became among other things an illustration of the thesis that the Church was a profession not below the dignity of men of talent and education and family." Moreover, he analyzes Walton's use of "Affliction" (I), "Content," and "The Pearl" as the source of material on Herbert's court–church conflict and concludes, "The seeming use of the poetry is to authenticate a generalization which Walton has made; in fact, particular verses are frequently used as evidence for generalizations which the verses themselves must originally have suggested."[9] If we were willing to assume that the poetry is straightforward autobiography, this procedure might seem to validate Walton's Herbert. But there are problems.

Walton's desire to portray a before-and-after Herbert defined by the poet's resolution of the problem of worldly ambition dictated his selection of "autobiographical" poems. The exposition of his thesis led Walton to choose poems whose speaker expresses an awareness of his consequence and his potential for rising in the world. Against these, Herbert's subsequent retirement to a country parsonage could shine more brilliantly. Had Walton wished to treat the subject of Herbert's vocation comprehensively, he would not have ignored the clearly labeled "Employment" poems. His omission is understandable: rather than evidence of Herbert's youthful ambition, he would have found expressed there a willingness to serve frustrated by uncertainty due to the lack of divine guidance. Perhaps Walton judged such concerns as the too-fine preoccupations of an exceptionally pious mind, or perhaps he simply did not wish to complicate his court-ambition/church-humility design. The point is that, having decided to use the poetry as a source of biographical information, Walton did not do justice to the complex problem of vocation as it is presented in *The Temple*.

Amy M. Charles's recent biography offers the reader many new insights into Herbert's life and, for our purposes, one especially valuable piece of information—the probable date of Herbert's ordination as deacon. Unfortunately, her exhaustive

9. Novarr, *Walton's Lives*, pp. 313, 333.

research indicates that there is no definitive evidence to answer all of the other questions surrounding his vocation. On these matters, however, her Herbert differs radically from Walton's. Charles attempts to discredit his ambition almost entirely, suggesting that from 1615 he progressed steadily, if slowly, toward his career in the Church: the poet "early expected not only to study divinity but to enter holy orders." In 1615—ten years before Walton said Herbert's court hopes died—Herbert stated, in a letter to Sir John Danvers, his intention to enter eventually "into a Benefice"; in 1618, another letter states that he is "now setting foot into Divinity."[10] Charles thinks there is no reason to believe that his plans ever changed: "Herbert's intention in his studies . . . is clearly stated at several times; and though the matter of holy orders is seldom mentioned directly, there is no reason that it should have been" (*A Life*, p. 89). Herbert became a major fellow of Trinity College on 15 March 1616. Because it was the rule for fellows, Charles suggests that his ordination as deacon seven years after proceeding Master of Arts was simply taken for granted by the young poet and his family: "Herbert would therefore have been expected to take orders as deacon in the spring of 1623" (*A Life*, p. 89). Certainly, the letters and the fellowship suggest that fifteen years before Herbert became a priest, he foresaw a religious vocation.

But Herbert's response to the statute governing the ordination of fellows raises questions. As stated above, Charles has established the probable date of Herbert's ordination as deacon, though its exact date is not known. This vital information reveals, if not the end of Herbert's secular ambitions, at least the date when he made official his commitment to the Church and, incidentally, when he could no longer hold civil employment. On the basis of the aforementioned dispensation granted on 3 November 1624 permitting Bishop Williams to ordain Herbert at any time, Charles concludes that the ordination probably took place "before the end of 1624" (*A Life*, p. 117). But even if we suppose that Herbert was ordained in

10. *A Life*, p. 88; *Works*, letter 5, pp. 366–67, and letter 3, pp. 364–65. See *A Life*, pp. 75, 88, for the dating of letter 5.

November 1624, still the event would have taken place some twenty months after March 1623, when he would "have been expected to take orders as deacon" to comply with the Trinity College statute.[11] Citing Sir Francis Nethersole's nine-year holding of a major fellowship (1610–1619) without ordination, David Novarr has shown that the statue was not strictly enforced (pp. 517–18). Notwithstanding the example of his predecessor as orator and the permissiveness of Trinity on this matter, Herbert's delay is not consistent with the figure of a man moving steadily toward a firmly defined goal. During those twenty months, the university orator addressed King James and Prince Charles and served in Parliament.

Of course, there were circumstances in Herbert's life that might explain his delay in taking orders. Charles suggests that his decision to stand for Parliament may have been influenced by the absence from England of his brothers, the "uncertain health" of his mother, and, possibly, the necessity of arranging care for three orphaned nieces, a responsibility that his ailing mother could not undertake (*A Life,* p. 104). There is no documentary evidence to indicate if or how much these considerations deterred Herbert. We do know that by November 1623, when he was named to Parliament, he had already delayed ordination beyond the statutory seven years by eight months—and that by November 1624, he had delayed it by twenty. Taken together, Herbert's postponement of his ordination and his activities during this period suggest that his early plan to enter into a benefice may have been modified, if only temporarily.

The letters that Charles cites may also reflect a modification of Herbert's plans rather than the unstated assumption about his future that she proposes. That phrase about the benefice from letter 5 (1615) implies a definite intention, but letter 3 (March 1618) refers only to Herbert's studies in divinity with no mention of an eventual living. Then there is letter 8 (Octo-

---

11. On the matter of time, there is not a very large difference between Walton and Charles. If we believe that Herbert was ordained immediately after the archbishop's dispensation, as Charles suggests, it would mean that he took the decisive step on 27 March 1625, only some five months before the time Walton says his court hopes died.

ber 1619), in which Herbert writes to his stepfather about the possibility of being named university orator and the reservations of Sir Francis Nethersole, the present orator:

> I understand by Sir *Francis Nethersols* Letter, that he fears I have not fully resolved of the matter, since this place being civil may divert me too much from Divinity, at which, not without cause, he thinks, I aim; but, I have wrote him back, that this dignity, hath no such earthiness in it, but it may very well be joined with Heaven; or if it had to others, yet to me it should not, for ought I yet knew. (*Works*, p. 370)

Charles admits that Herbert sounds "equivocal" here, but suggests that "the wording 'Divinity, at which, not without cause, he thinks, I aim' may be taken almost as a bit of rueful humor" (*A Life*, p. 89). Another plausible interpretation, however, is more consistent with Herbert's session in Parliament and his delay of ordination until the end of 1624: whatever he might have thought about his eventual vocation in 1615, by 1619 his prospects at Cambridge made him think that his divinity studies could lay the foundation for a prominent civil career.

Indeed, we should have to assume an astounding otherworldliness to suppose that, on his accession to the oratorship in 1620, Herbert was unaware of the advancement of his two predecessors. As Hutchinson remarks, Sir Robert Naunton and Sir Francis Nethersole used the oratorship as "a stepping-stone to a career as a secretary of state" (*Works*, p. xxviii). It was possible, also, to combine divinity with a secular career, as did Herbert's friend John Williams, who by 1624 was Lord Keeper, Dean of Westminster, and Bishop of Lincoln. But, judging from his predecessors' careers, the future seemed to point to secular preferment. Herbert may well have thought it imprudent to debar himself from civil employment by premature ordination.

Herbert's ambition to be a Christian statesman was posited some years ago by Joseph Summers: "There is no evidence that at any time during his life Herbert abandoned his early plan to base his career on 'Divinity,' to further the cause of religion; there is also no evidence that before [his ordination as deacon] he abandoned his hope for great place in civil affairs."[12] The ambition for a prominent secular position would not have seemed unworthy to Herbert, who wrote in 1631 to a friend concerned about his own vocation: "Higher opportunities of doeing good are to be preferred before lower, euen where to continue in y$^e$ lower is no sinn. by y$^e$ Apostles rule" (*Works*, p. 380). A secular career in his country's employ might well have seemed to offer a broad scope for Christian service, especially if Herbert considered himself "a man of suitable gifts and personality who . . . had influential friends and kinsmen" (*Works*, p. xxxi). The practical attitude expressed to this friend in 1631 was already in evidence about 1614, when Herbert wrote to his younger brother:

> Let there be no kind of excellency which it is possible for you to attain to, which you seek not; and have a good conceit of your wit, mark what I say, have a good conceit of your wit; that is, be proud, not with a foolish vanting of yourself when there is no caus, but by setting a just price of your qualities: and it is the part of a poor spirit to undervalue himself and blush. (*Works*, p. 366)[13]

Considering his advice to others, it seems unlikely that Herbert undervalued himself or the talents and opportunities given him.

A combination of circumstances may have persuaded Herbert that his opportunity to serve was not to be, like Naunton's and Nethersole's, in civil affairs: the fact that after a promising beginning his career was at a standstill; his awareness that the oration made to Prince Charles (October 1623) was impolitic; and his experience as a member of Parliament (February–May 1624). Herbert had not advanced as much as his earlier career had probably led him to expect. In the four years from 15 March 1616 to 21 January 1620, Herbert was elected to or was given five appointments at Cambridge. But after that steady succession, other appointments did not follow. That must have been a growing disappointment as time passed. When he

12. *Herbert: Religion and Art*, p. 37.
13. Charles suggests (*A Life*, pp. 77–78) that letter 4 dates from the spring of 1614 rather than 1618, the date Hutchinson gives it.

faced the consequences of speaking from personal conviction on official occasions, that was another discouragement.[14] His speech to the prince attributed a praiseworthy peaceful attitude to him at a time when Prince Charles wanted war; Herbert probably realized that it would destroy "an essential bridge to any future favor at court."[15] This experience must have made him keenly aware of the problems that public life poses for a man of conscience. As for his participation in Parliament, Herbert may have been disappointed in himself: a member, he wrote later, "must not only be a morning man, but at Committees also; for there the particulars are exactly discussed, which are brought from thence to the House but in generall" (*Works*, p. 277). However this opinion was formed, he had a standard by which to measure his own performance: when his brother Edward was a member, he served on ten committees; Herbert served on one. Furthermore, as Charles remarks, the parliamentary experience also disillusioned Herbert on another level. He had an "idealistic view of the undertaking" of the Virginia Company and a personal interest because Sir John Danvers and the Ferrars were very much involved in its affairs (*A Life*, pp. 106–7). After divisive struggles, the charter of the company was revoked before the session ended.

Herbert's application for permission to be ordained at any time followed his one parliamentary session. Considering his earlier postponement of this important step, his urgency at that particular time is suggestive. In her account, Charles is aware of the implications of his serving in Parliament. She describes the experience as decisive although, according to her interpretation, no such decision could have been necessary or even relevant: "Any 'Court-hopes' that may have existed when the session of Parliament opened had surely been dispelled before it closed" (*A Life*, p. 111).[16]

14. As Summers remarks, "Herbert had strong reasons for the intensity of his attitude" about war: his brothers William and Richard were both killed in military service, Richard in 1622 (*Herbert: Religion and Art*, p. 41).

15. Charles, *A Life*, p. 106.

16. Herbert's application for ordination as deacon, according to Charles, was made "during his six-month leave from the oratorship at Cambridge" (*A Life*, p. 113), sometime between 11 June and 3 November 1624, when the permission was granted. As Charles remarks, on 29 May 1624 Parliament was

As the summaries of Walton's and Charles's biographies indicate, the material allows for a different theory. Herbert's remarks in his letters, his delay of ordination twenty months beyond the prescribed period, his service in Parliament, and his subsequent request to be ordained by Bishop Williams suggest the possibility that between 1615 and November 1624, Herbert's thoughts on his vocation moved full circle. Initially, he intended to go into orders, but he came to aspire to an eminent position as a religious statesman. When attainment of that goal seemed improbable and unpalatable, he reverted to his original plan. The ill-fated hope for a civil career in no way represented a turning away from Herbert's unwavering ambition, to serve God in the highest capacity that he could obtain. One stanza of "Submission" will put pious ambition in its right perspective. The speaker of the poem, whose pride we can characterize for the moment as ignorance, addresses God:

> Were it not better to bestow
> > Some place and power on me?
> Then should thy praises with me grow,
> > And share in my degree.
>
> (5–8)

Christian ambition is not motivated by self-aggrandizement or a longing for prestige. It is the desire to use God's gifts as efficiently as possible so that his people benefit by his servants' endeavors, so that his influence and power be perceived in his congregation, so that he be praised. God did not circumscribe the sphere of acceptable service to the clerical life. Statesman, poet, priest: all can serve in the different vocations for which their respective talents best equip them.

Experience and circumstance taught Herbert to relish less the sort of prominence he sought by pursuing the university oratorship, "the finest place in the University," as he described it (*Works*, p. 369). He took deacon's orders, positively turning away from a civil career. The priesthood was still some years in the future, and on the cause of this last delay (if not on

---

prorogued until 3 November 1624. However, on 1 October the session was postponed until 25 February 1625, and on 19 January, postponed again. This second session of Parliament never sat.

its approximate date or length) Charles agrees with Walton. In the church at Dauntesey, she writes, "and in that at Edington, which became his parish church at the time of his marriage in the following year, Herbert would undergo and resolve some of the conflicts that must be overcome before he could eventually proceed to Bemerton and to the priesthood" (*A Life*, p. 138). A substantial number of Herbert's lyrics reflect these conflicts, treating them in the context of grace and charity.

    \*    \*    \*

Little is known about the prepublication history of *The Temple*. Apparently irrecoverable, for example, is the precise date when Herbert wrote the 164 poems that are the whole of his English verse, save for a few poems excluded from the volume.[17] But the doctrines of the seventeenth-century Church of England are not irretrievable, though it is impossible to abstract Herbert's detailed personal creed from his work: he seems perversely quiet in an age engaged in frequent religious disputes and dominated by outspoken personalities like John Donne. As Helen C. White observes while explaining why "religious controversy as such held no fascination" for Herbert, "there is no sign anywhere in his life or writings of any question as to which was the right church, and where the path of salvation was to be found." Herbert was an Anglican; evidently, he felt no need to defend the doctrine of the Church publicly.[18]

Another reason for Herbert's silence was his opinion that "Curiosity in prying into high speculative and unprofitable questions, is another great stumbling block to the holinesse of Scholars." This curiosity he classified as one of several "spir-

17. Hutchinson includes eleven such poems (*Works*, pp. 200–207). These include some earlier versions of poems that appear in *The Temple* considerably altered (such as "Even-song") and the two sonnets that Herbert sent to his mother on New Year's Day 1610.

18. White, *The Metaphysical Poets*, p. 166. Summers and Pebworth argue persuasively that poems such as "Divinitie," "The British Church," and "Church-rents and schismes" "participate in the religious controversies they decry." See Claude J. Summers and Ted-Larry Pebworth, "Herbert, Vaughan, and Public Concerns in Private Modes," p. 2. Though Herbert implicitly and subtly indicates his partisan, pro-established-Church position in these poems, he does not participate more openly in the disputations that taxed so many religious thinkers.

ituall wickednesses" that must be fought with "the shield of
faith" (*Works*, p. 238). Besides, controversy did more than
harm contentious scholars. This is certainly the poet's opinion
in "Church-rents and schismes" as he addresses the "Brave
rose," the Church of England:

> But when debates and fretting jealousies
> Did worm and work within you more and more,
> Your colour faded, and calamities
>     Turned your ruddie into pale and bleak:
>     Your health and beautie both began to break.
>                                              (16–20)

The Church, weakened from within by controversy, seems so
pathetic to him that he wishes he had "eyes enough to weep, /
As many eyes as starres." Obviously, strife and open disputa-
tion had no appeal for Herbert. As a clergyman, he assented to
the Thirty-Nine Articles of the Church, but he did not directly
comment on the theology they teach. Consequently, to outline
the positions of the Anglican Church within which Herbert
worked, it is necessary to turn to other divines for information
or elaboration when Herbert's poems or prose works are silent
about the doctrinal assumptions on which they rest.

   The concepts of grace and charity involved the nature of God
and mankind, the relationship between the two, and the relationships between men. On these broad and essential matters,
seventeenth-century Protestants all disagreed with Roman
Catholics on several points of doctrine, and, among themselves, disagreed mainly (and vigorously) about the nature of
God's grace. The disagreement among English Protestants
was not about the doctrine as a whole, but about whether man
could resist or work with grace. Still, this quarrel was among
men who worked from common premises. Protestants shared,
along with many beliefs, a great reverence for Augustine.
Second only to the Bible, his writings were studied closely by
Luther and Calvin as well as by men like Donne and Herbert,
who mentioned "St. Augustines workes" in his will (*Works*, p.
382).

   "Miserable man! A Toad is a bag of Poyson, and a Spider is a
blister of Poyson, and yet a Toad and a Spider cannot poyson

themselves; Man hath a dram of poyson, originall-Sin, in an invisible corner . . . and he cannot choose but poyson himselfe and all his actions with that."[19] John Donne did not startle or particularly insult his auditors with this description of their natural state. Toads, spiders, worms—the English Protestant of the seventeenth century often had images of these or similar creatures evoked for his edification. George Herbert's swine in "Miserie" are not quite so repugnant as Donne's toad or spider, but the point is the same. "Man cannot serve thee," the speaker tells God,

> let him go,
> And serve the swine: there, there is his delight:
> He doth not like this vertue, no;
> Give him his dirt to wallow in all night:
> These Preachers make
> His head to shoot and ake.
>
> (43–48)

Delight in serving the swine transforms into a mirror image of them the self-destructive man who is so depraved that reprimand only gives him a headache.

By this emphasis on man's depravity, preachers reminded Christians of their natural sinfulness and their human inheritance of shame and guilt. Christendom agreed that Adam's fall had the far-reaching consequence of enslaving humanity to sin. In this Augustinian view, all were tainted and, therefore, unable to help themselves out of the mire of their own degradation. The seventeenth-century preacher's explicit descriptions of man's putrid state were intended to destroy or at least subdue his pride, to make him abhor the dirty lump of death sin had made of him, and to make him see his need to turn to God. For despite his weakened condition, man did have a small remnant of reason. Augustine called this "the intellectual light, by which we distinguish between right and wrong." But "this light of reason that is in thee, this poore snuffe, that is almost out in thee," as Donne described it, was certainly not capable of effecting what man most desired—salvation.[20] In-

19. *Sermons of John Donne,* 1:293.
20. *Concerning the City of God against the Pagans,* p. 474; Donne, *Sermons,* 3:360.

deed, as Herbert says in "Divinitie," thanks to man's foolish-
ness, sometimes "Reason triumphs, and faith lies by" (line 8).
Whatever his natural capacities, man's corruption deserved
eternal damnation. At the same time, it made it impossible that
in or by himself man should be able to save himself by reconciliation to God. He might earnestly wish to be saved, he might
act as if he were saved, but all his efforts would come to
nothing. In the matter of salvation, man was powerless.

Christianity agreed that this impotence is man's condition
and that at this uncomfortable juncture, God's love intervenes.
Richard Hooker wrote:

> Sin both *original* and *actual* committed before belief in the prom-
> ise of salvation through *Jesus Christ*, is through the mere mercy
> of God taken away from them which believe, justified they are,
> and that not in reward of their good, but through the pardon of
> their evil works. For albeit they have disobeyed God, yet our
> Saviour's death and obedience performed in their behalf doth
> redound to them, by believing it they make the benefit thereof
> to become their own.

Hooker explains that this divine intervention in human affairs
is grace: "*Remission of sins* is grace, because it is God's own free
gift; faith which qualifieth our minds to receive it is also grace,
because it is an effect of his gracious spirit in us; we are
therefore justified by faith without works, by grace without
merit." The force that makes salvation by Christ's death possible, then, "from the standpoint of God, the giver, . . . is grace;
from the standpoint of man, the receiver, . . . is faith."[21]
Article 11 (1563) of the Church of England affirms that faith
alone justifies the sinner:

> We are accounted righteous before God, only for the merit of
> our Lord and Saviour Jesus Christ by Faith, and not for our own
> works or deservings. Wherefore that we are justified by faith
> only is a most wholesome doctrine, and very full of comfort.[22]

21. Richard Hooker, "Fragments of an Answer to the Letter of Certain
English Protestants," in *Of the Laws of Ecclesiastical Polity*, 2:504; Charles H. and
Katherine George, *The Protestant Mind of the English Reformation*, p. 44.

22. E. J. Bicknell, *A Theological Introduction to the Thirty-Nine Articles of the
Church of England*, p. 254. This Article reflects the Pauline emphasis on justification by faith alone: "Where is boasting then? It is excluded. By what law? of

Herbert echoes this doctrine when he writes, "Faith needs no staffe of flesh, but stoutly can / To heav'n alone both go, and leade" ("Divinitie," lines 27–28). Since the free gift of grace makes faith possible, grace and faith are the essentials of salvation.

Seventeenth-century Protestants stated and restated the principle of justification by faith alone because it opposed the Roman Catholic doctrine that seemed to them to give too large a role in salvation to man and his works. A sermon preached about 1625 by John Preston includes these remarks: "The Papists, they teach that workes are the maine, and many things they prescribe that men must doe: our Doctrine is, you see, that faith onely is required: Indeede, many things follow vpon faith, but faith is that you must onely labour for, and then the rest will follow vpon it." Preston stresses the human effort of the Roman Catholic way to salvation; Thomas Rogers, the late sixteenth-century commentator on the Articles, emphasizes the transaction implicit in the doctrine of justification by works for a more combative summary: "The pharisaical Papists do hold a justification by merits . . . [and] teach, besides, that life eternal is due unto us of debt; because we deserve it by our good works. They teach, finally, that by good works our sins are purged."[23] The idea that salvation could be any man's due—that God could owe it to anyone—was preposterous to Preston, Rogers, and their coreligionists. Protestantism could not allow such a diminution of Christ's role in salvation or such an enlargement of man's. Christ redeemed mankind by his sacrifice, and his righteousness was imputed to undeserving man. The individual's works—his acts of charity or the commendable labors of his daily occupation—counted for nothing in gaining salvation.

Not that the Anglican of Herbert's time had nothing to do. English preachers insisted that good works were the fruit of justifying faith:

---

works? Nay: but by the law of faith. Therefore, we conclude that a man is justified by faith without the deeds of the law" (Romans 3:27–28).

23. Preston, "Of Faith," in *In God's Name: Examples of Preaching in England, 1534–1662*, ed. John Chandos, p. 295; Thomas Rogers, *The Catholic Doctrine of the Church of England: An Exposition of the Thirty-Nine Articles*, p. 116.

It is a childish cavil wherewith in the matter of justification our adversaries do greatly please themselves, exclaiming, that we tread all Christian virtues under our feet, and require nothing in Christians but faith; because we teach that faith alone justifieth: whereas by this speech we never meant to exclude either hope and charity from being always joined as inseparable mates with faith in the man that is justified; or works from being added as necessary duties required at the hands of every justified man.

First the justifying faith of grace, and then works: the stress on this order was to insure that no one made the supposed Roman Catholic error of attributing merit to the individual or his works. Article 12 (1563) defined the Church's position:

Albeit that Good Works, which are fruits of Faith, and follow after Justification, cannot put away our sins, and endure the severity of God's Judgement; yet are they pleasing and acceptable to God in Christ, and do spring out necessarily of a true and lively Faith; insomuch that by them a lively faith may be as evidently known as a tree discerned by the fruit.[24]

The Protestant did good works not hoping to earn justification, but striving to please God. The true faith actuated him, and subsequently his works identified him as one of the justified. As we shall see later, the concept of works is intimately related to charity.

Sin, grace, faith, justification, and works: thus far all seems Protestant unity against the common antagonist, Roman Catholicism. But before we can consider grace in more detail, we must turn our attention to grace in the specific context of predestination. On this point, the seventeenth-century Protestant might discover his adversary to be a Protestant of a different persuasion. The problem was not predestination itself, for Protestants agreed that not every man was destined to be saved. The problem was in the conceptions of God, grace, and free will that Calvin's doctrine carried with it. In brief, Calvin taught that man is totally corrupt and devoid of moral freedom: "I assert that the will, being deprived of its liberty, is

24. Richard Hooker, "A Learned Discourse of Justification, Works, and How the Foundation of Faith Is Overthrown," in *Ecclesiastical Polity*, 1:59; Bicknell, *Thirty-Nine Articles*, p. 264.

necessarily drawn or led into evil."[25] If God had chosen to abandon man in his degenerate condition, incessant and inevitable sin (with its eternal consequence) would have been his lot. Fortunately, God's mercy decreed that some of the undeserving would be saved. The elect are those "particular individuals, to whom God not only offers salvation, but assigns it in such a manner, that the certainty of the effect is liable to no suspense or doubt . . . In the members of Christ there is a conspicuous exhibition of the superior efficacy of grace; because being united to the head, they never fail of salvation" (*Institutes*, 2:179–80). Calvin insisted on the irresistible nature of redeeming grace, which "is not merely offered by the Lord to be either received or rejected, according to the free choice of each individual, but . . . is grace which produces both the choice and the will in the heart" (*Institutes*, 1:332). God's grace does everything; man cannot be said even to cooperate with it: "It is wrong to attribute to man a voluntary obedience in following the guidance of grace" (*Institutes*, 1:322–23). The elect are blessed with the gift of irresistible grace.

As God predestined the elect to receive his unfailing grace, he predestined the reprobate to lack it. "Those, therefore, whom he has created to a life of shame and a death of destruction, that they might be instruments of his wrath, and examples of his severity, he causes to reach their appointed end, sometimes depriving them of the opportunity of hearing the word, sometimes by the preaching of it, increasing their blindness and stupidity" (*Institutes*, 2:232). Calvin did not evade the obvious, distressing question: "Why, then, in bestowing grace upon some, does he pass over others? . . . Let us not hesitate to say with Augustine, 'God could convert to good the will of the wicked, because he is omnipotent. It is evident that he could. Why then does he not? Because he would not. Why he would not, remains with himself' " (*Institute*, 2:233).

The cool certainty with which Calvin and his followers described the wretched fate of most men inspired barbs like John Hales's: "Nobody would conclude another man to be damned if he did not wish him to be so." But there were implications

25. John Calvin, *Institutes of the Christian Religion*, 1:318 (hereafter cited as *Institutes*).

more serious than the uncharitableness of the hearts that taught the doctrine of election. Many of Herbert's contemporaries who considered this system objected that if helpless men were to be damned solely for lack of God's grace, then he was responsible for their sin, and he was cruel. This idea was abhorrent to those Anglicans like John Donne (and George Herbert) who drew back from extreme Calvinism: "Our sinnes are our owne, and our destruction is from our selves. We are not as accessaries, and God as principall in this soul-murder: God forbid."[26]

Donne's ringing claim that our sins are our own may seem strange, but it expresses negatively a belief in man's free will and, consequently, a disbelief in Calvin's irresistible grace. In another sermon, Donne explains more fully:

> Christ saves no man against his will. There is a word crept into the later School, that deludes many a man; they call it *Irresistibility;* and they would have it mean, that when God would have a man, he will lay hold upon him, by such a power of grace, as no perversness of that man, can possibly resist. There is some truth in the thing, soberly understood: for the grace of God is more powerful than any resistance of any man or devil. But leave the word, where it was hatcht, in the School, and bring it not home, not into practice: for he that stays his conversion upon that, God, at one time or other, will lay hold upon me by such a power of Grace, as I shall not be able to resist, may stay, till Christ come again, to *preach to the Spirits that are in prison.* Christ beats his Drum, but he does not Press men; Christ is serv'd with Voluntaries.

26. Hales is quoted in *The English Sermon, 1550–1650*, ed. Martin Seymour-Smith, 1:391; Donne, *Sermons*, 9:65. The extent of Herbert's Calvinism or "Puritanism" is disputable. Richard Strier finds a localized Puritanism in " 'To all Angels and Saints': Herbert's Puritan Poem," and A. D. Nuttall asserts that the poetry "overthrows Calvinism by subjecting it to the test of ingenuous loyalty" (*Overheard by God: Fiction and Prayer in Herbert, Milton, Dante and St. John,* p. 81). In " 'With Winges of Faith': Herbert's Communion Poems," pp. 57–58, Jeanne Clayton Hunter suggests that the interpretation of the sacrament in *The Temple* is "closely allied to the eucharistic teachings of John Calvin." However, she goes on to add a vital reminder of Anglican latitude: "Given the interpretive allowance made under Elizabeth, Herbert's position naturally is not out of consonance with the prayer book or with Richard Hooker's position as set forth in *Of the Laws of Ecclesiastical Polity.* Nor did Herbert and Hooker hold differing views." Even while noting any Calvinist

The truth of the matter was found by apologists for the Church of England to reside in a paradox. The power of God to effect by grace whatever he would was affirmed, but at the same time, the freedom of the individual will was also affirmed. This paradox accommodated both man's belief in God's omnipotence and his experiential sense of himself as a self-directed, willing individual. That formulation, for which Herbert and his coreligionists were indebted to Augustine, was essential if the central problem of salvation and damnation was to have real significance or to influence the way Christian life was lived. Jeremy Taylor explained to his congregation, "If, after the fall of Adam, it be not by God permitted to us to choose or refuse, there is nothing left whereby man can serve God or offer Him a sacrifice. It is no service; it is not rewardable if it could not be avoided, nor the omission punishable if it could not be done."[27]

If the doctrine of strict predestination by irresistible grace had been, in practice, the basis of seventeenth-century English Protestantism, the constant exhortations to repentance and piety that thundered from the pulpits would have been pointless. Even James Ussher, "an exemplary Calvinist mind, having repudiated the concept of human 'free will to good,' appears constrained in practice to treat the same concept as an inescapable element of reality" when he admonishes, "Yet it shall be *easier for Sodome and Gomorrah then for you*, if you repent not while you may, but goe on to despise God's grace."[28] If there is

---

elements in Herbert's theology, it is well to remember that the orthodox Anglican position sometimes overlaps with them; that Herbert endorsed high-church rituals, as Leah Sinanoglou Marcus points out ("George Herbert and the Anglican Plain Style," in *"Too Rich to Clothe the Sunne": Essays on George Herbert*, ed. Claude J. Summers and Ted-Larry Pebworth, p. 184); and that "the exaltation of the English establishment and the destruction of Roman Catholicism and of Genevan Calvinism" are set forth by the Biblical allusions in "The British Church" (Summers and Pebworth, "Herbert, Vaughan," p. 8).

27. Donne, *Sermons*, 7:156; Taylor, from *Unum Necessarium . . .*, in *Anglicanism: The Thought and Practice of the Church of England, Illustrated from the Religious Literature of the Seventeenth Century*, ed. Paul E. More and Frank L. Cross, p. 652.

28. Chandos, *In God's Name*, p. 228.

no free will, there is no reason to castigate sin or urge its amendment.

The Church of England had truly found the via media on this issue, according to one of its divines, George Bull:

> Whilst we avoid Pelagianism by acknowledging the necessity of grace, let us take care, on the other hand, that we fall not into the abyss of Manichaean folly, by taking away free will and the co-operation of human industry. The middle, the royal way must here be chosen, so as to turn neither to the left hand nor to the right, which will be done if we suppose that with grace, but in subjection to it, the freedom of the will amicably unites. This saying of Augustine is common and well known: "If there be no grace of God, how can He save the world? and if there be no free will, how can He judge it?"

Bull might have chosen many other passages, since Augustine insisted on the freedom of the will. His one qualification was the balancing one that Bull (and others) made: "And the will owes its freedom in no degree to itself, but solely to the grace of God which comes by faith in Jesus Christ; so that the very will, through which we accept all the other gifts of God which lead us on to His eternal gift, is itself prepared of the Lord, as the Scripture says."[29] Some lines in Herbert's "Providence" express the idea:

> We all acknowledge both thy power and love
> To be exact, transcendent, and divine;
> Who dost so strongly and so sweetly move,
> While all things have their will, yet none but thine.

For the gift of free will, man is indebted to God's grace. It is God's will that "all things have their will."

Just as it is grace that makes faith possible in the first place, so it is grace that makes the Christian activity of good works possible after man's justification by faith. "Of free will" is the title of the tenth Article of the Church of England (1563):

> The condition of man after the fall of *Adam* is such that he cannot turn and prepare himself of his own natural strength and good works, to faith and calling upon God: Wherefore we

29. Bull, from *Harmonia Apostolica,* in *Anglicanism,* p. 312; *The Enchiridion on Faith, Hope and Love,* pp. 124–25.

have no power to do good works, pleasant and acceptable to God, without the grace of God by Christ preventing us, that we may have a good will, and working with us, when we have that good will.

Thomas Rogers reads the latter part of the Article to mean that "man may perform and do good works, when he is prevented by the grace of Christ, and renewed by the Holy Ghost." He uses as one scriptural proof the same verses that Augustine, Bull, and many others referred to in the context of works and free will: "Work out your own salvation with fear and trembling. For it is God which worketh in you both to will and to do his good pleasure" (Philippians 2:12–13).[30]

Anglican theologians and priests like George Herbert referred to *prevenient* and *subsequent* grace to distinguish between the stages of willing and of doing good, and to emphasize once again that all initiative and credit belong to God. Prevenient grace, explained Hooker, "shall put in us good desires, and the second shall bring them to good effect." John Donne made the same distinction in a sermon: "No man can prepare that worke, no man can begin it, no man can proceed in it of himselfe. The desire and the actuall beginning is from the preventing grace of God, and the constant proceeding is from the concomitant, and subsequent, and continuall succeeding grace of God." But if Donne made sure that God's initiating and continuing grace was acknowledged, he as carefully made sure that man's cooperation was also acknowledged: "Man is that creature, who onely of all other creatures can answer the inspiration of God, when his grace comes, and exhibit acceptable service to him, and cooperate with him."[31]

Of course, man was free to follow or to refuse the promptings of prevenient grace, as we see in the fanciful "Artillerie":

> As I one ev'ning sat before my cell,
> Me thoughts a starre did shoot into my lap.

30. Bicknell, *Thirty-Nine Articles*, p. 219; Rogers, *Articles*, p. 106; Augustine, *Enchiridion*, p. 39; Bull, from *Harmonia Apostolica*, in *Anglicanism*, p. 313.

31. Richard Hooker, 2:497. The distinction was one made by Augustine: "The whole work belongs to God, who both makes the will of man righteous, and thus prepares it for assistance, and assists it when it is prepared" (Augustine, *Enchiridion*, p. 40). Donne, *Sermons*, 2:305; 1:271.

I rose, and shook my clothes, as knowing well,
That from small fires comes oft no small mishap.
　　When suddenly I heard one say,
　　*Do as thou usest, disobey,*
　　*Expell good motions from thy breast,*
*Which have the face of fire, but end in rest.*

(1–8)

The ironic urging and exasperated tone in the speech of the
star to the narrator ("who had heard of musick in the spheres, /
But not of speech in starres") tell the whole story. Here is a
phlegmatic creature who habitually expels good "motions"
("inward promptings" or "impulses," *OED*) that seem too
arduous or liable to "mishap." Because of his laziness or caution, he fails to see that by undertaking the good that the
shooting star represents, he would find not difficulties but
"rest." Precisely because he is free, man can refuse his own
good.

　　The cooperation of man with grace in the "acceptable service" of good works was very important in the Christian
scheme. Elucidating a scriptural text, Augustine wrote that the
purpose of virtuous action "is not 'to be seen of them' [other
men], that is, with the intention that they should be converted
to *you*, because by yourselves you are nothing, but 'so that they
may glorify your Father, who is in Heaven,' and so that they
may be converted to *him*, and become what you are." This
effect is what Donne had in mind when he explained what he
called *Lux Repercussionum:* "That is, when Gods light cast upon
us, reflecteth upon *other men too*, from us; when God doth not
onely accept our works for *our selves*, but imployes those works
of ours upon *other* men . . . our good works shall not onely
profit *us*, that *do* them, but *others* that *see them* done."[32] This
desire to glorify God by being of service to other men, so that
they also might know and love God, is charity.

　　In Herbert's day, *charity* still meant specifically Christian
love. God's love to man and man's love to God and to his
neighbor were all included in the meaning of the word, though
then as now the word was used most often to refer to a man's

32. Augustine, *City of God*, p. 204; Donne, *Sermons*, 3:373–74.

concern for other men. Charity was an attitude, a particular point of view that guided the Christian in all his relations to others. Charity could be discussed in the loftiest terms by John Donne:

> Charity desires not her own, sayes the Apostle; but much lesse doth charity desire no more than her own, so as not to desire the good of others too. True love and charity is to doe the most that we can, all that we can for the good of others. So God himself proceeds, when he says, *What could I doe, that I have not done?*

But charity could also be invoked by Joseph Hall to answer the question "Whether it is lawful for me, to raise any profit by the loan of money?":

> Shortly, for the guidance of our either caution or liberty, in matter of borrowing or lending, the only cynosure is our charity. For in all human and civil acts of commerce, it is a sure rule that whatsoever is not a violation of charity cannot be unlawful, and whatsoever is not agreeable to charity can be no other than sinful. And as charity must be your rule, so yourself must be the rule of your charity: Look what you could wish to be done to you by others, Do but the same to others,—you cannot be guilty of the breach of charity. The maxims of traffic are almost infinite; only charity, but ever inseparable from justice, must make the application of them. That will teach you that every increase by loan of money is not usury, and that those which are absolutely such are damnable.[33]

A broad concept familiar to all, charity was by no means understood to refer only to almsgiving.

Divine love provides the inspiration, the example, and the power of human love. God's love, like his grace, precedes any desire or motion of man's. He gave the greatest manifestation of his love of mankind in the gift of his Son. The redemption by Christ's sacrifice showed love that was not evoked by any merit or intrinsic lovableness in humanity; indeed, the Crucifixion simultaneously demonstrated divine charity and the just punishment for human sin. Loving man while he was yet a

33. Donne, *Sermons*, 5:278; Hall, from *Resolutions and Decisions of Divers Practical Cases of Conscience, in Continual Use among Men*, in *Anglicanism*, p. 678.

sinner, God made possible man's redemption through the Crucifixion.

"As the Father hath loved me, so have I loved you: continue ye in my love. If ye keep my commandments ye shall abide in my love; even as I have kept my Father's commandments, and abide in his love" (John 15:9–10). With these words at the Last Supper, Christ indicated that his endeavors were a conscious obedience to the will of God, and that his love for humanity sprang from the Father's love for him. God's love evoked a corresponding love that was expressed primarily by obedience to his will and by love to mankind. As a modern commentator observes, "Jesus saw no problem or conflict between love to God and love to Man. Not because he fused them into one, but because for him love to God inspired love to man. He recognized direct love to God as expressed in prayer and worship as well as in the service of our fellow-man."[34]

It is the same for man. The experience of God's love creates in him the love with which to obey Christ's commandments to √love God and his fellow man. Isaac Barrow thus describes the creative power of divine love: "That God thus should *love us, sending His Son to be a propitiation for our sins,* in so dismal a way of suffering, how stupendous is that goodness! How vast an obligation doth it lay upon us to reciprocal affection!"[35] Though man is imperfect, and therefore incapable of perfect charity, Christ is the inspiration and pattern for the Christian love that is obedience and service. We need only consider the divine pattern to realize how demanding is the command to "Love thy neighbor as thyself." As Donne said simply, "True love and charity is to doe the most that we can, all that we can for the good of others." The Christian's duty is to do good works, to help his neighbor in physical need, in spiritual need, in everything.

Herbert also stressed the awesome obligations of charity. Twice in his prose writings he calls the reader's attention to Philippians 4:8. Writing on the parson's charity in "The Country Parson," Herbert paraphrases the verse: "For the Apostles

34. James Moffatt, *Love in the New Testament,* p. 124.
35. Barrow, from *Sermons,* "Upon the Passion of Our Blessed Saviour," in *Anglicanism,* p. 293.

rule *Philip.* 4. being admirable, and large, that *we should do whatsoever things are honest, or just, or pure, or lovely, or of good report, if there be vertue, or any praise;* and Neighbourhood being ever reputed, even among the Heathen, as an obligation to do good, . . . therefore he satisfies this duty also" (*Works*, p. 253). He refers to the same text in his notes on Valdesso's *Considerations.* Valdesso wrote that in aid to others, Christians ought to remain "quiet, when they doe not perceive any motion, understanding it, that God would haue them to remain quiet." Herbert's comments are enlightening:

> In indifferent things there is roome for motions and expecting of them; but in things good, as to relieve my Neighbour, God hath already revealed his Will about it. Therefore wee ought to proceed, except there be a restraining motion (as *S. Paul* had when hee would have preached in Asia), and I conceive that restraining motions are much more frequent to the godly, then inviting motions; because the Scripture invites enough, for it invites us to all good, according to that singular place, *Phil.* 4.8. A man is to embrace all good, but because he cannot doe all, God often chuseth which he shall doe, and that by restraining him from what he would not have him doe. (*Works*, p. 313)[36]

Not only do "the godly" understand that they are commanded to do "all good" for others; in the absence of "restraining motions," they attempt to do all good.

The New Testament emphasizes the divine paradigm, and hence the active nature of charity: "Hereby perceive we the love of God, because he laid down his life for us: and we ought to lay down our lives for the brethren. But whoso hath the world's good, and seeth his brother have need, and shutteth up his bowels of compassion from him, how dwelleth the love of God in him? My little children, let us not love in word, neither in tongue; but in deed and in truth" (I John 3:16–18). Not in word, but in deed. Because charity is not merely a loving attitude but, like Christ's, is necessarily expressed in activity, we are once again in the province of good works and, ✓ consequently, of grace.

The theological contexts that Herbert took for granted are a

36. See also Herbert's letter to Arthur Woodnoth (*Works*, p. 380).

passport into territory that is remote to most of us, a world where the Christian's emotional, moral, and spiritual state means everything. They are vital in the understanding of the Christian speaker's assumptions about his nature and condition, his moral situation, and his spiritual responsibilities. As the next chapter will demonstrate, the concepts of grace and charity are essential also to our understanding of the nature of Herbert's poetry.

# 2

# "The Temple" and the Typical Christian

The most accurate proposition regarding the unity of *The Temple* has been made by Joseph Summers, who says that the volume is "the symbolic record, written by a poet, of a 'typical' Christian life within the Church."[1] His argument is just: the poems range over all the essential Christian concerns between baptism and the soul's reception into heaven, and the speaker exists within the framework of an institution that defines him and shapes his experience in certain patterns. The Christian and his life claim universality because of this definition of the individual man in terms applicable to the entire community of believers, and because of the shared experience imposed on its adherents by the institution's tenets. As Heather Asals remarks, "The experiences related in 'The Church' are the experiences of all its members throughout all time."[2]

1. Joseph H. Summers, *George Herbert: His Religion and Art*, p. 86. Helen C. White compares the Williams manuscript (the earliest known, which consists of 69 of the 164 *Temple* poems) to the 1633 edition (the first) of *The Temple*. She speculates that Herbert may have been ordering the poems when ill health stopped him "so that what we have now is but a partially organized whole" (*The Metaphysical Poets: A Study in Religious Experience*, p. 162). Other critics propose various narrative unities for *The Temple*. In *Five Metaphysical Poets: Donne, Herbert, Vaughan, Crashaw, Marvell*, p. 56, Joan Bennett suggests that it is Herbert's spiritual autobiography; in *The Poetry of Meditation*, p. 289, Louis L. Martz sees the book as a structure reflecting the movement of the "threefold division of the Christian life" (the active, the contemplative, and the newly active). Charles A. Pennel and William P. Williams see the pilgrimage of the soul as the dominant theme of "The Church" ("The Unity of *The Temple*," pp. 38–39); Elizabeth Stambler suggests that *"The Temple*, considered as a whole, *symbolizes*, in a peculiarly *literal* sense, its protagonist's life" ("The Unity of Herbert's 'Temple,' " p. 261).

2. Heather Asals, "The Voice of George Herbert's 'The Church,' " p. 526. See also Asals's chapter "The Sacramental Voice: Distance Related" in her *Equivocal Predication: George Herbert's Way to God*.

31

But Summers's formulation seems frigid. It does not indicate that what is most vital within the Church is the Christian's personal relation to God. Though he is typical, the Christian speaker of *The Temple* lives and feels the Christian experience as a particular personality involved with God in a close, developing, and individual relationship. An adequate description of Herbert's book must include the Christian's spontaneous and personal dealings with the Deity, his awareness of the historical God, and his participation in the community of believers. *The Temple* is the symbolic record of the life of a Christian engaged in an intimate and personal relationship with God. It is "intimate and personal" both in the sense that it consists of an ongoing interaction whose focal point is the speaker's daily joys, troubles, and reflections, and in the sense that frequently its dramatic immediacy seems unmediated (or uninhibited) by the distance, formalities, and distinctions that would seem to obtain between beings of radically different natures. Intimacy identifies the Christian with the entire congregation of the faithful and demands his efforts to assimilate in personal terms God's history, standards, feasts, and sacraments as they are promulgated by the Scriptures and the Church.

Notwithstanding the importance of the Christian speaker's intimate relationship with God, our study of *The Temple* must begin with the concept of the Christian community, because that is fundamental to our understanding of Herbert's approach to poetry, of the speaker's perspective on the world and his fellow man, and of the modes of grace, of God's active participation in the Christian life. The latter topic is complex; it will recur throughout the following chapters as we concentrate on the relationship between the speaker and God. Its treatment in this study reflects Herbert's treatment of it throughout *The Temple:* grace is available to each member of the Christian community in the same ways that it is accessible to the speaker of the poems. The universal availability of grace is a corollary of heavenly charity: throughout divine history and in the present instant, the innumerable manifestations of God's love aim at all of his people.

\*      \*      \*

Charity, the Christian's best effort to reproduce Christ's love for him in his love to other men, is essential and powerful, as Herbert observed:

> For many and wonderfull things are spoken of thee, thou great Vertue. To Charity is given the covering of sins, I *Pet.* 4.8. and the forgivenesse of sins, *Matthew* 6.14. *Luke* 7.47. The fulfilling of the Law, *Romans,* 13.10. The life of faith, *James* 2.26. The blessings of this life, *Proverbs* 22.9. *Psalm* 41.2. And the reward of the next, *Matth.* 25.35. In brief, it is the body of Religion, *John* 13.35. And the top of Christian vertues, I *Corin.* 13. (*Works*, p. 244)

The poet was very conscious of the power of charity, through God's grace, to accomplish a great deal. In addition to giving the Christian the initial desire to love, God also gives him the *charismata*, "grace-gifts," talents and abilities to be used for service to others in the Christian fellowship. Herbert quotes one of Paul's references to grace-gifts, Romans 12:4–6, in "The Country Parson": "For as we have many members in one body, and all members have not the same office: So we, being many, are one body in Christ, and every one members one of another. Having then gifts differing according to the grace that is given us, whether prophecy, let us prophesy according to the proportion of faith" (*Works*, p. 226). The apostle then mentions other grace-gifts such as ministering and teaching. James Moffatt remarks on this passage, "The experience of grace within the Christian communities involves capacities and responsibilities . . . Grace means for the Christian a certain ministry to others, and to this end 'grace-gifts' are bestowed."[3]

*The Temple* is George Herbert's artistic expression of charity. As Joseph Summers comments, Herbert "intended the poems . . . as expressions of his love for God as well as his neighbour."[4] This love is expressed primarily through in-

3. James Moffatt, *Grace in the New Testament*, p. 107.
4. *Herbert: Religion and Art*, p. 84.

structing the reader with poetry that exploits its didactic possibilities with varying degrees of subtlety. The same poetry, insofar as it praises God and thereby seeks to move others to praise and love him, is also an expression of the author's love for God. If the poems themselves did not consistently indicate it, the author's altruistic intention would be immaterial. As it is, the reader's awareness that Herbert means to instruct him alerts him to the devices the poet uses to achieve his aim. This utilization of his *charismata* must have seemed only appropriate to Herbert, who wrote that "every gift or ability is a talent to be accounted for, and to be improved to our Masters Advantage" (*Works,* p. 274).

Seen in this light, Herbert's poems are not "private," despite Helen Vendler's assertion: "An expressive theory of poetry suits *The Temple* best: no matter how exquisitely written a poem by Herbert is in its final form, it seems usually to have begun in experience, and aims at recreating or recalling that experience. To approach such private poetry as an exercise in public communication with an audience is to misconstrue its emphasis." Vendler ignores Summers's persuasive argument about "Herbert's view of the proper relationship between language and experience," which reads in part, "The expression of individual experience was valued not for the sake of self-expression but for its didactic effectiveness," and which concludes, "Even without an obviously didactic aim on the part of the speaker, the relation of Christian experience inevitably functioned didactically."[5]

Vendler's "expressive theory" does not allow for the various kinds of poems in *The Temple.* Roughly 95 of the 164 poems do seem to describe the speaker's experience, but there are also liturgical poems, allegories, emblem poems, poems of direct exhortation addressed to the "thou" who reads them, and reflective poems on the nature of God or man that seem to be

5. Vendler, *The Poetry of George Herbert,* p. 5; Summers, *Herbert: Religion and Art,* pp. 102–3. Arnold Stein's emphasis differs from Summers's, but he expresses a similar awareness of the personal and public aspects of Herbert's poetry. Herbert aspires, Stein suggests, "to an art of plainness . . . that can reveal impersonal truth without distortion, even while it registers the felt significance and force of a personal apprehension of that truth" (*George Herbert's Lyrics,* p. 2).

occasional syntheses of the thought and experience of the speaker. Those poems show that *The Temple* does not consist of "private poetry" as Vendler defines that phrase. Poems that seem to record experience are as much a part of Herbert's didactic method as are those like "Whitsunday," "Sunday," or "Lent," which illuminate the meaning of the Church feasts. They are private poems only in the sense that they aim to reveal the Christian reader to himself.

While Herbert's intent to instruct his reader is constant, the art with which he does so varies from poem to poem. In "The Church-porch," the reader is told what he ought to do to improve himself:

> Scorn no mans love, though of a mean degree;
> Love is a present for a mightie king. . . .
> Restore to God his due in tithe and time:
> A tithe purloin'd cankers the whole estate.
>
> (349–50, 385–86)

The poem consists of seventy-seven stanzas of such practical or pious bits of advice. Though often surprising in its witty appeals to pragmatic self-interest, the length of "The Church-porch" vitiates its impact. It resembles a collection of maxims whose individual pith is subverted by their proximity to each other.[6]

"The Church" section of *The Temple* also holds a few poems characterized by undisguised exhortation on the nature and condition of man. "Businesse" is one of these: "Canst be idle? Canst thou play, / Foolish soul who sinn'd to day?" If the lazy soul addressed were only the speaker's, his patient air of leading a dullard to obvious conclusions might not be so unattractive. But "Foolish soul who sinn'd to day" also accuses a multitude of willful idleness in the work of repentance.

> He that loseth gold, though drosse,
> Tells to all he meets, his crosse:

6. But see Joseph H. Summers, ed., *George Herbert: Selected Poetry*, pp. xiii–xxvii. As Summers's remarks indicate, "The Church-porch" has its admirers. John Ruskin wrote to a friend in enthusiastic terms: "Seriously, I admire George Herbert above everything, and shall learn 'The Church-porch' by heart as soon as I have time." See John L. Idol, Jr., "George Herbert and John Ruskin," p. 11.

He that sinnes, hath he no losse?

He that findes a silver vein,
Thinks on it, and thinks again:
Brings thy Saviours death no gain?
(31–36)

Though we acknowledge that the speaker's simple diction, his obvious questions and answers, and his repetitive approach are appropriate to his "foolish" auditor, who lacks rudimentary judgment and common sense, the poem inspires little interest. Such straightforward instruction has the advantage of being understood easily but has the disadvantage of being very like the sermons Herbert suspected of lacking universal appeal.[7] "A verse may finde him, who a sermon flies," he wrote in the first stanza of "The Church-porch," before he went on in that poem to write the many lines, which as a whole have the effect of a long, disjointed, and worldly sermon.

However, the poems that praise artlessly or that openly accuse the reader or urge him to do (or not to do) something specific are very few in "The Church." Herbert's best poems praise God and instruct the reader without alienating by direct assaults such as the one that mars "Businesse." It is not that the poet flatters his audience; "Sepulchre" is typical in its frank appraisal of man. As though he were present in the mysterious period between Christ's death and the Resurrection, the speaker of that poem addresses the "Blessed bodie" in the tomb. Inasmuch as Christ died for all repentant sinners from the beginning to the end of time, there is a sense in which the speaker was present at the Crucifixion, death, and Resurrection. His dramatic tactic is not as surprising as his concentration on a period about which the Gospels are silent, the period during which the Savior lay dead.

Ignoring the appropriate burial given Christ by Joseph of Arimathaea (Matthew 27: 57–60), the speaker feels compassion for the body "thrown" as carelessly as a useless object might be discarded:

7. Sharon Cadman Seelig remarks about "Businesse" that its "form militates against the emotional experience of the truths it appears to convey." See *The Shadow of Eternity: Belief and Structure in Herbert, Vaughan, and Traherne*, p. 21.

> O Blessed bodie! Whither art thou thrown?
> No lodging for thee, but a cold hard stone?
> So many hearts on earth, and yet not one
>                         Receive thee?
>                                 (1–4)

The shocked disbelief of the witness before the open tomb is emphasized by the medial caesuras of the first lines. Imagination and indignation render stone sepulchre and heart as contrasting lodgings—one uncomfortable, the other warm and soft. The speaker's implication of the honor due the unresurrected body insists on the magnitude and value of the sacrifice in itself. (Literally, he laments that the death of the Son is taken to heart by no one.) From being potential lodgings, the roomy hearts advance to consciousness—and guilt: "Thousands of toyes dwell there, yet out of doore / They leave thee." Admitting a population of trifles and "transgressions," the hearts are reprehensible innkeepers who shut their doors on Christ.

Trying to understand why not one heart will take the office of the tomb, the Christian discovers why none *can* do so:

> But that which shews them large, shews them unfit.
> What ever sinne did this pure rock commit,
> Which holds thee now? Who hath indited it
>                         Of murder?
> Where our hard hearts have took up stones to brain thee,
> And missing this, most falsly did arraigne thee;
> Onely these stones in quiet entertain thee,
>                         And order.
>                                 (9–16)

The implied contrast between the stone and the hearts in the first lines of the poem is displaced by the true contrast. The Christian pronounces it with leaden conviction, accusing the hearts first as failed murderers of Christ, then as murderous false witnesses against him. All are here identified with the men who took up stones against Jesus (John 10:31) and with those who testified falsely against him (Matthew 22:60). Herbert blends gospel truth with the dramatic situation to stress the responsibility of all sinners for the Son's suffering and death. Against the hearts' obdurate and senseless hatred, the

innocent welcome of the stones proclaims the sepulchre to be
the superior lodging.

The association of "stones" and "order" reminds the
mournful speaker of an analogous situation that hints at the
propriety of the Savior's rocky tomb. Just as the Old Testament
law was written by the finger of God on the stone tablets
(Exodus 31:18), so Christ, the fulfillment of the law, must dwell
in the stone sepulchre because he finds "no fit heart" to hold
him. When the Christian realizes that his analogy also discloses mankind's unregenerate sinfulness through the centuries, his melancholy deepens:

> Yet do we still persist as we began,
> And so should perish, but that nothing can,
> Though it be cold, hard, foul, from loving man
>              Withhold thee.

                                                              (21–24)

From compassion for a seemingly needy Christ, the speaker
has advanced to a grim awareness of the vulnerability of man
steeped in conscious and damning sin. His insight is the more
startling for being unsought: lodging foul, death-dealing
transgressions, the unreceptive human heart is a genuine
sepulchre.

The poem has progressed as if it were up to the human heart
to take in Christ, but in the end, as Stanley Fish remarks, it is
evident that "the active force in this situation . . . is not the
heart but Christ."[8] The Savior will not be withheld from man
though his heart be a cold and hard sepulchre, foul with sin.
This comforting thought ends an extremely accusatory poem,
but it does not mitigate the accusations of inhospitality and sin.
Man's nature is more forcefully depicted by comparison with
Christ's initiative and great countervailing love. Herbert takes
the reader to the sepulchre not when the discovery is made
that it is empty, with Christ having risen in triumph, but when
the reader can "see" the body, dead in the service of those who
still reject it. The poem then moves yet further back in time to
suggest that the reader participated in the indignities against

8. *Self-Consuming Artifacts: The Experience of Seventeenth-Century Literature*, p.
172.

the living Christ and stands "indited . . . / Of murder." Christ's refusal to withhold himself from man for any consideration is most striking against the background of this guilt, of this persistence in sin.

The accusations that "Sepulchre" makes are much more severe than the spiritual idleness with which "Businesse" charges the reader. Yet, though "Sepulchre" is more censorious, it succeeds because it avoids the intrusive preaching tone of the other poem. It does this partly by addressing not the reader but Christ. Moreover, the reader overhears a speaker who includes himself in his accusations, which thereby gain further validity. The "we" that the Christian uses implicates the reader, of course, but it avoids alienating him as does the pointing finger of "Businesse." Furthermore, the speaker of "Sepulchre" does not tell the eavesdropper that he ought to rectify the faults the poem reveals. To participate with the Christian in the sorrowful awareness of self-accusation may be the first step in rectification—but Herbert's art is to show only the uninviting human hearts and the persistently loving Christ. The reader is left to draw his own conclusions.

"Sepulchre" is more effective than "Businesse," but both share with all the *Temple* poems, whatever their particular excellencies or failures, the same theological concepts and a common religious purpose. Whether he wrote simple praise or exhortation, created imaginary situations or monologues for strategic points of the Christian past, Herbert's objective was the same. The allegories, liturgical or emblem poems, reflective poems, and poems describing the speaker's particular experience all praise God and enlighten the reader, encouraging him to turn to God in the different attitudes or for the different reasons indicated by the poems. The spirit of charity pervades *The Temple*.

\*       \*       \*

As "Sepulchre" demonstrates, the Christian's relationship with the eternal Deity does not operate within the usual limitations of time. Though it is unique in its particular details, it is not singular or exclusive. This nonexclusiveness has various implications, one being that many of the specific forms and

occasions of the Christian's devotion have been predetermined by the Scriptures and the Church. In such poems as
"The H. Communion," "H. Baptisme" (I) and (II), "Lent,"
"Sunday," and "Whitsunday," the speaker proclaims his
adherence to the rituals and observances that belong to the
entire family of God. His awareness of this nonexclusiveness is
also evident in poems that address, exhort, or describe man.
Underlying these poems are all or some of the following
assumptions: that there is a proper relationship between man
and God; that the laws and conditions of that relationship have
been revealed and apply to each member of the community;
that allegiance to the Almighty immediately identifies the
Christian with the larger body whose history defines each
member and his relationship to God; and that the love of God
places the Christian in a loving and responsible relation to his
fellows.

Poems like "Businesse," "Avarice," "Mortification," and
"Vanitie" (I) and (II) reflect the communal aspect of the Christian's perspective, as does "Ungratefulnesse":

> Lord, with what bountie and rare clemencie
> Hath thou redeem'd us from the grave!
> If thou hadst let us runne,
> Gladly had man ador'd the sunne,
> And thought his god most brave;
> Where now we shall be better Gods then he.
>
> (1–6)

Immediately, the speaker's initial exclamation to God challenges the relevance of the title of the poem. Wonder and a
dash of pardonable pride resound in his voice as he considers
the rare generosity that will eventually clothe him in eternal
radiance. Only one dark thread intersects his thankfulness and
confidence: God's bounty expresses itself in saving man despite his ignorance and inclination to error. But this strand is
"hidden," enclosed within happy gratitude on the one hand
and joyous expectation on the other.

Indeed, the inharmonious strand of thought disappears entirely. The reflecting Christian, implying by "betroth" (line 10)
the traditional imagery of the bridegroom and his bride, expands on the bounty of God. The bridegroom gives his bride

the promise of eternal pleasure and his two cases of jewels in token of their anticipated union. Thoughtfully, he provides for the bride's future delight by withholding a part of one treasure chest:

> The statelier cabinet is the *Trinitie*,
>> Whose sparkling light accesse denies:
>> Therefore thou dost not show
> This fully to us, till death blow
>> The dust into our eyes:
> For by that powder thou wilt make us see.
>
> (13–18)

As Richard E. Hughes comments, this is Herbert's "protestation . . . that he will not, and can not dilate on the doctrine of the Trinity in his poetry."[9] But the self-imposed limitation is artfully turned to advantage as a divine provision for future bliss. Similarly, the dust of decomposition undergoes a positive transformation: it becomes a sight-giving powder, somehow losing its irritating grainy essence to admit the excess of light, the Trinity. The bridegroom sets aside that awesome "cabinet," but gives the more alluring one, the Incarnation, in order to entice the bride with something familiar: "Because this box we know; / For we have all of us just such another."

By now, the reader's expectation of ungratefulness has been frustrated for the duration of twenty-four lines. But at last the dark thread is taken up again to fulfill the promise of the title:

> But man is close, reserv'd, and dark to thee:
>> When thou demandest but a heart,
>> He cavils instantly.
> In his poore cabinet of bone
>> Sinnes have their box apart,
> Defrauding thee, who gavest two for one.
>
> (25–30)

The bride, in a fine show of ungratefulness, does not bestow a reciprocal gift graciously, or even willingly. For the two treasure chests she receives, she hesitates to give her own paltry coffer. The contrast could not be more extreme. God has two

---

9. "George Herbert and the Incarnation," in *Essential Articles for the Study of George Herbert's Poetry,* ed. John R. Roberts, p. 53.

rare cabinets; man *is* two poor cabinets, his mere body and the heart within, a rich hoard of sin. The shabby box within the shabby box is withheld from a bridegroom so generous that he wants it as the complement to his own glorious present.

By virtue of his subject and point of view, the speaker of "Ungratefulnesse" becomes a Christian Everyman whose voice spans the ages. There is not a single *I* in the poem. We understand, of course, that in referring to "man" the speaker distinguishes between his present grateful self and a past (and future) self only too much inclined to ingratitude. His praise to God with its acknowledgment of ungratefulness might seem to set him apart from the errant community, but the poem defines gratefulness as the willing return to God of the heart rather than the reservation of it as a box in which to treasure sin. This gratitude can be maintained only temporarily by man. Though God can certainly dispel the heart's sin, the sinner is not always disposed to subject his heart to scrutiny and cleansing. The Christian describes the plight of fallen mankind, which has no hope of transcending its limitation and doom by itself. He meditates, therefore, on the nature and status he shares with all men and on the characteristic stance he and all others take before God. He is grateful for the divine generosity extended to him—even when he is all ungratefulness.

Sometimes Herbert uses typology to stress the individual's identity with the age-old community. Barbara Lewalski points out that seventeenth-century "Christians were invited to perceive the events and personages of Old and New Testament salvation history not merely as exemplary to them but as actually recapitulated in their lives, in accordance with God's vast typological plan of recapitulations and fulfillments." In poems such as "Josephs coat" and "The Bunch of Grapes" the Christian sees himself as an antitype of Joseph and of the Israelites journeying to the Promised Land. [10] His awareness of partaking of the communal identity also informs poems like "Ungratefulnesse," though they do not refer to any Biblical

10. *Protestant Poetics and the Seventeenth-Century Religious Lyric,* p. 131. On "The Bunch of Grapes" and "Josephs coat," see pp. 312–13.

personage, but instead refer to the typical imperfect man as he is defined by Christianity.

Just as the Christian shares in the human flaws, he also shares in the benefits the Deity extended to mankind in the distant past. God's long history of interaction with his people predates but nevertheless belongs to this speaker, having immediate and personal implications for him. In his consideration of historical events, he usually works just outside the realm of typology. In poems such as "Sepulchre," "Easter," and "Christmas," the events he describes do not repeat themselves symbolically in his own life, nor does his experience parallel that of any particular participant in those events. His strategy is much closer to the "composition of place" in which the meditator tries to imagine himself "present in the very spot where the event occurred."[11] The gains of immediacy and drama for the reader are important. Primarily, however, the Christian's imaginative device has a personal and spiritual aim. All religious feasts and holy days and a host of Scriptural events, together with the sacraments and the other observances and rituals of the Church, compose his spiritual inheritance. Inasmuch as it has a vital and present importance for him, he must regenerate that complex of revelation and tradition in personal and experiential terms.

The possession of the inherited past depends on its imaginative re-creation, as "Christmas" shows:

> All after pleasures as I rid one day,
>> My horse and I, both tir'd, bodie and minde,
>> With full crie of affections, quite astray,
> I took up in the next inne I could finde.
> There when I came, whom found I but my deare,
>> My dearest Lord, expecting till the grief
>> Of pleasures brought me to him, readie there
> To be all passengers most sweet relief?
>
>                                         (1–8)

---

11. Martz, *Poetry of Meditation*, p. 30. See also Martin Elsky, "History, Liturgy and Point of View in Protestant Meditative Poetry," p. 68: "In both the Old and New Testaments . . . *anamnesis* signifies the principle of ritual renewal of past events in sacred history through their representation in the present."

The absence of any reference to the Nativity and the speaker's self-characterization combine to create an interesting but unsettling effect. We listen to an anecdote that happened "one day" to a hunter so inept he got lost, so troubled his raging emotions yelped like hounds in full pursuit. Why he claims his horse was in the same condition of bodily and mental fatigue is not immediately clear, but "astray" especially confirms the allegorical quality of the tale. The strayed rider is the speaker in his past sinful identity. Quite unknowingly, he rode into the innyard where the host waited for him, but also for "all passengers" in need of relief. Given the title of the poem, the convenient inn with a host so eagerly receptive of course reminds the reader of the different circumstances that led Mary and Joseph to the manger. Even before Herbert brings the Nativity into the poem, he suggests with a fine subtlety the contrast between the welcome that the world gave to the Son and the one that the Son gives to man. Obviously, this is a story of redemption, very appropriate at Christmas when God came "to seek and to save that which was lost." The Christian remembers and celebrates his entrance into a new life together with Christ's entrance into human life.

The speaker's creative manipulation of his actual and inherited pasts and of his individual and typical identities makes "Christmas" a remarkable poem. The theatrical Christian seems matter-of-fact as he recounts a past experience, but just when his tone intensifies to wonder as he reaches the story's climax, it becomes apparent that he has recast experience into allegory. The figurative language acknowledges the universality of his experience and emphasizes the drama of the unexpected rescue. Though he already knew the outcome, his story's climax thrills him anew. When the refashioned and relived past dissolves into present ardor, the allegory, having served its purpose, is discarded. Having reexperienced ignorance, humility, and gratitude, the Christian expresses his joy that Christ came into his life.

In the sestet of the sonnet, his gratitude for past mercy inspires a petition for the continued indwelling of the Son:

> O Thou, whose glorious, yet contracted light,
>     Wrapt in nights mantle, stole into a manger;

> Since my dark soul and brutish is thy right,
> To man of all beasts be not thou a stranger:
>     Furnish & deck my soul, that thou mayst have
>     A better lodging then a rack or grave.
>
>                                          (9–14)

He alludes, with "Wrapt in nights mantle," to the tradition that the Infant was born at night, to his adoption of mortal flesh, and to the modesty of the event. The humility of the Savior, voluntarily assumed, recalls to the Christian his own true lowliness. His fervent prayer simultaneously explains and acknowledges his kinship to the horse, expands that kinship to include all (in the needy guise of unregenerate man), and evokes the traditional Nativity scene with the animals in the background. Just as the heart in "The Altar" and in "Ungratefulnesse" was an altar or a lodging only if God sanctified it for his use or habitation, the Christian's soul is a suitable lodging only if it is furnished and decorated by the invited guest. Decked by the desired guest according to his own taste, certainly the soul would excel hayrack or grave as a habitation.

The speaker's sinful past makes him concentrate on the benefits of the Incarnation. He refers to the Nativity across the distance of centuries, with Christ's grave as present to his mind as the manger. But in the second part of the poem, he actually participates in the Nativity:

> The shepherds sing; and shall I silent be?
>     My God, no hymne for thee?
> My soul's a shepherd too; a flock it feeds
>     Of thoughts, and words, and deeds.
> The pasture is thy word: the streams, thy grace
>     Enriching all the place.
> Shepherd and flock shall sing, and all my powers
>     Out-sing the day-light houres.
> Then we will chide the sunne for letting night
>     Take up his place and right:
> We sing one common Lord; wherefore he should
>     Himself the candle hold.
> I will go searching, till I finde a sunne
>     Shall stay, till we have done;
> A willing shiner, that shall shine as gladly,
>     As frost-nipt sunnes look sadly.

Then we will sing, and shine all our own day,
　　　　And one another pay:
His beams shall cheer my breast, and both so twine,
Till ev'n his beams sing, and my musick shine.

　　　　　　　　　　　　　　　　　　　　(15–34)

The Christian poet is present at the Nativity the instant he says
"The shepherds sing," thinking perhaps of their "glorifying
and praising" in Luke 2:20. He is present as a competing
singer, since he identifies his soul as another shepherd whose
"flock" attests both to the complexity of the speaking "I" and
to the dependency of all on the Lord, who provides the pas-
tures and streams. Cleverly, the speaker rigs the competition
he sets up with the innocent shepherds: he must win with
praise sung not only in words but in thoughts and deeds as
well. As John T. Shawcross suggests, the second part of
"Christmas" "is concerned with the metaphor of the Christ
child as the sun of day."[12] But Herbert's pun on sun/son
enables the speaker to project his playful contest onto a screen
of heroic proportions—and to convey his exuberance. Looking
about for a worthier competitor, the Christian would not find
one since even the sun must stop its praise by giving way to
night. After the soul's trio of choristers scolds the undutiful
"shiner," the Christian will dash off to explore the heavens in
search of a more dependable sun, one who will last out the
everlasting song merited by the Incarnation. This glad endless
light found, the Christian images the universal harmony ringing so gloriously that sunbeams sing and music shines in a
resplendent hymn of adoration.

The Christian regenerates the centuries-distant past with a
fantasy that grows from a brief projection of himself into the
scene. He hears the shepherds sing, and that is all he needs to
fire his imagination and emotions. He experiences a keen
desire to give the joyful event the kind of praise it merits. For
that reason, he imagines himself as a celestial impresario,

12. John T. Shawcross, "Herbert's Double Poems: A Problem in the Text of
*The Temple*," in *"Too Rich to Clothe the Sunne": Essays on George Herbert*, ed.
Claude J. Summers and Ted-Larry Pebworth, p. 217. Shawcross does not
believe that "Christmas" is one two-part poem, and reviews the evidence on
pp. 217, 228n.

bringing back the best accompaniment for the joyful song. The Son's light may have been "contracted" for his stay on earth, but the expansive shepherd-singer would provide cheerful sunbeams for the duration of his lengthy praise. The Nativity becomes his own by his experience of the emotions that he thinks the actual scene would have evoked. It is inaccurate to say that his experience parallels that of the shepherds. He invents their song, judges it inadequate, and describes his plan to surpass it; he creates a past in which his presence is as real as that of the other participants. Imagination enables him through an out-of-time experience to shed the human limitations that would have frustrated his desire to praise as his heart dictated. The endlessly singing soul, flock, and sun seem prettily naive, but they clearly indicate both the personal and immediate and the universal and eternal praise that are the Redeemer's due.

Thus, the Christian speaker at once acknowledges and regenerates his inherited past. The various stances and perspectives he adopts in *The Temple* depend upon his awareness of the long and continuing bond between God and humanity. He takes for granted that his individual identity partakes of the age-old Christian community. The possibilities of his relationship with God have been defined by the history of mankind's dealing with the Creator, and his with them. Wishing to draw close to God, the Christian must discover—or recover—the personal significance of Biblical events and of God's interactions with his people.

\*     \*     \*

Lamenting the "Decay" of the world, the Christian recalls for God the ancient days when "One might have sought and found thee presently / At some fair oak, or bush, or cave, or well." "Sepulchre" and "Christmas" demonstrate how devout acts of imagination enable the speaker to participate in some of these long-past days. But this essential effort is reciprocal communication between God and man only in an indirect way. Typically, the Christian's part of the interaction with God is carried out in thought and deed, though prayer is his most straightforward method of communication. As we might expect, he reports his actions, meditates, and expresses emotions in poems addressing God. But Herbert portrays a relationship including one partner who is not seen or heard in any ordinary sense. His problem is to convey God's presence and his grace, his active but invisible participation in the Christian life.

Notwithstanding the cessation of miracles, there are various strategies by which Herbert succeeds in making his Lord manifest himself. The Father or the Son speaks an occasional word or favors the speakers of the poems with lengthier comments when they are warranted by the situation. The finally regularized rhyme in "Deniall" is an indication of God's presence. (Indeed, "The Quidditie" asserts that verse "is that which while I use / I am with thee, and *most take all*.") But in *The Temple* God most frequently *shows* himself in the natural world and in the Christian speaker's claims of divine participation in his inner life. The speaker assumes that nature conveys divine messages for man that can be interpreted in a plausible way. He also implies, by persistently iterated requests that God reform him, that the shadowy omnipresence constantly acts to improve him. His imperfections establish the need for God's action; his prayers assume that such action is possible and forthcoming. Overhearing such petitions, the reader must accept what the speaker takes for granted: his divine auditor's intervention in his life.

Usually, the Christian of *The Temple* does not dwell on fine descriptions of nature. Certainly he looks out on the large world to praise its Creator, but he considers nature mostly as a medium that expresses God, a means God uses to communicate with mankind. The speaker almost ignores "The Storm," for instance, except as a reminder of repentance:

> If as the windes and waters here below
> Do flie and flow,
> My sighs and tears as busie were above;
> Surely they would move
> And much affect thee, as tempestuous times
> Amaze poore mortals, and object their crimes.

(1–6)

The reader knows this is more than a windy little shower only because the Christian wishes his sighs and tears were as energetically flying and flowing upward. Though the link between storm and repentance seems to be a personal association made by the conscientious speaker, this interpretation does not outlast the stanza. Tempests remind and accuse "poor mortals" of their misdeeds and need of repentance. Because they convey a divine message and set in motion a vital spiritual process, they merit praise: "Poets have wrong'd poore storms: such dayes are best; / They purge the aire without, within the breast." The objective particularities of the storm occasioning the poem are so unimportant that, finally, the speaker makes no distinction between outer and inner weather. The natural occurrence and the spiritual condition it inspires are smooth cause and effect in the providential scheme. Often the speaker of *The Temple* thus treats the natural world as the Creator's eloquent countenance.

Most frequently, the active divine presence is implied by the Christian's assumption that God can respond to his petitions, as we see in "The Sinner":

> Lord, how I am all ague, when I seek
> > What I have treasur'd in my memorie!
> > Since, if my soul make even with the week,
> Each seventh note by right is due to thee.
> I finde there quarries of pil'd vanities,
> > But shreds of holinesse, that dare not venture
> > To shew their face, since crosse to thy decrees:
> There the circumference earth is, heav'n the centre.
> In so much dregs the quintessence is small:
> > The spirit and good extract of my heart
> > Comes to about the many hundred part.
> Yet Lord restore thine image, heare my call:
> > And though my hard heart scarce to thee can grone,
> > Remember that thou once didst write in stone.

Against the reader's expectations, a penitent addresses God. Until his final hopeful petition, the speaker (who casts himself successively as the heart's explorer, prospector, cartographer, and alchemist) is abashed and distressed. Self-examination sickens him. His fearful awareness of the law is implicit in the standards he sets for his soul. Searching for the acceptable fraction of treasure within the ore, he finds instead heaps of jaggedly destructive rock. To reserve one-seventh part of the soul for God may not seem an ambitious goal, but the Christian is chagrined to find no such reassuring (if legalistic) proportion. His fear of retribution and the correction of his mathematical approach are implicit in the light personification of the frightened shreds of his heart, which hide because they are opposed to God's decree: "Thou shalt love the Lord thy God with all thy heart, and with all thy soul, and with all thy mind" (Matthew 22:37).

The Christian's shocked need to admit his failings, to make a full confession, causes him to restate his findings three times, using different metaphors. Like a disheartened but grimly fascinated prospector, he assesses again and again the small worth of what he labored to extract and amass. Distillation no less than quarrying requires time and effort, but the speaker's exertions yield little. The demoralized failure turns for help to the power that once wrote on stone. The fearsome lawgiver is also the willing artist in stone: God is asked to hear, restore, and help. The petition asserts the faith that God will act to bring the penitent, though undeserving, back to himself. "The Sinner" is the loving partner who discovers he has unknowingly or unwillingly caused a rift. (As the title characterizes the speaker, it also defines a type: the Christian who treasures a heap of vanity, believing it a store of sanctity.)[13]

Sometimes, thanks to Herbert's sleight of hand, God has an appreciable effect on the Christian, and the reader must infer that the Almighty has acted in response to a petition. "Assurance" is of the same order of subtlety as "Deniall": it demonstrates that God answers prayers. Herbert uses a strategy of

13. In general, I agree with Barbara Leah Harman that "the attention . . . to inherited and shared meanings" should not and need not result in a "dismissive attitude . . . toward that origin of idiosyncratic meaning—the self" (*Costly Monuments: Representations of the Self in George Herbert's Poetry*, p. 28). But I think she overestimates the power of the past to transform "individuals into a collectivity" (p. 21) as well as the desirability of such a transformation from the Christian perspective. As my remarks indicate throughout, but especially on poems like "Christmas" and "The Sinner," the "collectivity" that is the Church, or the Christian community, does not deprive the individual self of its experience or of its particular perception of that experience.

inconsistency to persuade the reader that he witnesses God's grace, his intervention, within the poem. Initially, the speaker "exposes the insufficiency of [his] mind to its task and so argues for the necessity of revelation."[14] The first part of the poet's strategy is to dramatize the Christian's helplessness and ask for God's aid. The second part is to present a radically altered man, a sudden change that is inconsistent with the initial characterization. The inconsistency is a transformation explicable only in terms of divine influence. Though the poem clearly depicts two states, before and after prayer, it is wholly in the present tense as if the petitioner were unaware that his prayer has been answered even as he speaks it.

This poem, though "ready . . . to change direction or to modify attitudes," is not an example of what Vendler calls "the reinvented poem" (p. 25). Its point is precisely that the speaker himself cannot change direction or modify his attitude. When these things happen, the poem insists that the cause is responsive grace in action. The reader does not quite see God, but he is encouraged to conclude that the Deity has been present because of his effect on the speaker. God acts between the lines of Herbert's poem; he is responsible for the change that seems initially to be a simple inconsistency. Adopting Vendler's language, then, we might say that the poet sometimes presents a "reinvented speaker," reformed or reinvented (with new, improved features) by God.

Using a favorite tactic in "Assurance," the Christian isolates one of his troubling aspects and accords it an illusory independent status by personification. He thus acquires an antagonist and invests his self-criticism with drama. Indeed, the speaker's complexity is such that his inner world seems populated by argumentative warring factions that include despairs, devils, and pensiveness locked up, for the present, behind a psychic door. Written in the present tense, "Assurance" develops dramatically as a straightforward narrative, related entirely through the Christian's speeches to a thought, to God, and to the thought again. His antagonist is a "Spitefull bitter thought." He exclaims against this merciless foe who tortures

14. Stanley Fish, *The Living Temple: George Herbert and Catechizing*, p. 44.

and attempts to poison him as punishment for some misdeed. "Wit," a combatant for the speaker's side, is no match for the enemy-thought with his "rank poison." The first stanza ends with the substance of the thought unspecified but its effects clearly delineated.

Continuing in a tone of injured disbelief, the speaker discloses in the second stanza that he inveighs and struggles against his own doubt, created by a self-detected wrong. We learn that the antagonist-thought's fleering contradiction of yet other more sanguine thoughts opened the hostilities: "Thou said'st but even now, / That all was not so fair, as I conceiv'd, / Betwixt my God and me." His fragmented self-perception, extreme though it is, reflects a psychological actuality: valuing his "league" with God and needing to believe in its security, he is yet capable of threatening the relationship with misdeeds that produce doubts and insecurity. Turmoil and agitation surface from the conflict within:

> And what to this? what more
> Could poyson, if it had a tongue, expresse?
> What is thy aim? wouldst thou unlock the doore
> To cold despairs, and gnawing pensivenesse?
>     Wouldst thou raise devils? I see, I know,
>     I writ thy purpose long ago.
>
> (13–18)

The rapid and reproachful questions reflect the Christian's agitated helplessness before the rebellious thought—the speaking poison who might marshal formidable allies in the war against peace of mind. Doubt, a serious matter for the Christian at any time, is a grave threat when, uncontrolled, it gathers strength and wins the day; awareness of this menace underlies his self-reproach.

Against such a foe, the speaker's helplessness is pathetic. His only recourse is childlike: he responds to the bully's threat with a threat of his own:

> But I will to my Father,
> Who heard thee say it. O most gracious Lord,
> If all the hope and comfort that I gather,
> Were from my self, I had not half a word,

> Not half a letter to oppose
> What is objected by my foes.
>
> But thou art my desert:
> And in this league, which now my foes invade,
> Thou art not onely to perform thy part,
> But also mine; as when the league was made
> Thou didst at once thy self indite,
> And hold my hand, while I did write.
>
> (19–30)

Attacked by an inimical thought with strong allies in readiness, the speaker petitions his only ally for help in the conflict. The prayer begins with his denial of any ability on his part to oppose the enemy. Anxiety prompts him to remind God of the terms of their league: however threatened by his wrongdoing, the covenant dictates that the divine hope, comfort, merit, and power must be deployed on his behalf. The image of the divine hand clasped over the writing human hand (which unaided cannot muster "half a letter") insists on the Christian's utter powerlessness alone and alludes (by the pun on indite/indict) to the Son's voluntary death, which made possible the new league between God and man.[15] In the course of moving from his own helplessness to the Father's "part," the speaker's tone grows firmer; a stirring conviction rings through the traditional images affirming God's protective might (line 35). Herbert may have recalled Psalms 18:2: "The Lord is my rock, and my fortress, and my deliverer; my God, my strength, in whom I will trust; my buckler, and the horn of my salvation, and my high tower."

Finally, there is evidence that the beleaguered Christian's prayer has been answered:

> Now foolish thought go on,
> Spin out thy thread, and make thereof a coat
> To hide thy shame: for thou hast cast a bone
> Which bounds on thee, and will not down thy throat:

15. See Heather Asals (*Equivocal Predication*, p. 18) for her discussion of the pun's importance and for an entirely different perspective on "Assurance." See also Jane A. Wolfe, "George Herbert's 'Assurance,' " p. 213, for the view that the poem expresses "no turmoil or distress."

> What for it self love once began,
> Now love and truth will end in man.
>                    (37–42)

The speaker is more than insouciant now in addressing the formerly "bitterly spitefull thought." A jubilant and smug Wit figuratively demotes the enemy-thought, which becomes an embarrassed spider advised to spin itself a concealing cocoon. The Christian's taunts show how thoroughly his doubts have been choked: God has responded to his prayer for help. The reader may object that the man has simply reminded himself of God's promise and power, and so only defeated his own doubts. But the terms of the poem refute this objection: the problem is referred to God precisely because the speaker discounts his own ability to deal with it. The first three stanzas show the accuracy of this judgment. The speaker seems to sputter as he characterizes the thought in the first two lines of the poem. He does not argue or remonstrate; he can only complain, repeat the content of the thought, and complain again before he makes his appeal. Before his prayer, he does not fight his doubt with "half a word, not half a letter." When he tells God, "Thou art not onely to perform thy part, / But also mine," the reader understands why this is necessary. The Christian first demonstrates and then avows his inability to suppress his own doubts and fears. When they are nevertheless suppressed, the logical conclusion is that God has answered the petition even as it is being formulated. The poem creates the illusion that a supernatural event occurs in the space between the last two stanzas: God acts to transform helplessness and doubt into "Assurance."

Herbert's creation of meaning from the space between two lines is reminiscent of Donne's similarly suggestive technique in poems like "The Canonization." Herbert's task seems more difficult because he implies the action of grace, which "drops from above" so softly that its advent may be imperceptible even to the man it touches. To demonstrate that grace has an immediate and appreciable effect on its recipient, Herbert uses inconsistency—two contradictory aspects of the Christian speaker that are bridged by the prayer that summons grace. (In "Assurance," as we saw, the helpless victim of the first three

stanzas is transformed into the confident victor of the final
stanza.) The strategy first calls into question the reason for the
speaker's abrupt change and subsequently demonstrates that
his prayer is answered by grace. His inconsistency is not the
result of "second thoughts [that] are everywhere" in Herbert's
poems, nor is it an example of the "successive and often
mutually contradictory expressions of the self as it explores the
truth of feeling."[16] The poem's complexity is of another order.
Successive and contradictory aspects of character or perspective, "Assurance" shows, may reflect more than the poet's
chameleon mind.

When a request made in one poem is answered in another,
questions of inconsistency or self-contradiction are less likely
to arise. In fact, the reader's awareness of the relation of the
two poems helps to explain matters incapable of clarification
by close reading alone. Pairs of the prayer-and-response pattern in *The Temple* include "The Priesthood" and "Aaron,"
"Man" and "Providence," and "The Crosse" and "The
Flower." "Longing" and "The Bag" are among the most interesting because the second poem includes a detailed description of how prayers are conveyed to God.

"Longing" is one of the most powerful poems in *The Temple.*
It is an anatomy, a naming of parts, whose images reflect the
Christian's pain and sense of incoherence when he feels abandoned by God. Literally, his center does not hold: eyes, knees,
bones, heart, soul, and other members break their silence to
proclaim their individual agony. Curiously, the speaker's fragmentation causes him to perceive God similarly—as the breast
and the "Bowels of pitie" whose inattentive eye and ear are
very much in demand. The resultant impression of violence is
so forceful that "Longing" seems more diatribe than prayer.
But it is a prayer, imploring, angry, exasperated, and urgent:

> With sick and famisht eyes,
> With doubling knees and weary bones,
>                 To thee my cries,
>                 To thee my grones,
> To thee my sighs, my tears ascend:
>                         No end?

16. Vendler, *Poetry of George Herbert,* pp. 27, 56.

> My throat, my soul is hoarse;
> My heart is wither'd like a ground
>             Which thou dost curse.
>             My thoughts turn round,
> And make me giddie; Lord, I fall,
>             Yet call.

                        (1–12)

The hungering eyes, the hoarse soul and throat suggest that
we overhear the final portion of a prayer that has been going
on for some time. The Christian's detailed description of his
pitiable condition implicitly reproaches a Lord so merciless
that he ignores bones and throats almost worn out for his sake.
Fragmentation, belied by the constant *ababcc* rhyme scheme, is
reflected in the truncated, shorter lines. Together with the
repetition in the first stanza of "To thee my," these give growing emphasis to the impatient petitioner's offerings. The
speaker insists that his remarkable spiritual hardiness deserves a more responsive attitude by pointing out that though
he falls, he calls. A fall focuses the faller's attention upon
himself—in a manner entirely foreign to this selfless soul.

God is reminded, in the third and fourth stanzas of the
poem, of his putative pity, but he is also addressed as "Lord of
my soul, love of my minde": the Christian's distress and confusion are evident in his rapid changes of tone and attitude.
Self-commiseration, reminders to God of his merciful attributes, accusations thinly disguised as baffled questions,
straightforward accusations, and commands to God to hear,
look, and "mark well"—all jostle each other in this robust and
unceremonious prayer. The reader, involved as he must be by
the Christian's articulate sufferings, can only wonder what
causes them. The sufferer is reticent only about the "past" that
precedes his utterance:

> Look on my sorrows round!
> Mark well my furnace! O what flames,
>             What heats abound!
>             What griefs, what shames!
> Consider, Lord; Lord, bow thine eare,
>             And heare!

                        (25–30)

The cause of the Christian's distress is buried in his allusion to the furnace that figures in several Biblical passages, as in Isaiah 48:10, where it is the refining "furnace of affliction." God declares in Ezekiel 22:18–22 that "dross" and impurities demand strong measures: "As they gather silver, and brass, and iron, and lead, and tin into the midst of the furnace, to blow the fire upon it, to melt it; so will I gather you in mine anger and in my fury, and I will leave you there, and melt you" (22:20). The speaker's "shames" abound for a reason, however unspecified; he demands God's ear nevertheless, because he thinks he has been forgotten in the uncomfortable furnace. "Bow down thine eare" and variants such as the one above are also frequent in the Bible, but Herbert may especially have had in mind Psalm 31:2, whose context (31:9–10) includes: "Have mercy upon me, O Lord, for I am in trouble: mine eye is consumed with grief, yea, my soul and my belly. For my life is spent with grief, and my years with sighing: my strength faileth because of mine iniquity, and my bones are consumed." The allusions remind us that the Christian's condition and his reaction to it are personal without being unique— and inform us that he knows this without deriving comfort from it.

Because he fails to get results, the speaker grows more insistent. It seems unbelievable to him that Christ, who died for mankind, should now be dead to his prayer for relief. Having created the ear, should Christ now not listen? The heavenly silence exacerbates the Christian's condition. He moves from fragmentation to disintegration in the seventh stanza: reduced to a "pile of dust," he suffers such pain that each crumb of that dismembered pile entreats its silent Maker for help. But entreaty gives way to something different:

> To thee help appertains.
> Hast thou left all things to their course,
> And laid the reins
> Upon the horse?
> Is all lockt? hath a sinners plea
> No key?
>
> (43–48)

To help is his characteristic activity, God is reminded with a certain amount of asperity, unless he has suddenly left off doing his duty. The allusions referring the reader to the Bible put these reproaches in perspective without dulling them. Imminent catastrophe threatens, according to the image of the Deity as rider of the universal horse allowed to take its own subrational way. It is a measure of the Christian's despair that he questions whether the whole universe—and not only his inner world—is abandoned by controlling Providence. The image of locked doors, like that of the dropped reins, stresses the Deity's willful desertion of the frantic petitioner.

When there is no respite, the speaker's tone grows yet sharper as he contrasts God's situation with his own ill-used state. He is bitter about what is usually taken for granted: God reigns in his heaven regardless of what misfortunes befall his creatures. But this is a very personal reproach, meant to make the apparently indifferent Creator feel guilty for ignoring the sufferer who, despite this undeserved neglect, still considers himself God's "childe." "Lord, didst thou leave thy throne, / Not to relieve?" When the divine will to succor (which is grace) does not descend but stubbornly stays "on high," the Christian is baffled. Did not the Incarnation once bring and thereafter promise loving relief? Insisting that within himself sin is dead, the speaker cannot understand his cold treatment. Indeed, it is difficult to comprehend.

His "Longing" has continued for some time now. Clearly, prayers are not like the magic spells of childhood that produce instantaneous results. Grace has delayed for at least the duration of seventy-two lines before the Christian concludes:

> Lord JESU, heare my heart,
> Which hath been broken now so long,
> That ev'ry part
> Hath got a tongue!
> Thy beggars grow; rid them away
> To day.
>
> My love, my sweetnesse, heare!
> By these thy feet, at which my heart
> Lies all the yeare,
> Pluck out thy dart,

And heal my troubled breast which cryes,
                        Which dyes.
                          (73–84)

At the extremes of pain and fragmentation, the Christian begs
at the divine feet for the removal of the divine dart and pleads
with the tongues of the wounded, broken heart. Though he
ends on a note less aggressive than he has previously used, his
request is the same made throughout: "heare!" And God
hears. The first line of "The Bag" reveals that grace has inter-
vened at last—his petition has been answered: "Away despair!
my gracious Lord doth heare." George Ryley, anticipating
F. E. Hutchinson, remarks, "The Poem seems to be Connected
to the former. As tho' he had obtain'd an Answer to his prayer
in the Last."[17] Because it marks a victory over the despair so
well described in the preceding poem, "The Bag" is a happy
poem, though it concentrates eventually on the image of
Christ wounded on the Cross. But before this, there is a declaration of faith and a cheerful flight of fancy:

Away despair! my gracious Lord doth heare.
          Though windes and waves assault my keel,
          He doth preserve it: he doth steer,
          Ev'n when the boat seems most to reel.
          Storms are the triumph of his art:
Well may he close his eyes, but not his heart.

Hast thou not heard, that my Lord JESUS di'd?
          Then let me tell thee a strange storie.
          The God of power, as he did ride
          In his majestick robes of glorie,
          Resolv'd to light; and so one day
He did descend, undressing all the way.
                          (1–12)

The first stanza might be the Christian's answer to his own
question in "Longing": "Hast thou left all things to their
course, / And laid the reins / Upon the horse?" Without de-

17. John M. Heissler, ed., *Mr. Herbert's Temple & Church Militant Explained
and Improved . . .*, 2:505. I use Ryley's remarks on Herbert's poems because his
is the first systematic commentary on them and because his perspective is that
of an English Protestant writing about eighty-two years after the publication of
*The Temple*.

nying this or the other thoughts and feelings that almost overwhelmed him, the speaker affirms his faith in Providence by
the image of the pilot steering his craft through stormy seas.
The speaker has experienced, in the space between the last line
of "Longing" and the first line of "The Bag," the relief for
which he begged. He happily asserts that God preserved him
through the crisis.

Typically, the speaker lectures his own defeated despair.
After waving it away somewhat brusquely, he relaxes into
good humor and imagination in the second stanza. As though
to a child who can be quieted with a striking statement, despair
is told what it evidently did not know, that Jesus died. Its
attention secured, the adult promises it a strange tale, an apt
description of the myth that follows of the voluntary, pre-
Incarnation divesting of Christ's celestial glory. By tone and
manner, the speaker characterizes his past emotion as immature and irrational: how can anyone despair who knows that
Christ gave up glory to suffer and die for his sake? The poem is
a cheerful admission of the absurdity of asking "Lord, didst
thou leave thy throne / Not to relieve?"

The story the Christian tells himself is strange also because it
has no middle. From its beginning, the tale moves quickly to its
end. Christ's side is pierced by a spear, "And straight he
turn'd, and to his brethren cry'd":

> If ye have any thing to send or write,
>   I have no bag, but here is room:
>   Unto my Fathers hands and sight,
>   Beleeve me, it shall safely come.
>     That I shall minde, what you impart,
> Look, you may put it very neare my heart.
>
> Or if hereafter any of my friends
>   Will use me in this kinde, the doore
>   Shall still be open; what he sends
>   I will present, and somewhat more,
>     Not to his hurt. Sighs will convey
> Any thing to me. Harke, Despair away.
>                                               (31–42)

In his joyful frame of mind, the speaker outdoes himself when he imagines the wounded Christ speaking. No time elapses between the "Christ-side-piercing spear" and the Savior's inventive idea for the usefulness of his wound to his brothers. He promises not only to carry and deliver the messages but also to make his own helpful additions to them. "Is all lockt? hath a sinners plea / No key?" is the question "Longing" poses; "The Bag" states, and itself proves, that the door near Christ's heart is and has always been open to receive prayers whether they consist only of sighs or of bitter and unwarranted reproaches. Considering the unmannerly and irritable prayer of the Christian, it is a small miracle that it was answered, much less so quickly. Perhaps the additions and loving intercession that Christ promises account for the petitioner's success.

The link with "Longing" explains some of the problems raised by "The Bag." Helen Vendler remarks that, oddly, "death is simply not permitted to happen" in this poem and wonders, "How can this tranquil narrative be reconciled with Herbert's expressed need for a medicine against despair? Where, for that matter, has his despair gone?"[18] The Christian complained in "Longing" that God was dead to his pleas (lines 31–34); now he realizes that Christ is not and never was dead to those who belong to him, certainly not when he was on the Cross. The speaker's despair has evaporated. Just as "Longing" is a thing of the past as soon as the reader turns to "The Bag," the Christian's despair is a thing of the immediate past. There is no need of a remedy—the remedy was given when God heard his prayer, in the instant before "The Bag" opens with "Away despair!" With these words, the speaker jauntily brushes aside the now-inappropriate emotion. His exempla enable him to correct the criticism implied in "Longing" that Christ fails to keep the promise of the Incarnation and Crucifixion. They dramatize scenes whose imaginary details emphasize the true and joyful implications, for himself, of the actual events. The poem is a celebration of grace and an exuberant jeu d'esprit inspired by the speaker's rediscovery that he is loved.

\*     \*     \*

18. Vendler, *Poetry of George Herbert*, pp. 175, 176.

George Herbert knew the power of shared expressions of faith to encourage and strengthen the individual heart:

> Though private prayer be a brave designe,
> Yet publick hath more promises, more love:
> And love's a weight to hearts, to eies a signe.
> We all are but cold suitours; let us move
>     Where it is warmest. Leave thy six and seven;
>     Pray with the most: for where most pray, is heaven.
>
>                              ("The Church-porch," 397–402)

His poetry aims to spark or rekindle the reader's awareness of his spiritual status and to alert him to the active presence of God in his life. Just as the whole history of the Christian community with God belongs to the speaker of *The Temple,* so Herbert indicates that the action of grace discernible in his experience is available to all. In this sense, "the 'I' of 'The Church' [is] the voice of One Man who is every man"; [19] consequently, it imparts valuable insight to others engaged in the Christian life. When Herbert uses the Christian's inconsistency within a poem and the consecutive placement of related poems to suggest God's participation in the speaker's life, he means not to imply that these are singular occurrences, but to remind or instruct the reader of the power available to him through prayer. In "The Storm," the speaker assumes that the weather has a directive for him—and for all others. Though the tempestuous sign is from God, the poem cannot be described as a personal communication. "Ungratefulnesse" is not a personal poem either, but a meditation on the timeless and characteristic human attitude toward God.

In spite of the inescapable typicality of his experience, however, the Christian has a personal relationship with God. The homage of "Christmas" represents his individual response to God's great gift. "The Sinner" suggests a type, but is also the Christian speaker standing ashamed before God. He depends on the power that inscribed stone tablets ages ago, but he prays for help now, in his present situation. At all times "The Bag" conveys petitions to the Creator from all Christians, but it also serves the speaker in his present experience of

19. Asals, "Voice of 'The Church,' " p. 516.

desolate "Longing." As Herbert depicts it, the Christian life is a unity of the personal and the communal, the particular and the typical, the immediate and the timeless.

# 3

# Self-Observation and Constant Creation

*The Temple* presents the praiseworthy and lovable nature of God, the nature and condition of man (which is to say, his need of God), and the relationship of man and God. In any poem one of these general subjects may predominate, but usually two or all three are treated together. Repeatedly, the poems broach these concepts and enliven them as the assumptions, insights, or struggles of one man: *The Temple* records the unfolding history of the protagonist who dominates the book. Furthermore, "we see another (even more dominant) figure" through him: God appears "very much as the beloved woman appears in . . . courtly lyrics, characterized indirectly, via the reactions of the protagonist."[1] Though other persons are briefly and infrequently mentioned, the world of *The Temple* is inhabited chiefly by two characters, the Christian speaker and God. Their drama is sharply focused: they pore over the man's constantly changing heart and their relationship. Because the zealous speaker laments or reveals his human flaws so often and so vividly, we may overlook the magnification of the Christian implicit in the dramatic situation of the volume. Vitalizing the concept of the personal Savior, God watches closely over this person's life, participating in it as if the sometimes-obstreperous creature were truly the apple of his eye, the one soul he cherishes and wants to take to himself. Since dramatic interaction between God and man characterizes Her-

1. Elizabeth Stambler, "The Unity of Herbert's 'Temple,' " pp. 253, 252. Stambler identifies some of the other similarities between Herbert's book and volumes of courtly love poetry in this article. See also Joseph H. Summers, "From 'Josephs coat' to 'A true Hymne,' " p. 11: "Herbert seems to have conceived of the entire volume as a living, changing image of the divine art of love."

bert's poetry, the theological concepts most emphasized in *The Temple* are grace and charity.

The exposition of the kind of interaction possible between a divine and a human personality, and of the nature of their loving relationship, started in the preceding chapter with the appearance of grace, God's participation in the Christian life. As soon as his actions are represented as correlating to the Christian's particular situation, their relationship is authenticated as interactive. When God does not act with specific reference to the speaker, the Christian acts and the relationship develops and progresses accordingly. Its dramatic impetus is usually provided by the human partner. Reflecting on his actions or spiritual condition, he also infers (and brings into play) God's attitudes or his reactions to the immediate circumstances. Since most of the noteworthy things that "happen" in this relationship occur within the speaker's heart and mind, it follows that he must analyze himself often and fully: that is how he experiences the relationship and determines its status. Self-scrutiny, for example, disclosed in "The Sinner" the offense against God and revealed the disinterested character of the love the speaker receives. Whether the Christian examines his conscience or remarks on man's fallen nature, self-analysis is imperative. The special conditions and limitations of private interaction between God and himself explain his frequent inwardness. His heart and mind are love's primary field of action; self-analysis enables him to apprehend and to conduct his personal relationship with God.

This chapter continues the analysis of grace and charity in *The Temple* with special emphasis on the character of the divine and human lovers and of their relationship. These topics are explored in the context of poems that enable us, at the same time, to observe two of Herbert's heuristic strategies: title-linked poems and the dispersed poetic sequence. These matters lay the foundation for our approach in subsequent chapters to the lengthy narrative sequence related to Herbert's choice of vocation.

\*     \*     \*

Many poems in *The Temple* indicate Herbert's interest in

emotional variability and justify Aldous Huxley's description
of him as the poet of "inner weather."[2] "The Temper" (I)
theorizes about what the speaker could do "if what my soul
doth feel sometimes / My soul might ever feel!" "The Temper"
(II) begins: "Where is that mightie joy / Which just now took
up all my heart?" Observation of his joys, griefs, and emotional fluctuations allows the Christian speaker to determine the
quality of his relation to God and helps him to maintain his
spiritual health. "The Familie" demonstrates the curious state
of affairs that makes self-observation vital. The reader might
expect the poet to record the emotions attendant upon an
experience or insight. Often, however, the speaker reverses
this cause-effect sequence: he feels the emotions and then
reads them for what they indicate about his standing with
God:

> What doth this noise of thoughts within my heart,
>     As if they had a part?
> What do these loud complaints and puling fears,
>     As if there were no rule or eares?
>
> But, Lord, the house and familie are thine,
>     Though some of them repine.
> Turn out these wranglers, which defile thy seat:
>     For where thou dwellest all is neat.
>
>                     (1–8)

The speaker's initial questions unmistakably place the responsibility for the inner state of affairs with the owner and paterfa-
milias of the house. In "Christmas," the more self-possessed
Christian asserted, "My soul's a shepherd too; a flock it feeds /
Of thoughts, and words, and deeds." But when the thoughts,
complaints, and fears, some of the family, are troublesome, he
disclaims any ties with them, let alone the title of responsible
caretaker. His surprise and mild annoyance cast him in the role
of a boarder dismayed to find he has moved in with a rambunc-
tious family lacking paternal discipline. Since he does not hint
at the cause of the family's clamoring, the reader cannot evalu-
ate this denial of responsibility. Nevertheless, the speaker

2. Aldous Huxley is quoted by Helen Gardner in her introduction to *The
Poems of George Herbert*, p. xv.

thinks the current status of his relationship with God is disclosed by the din; it also causes him to bring into play what he supposes, under the circumstances, to be his Lord's attitude toward himself. The clamor means that God cannot possibly be close, in residence; the Master rejects the unattractive man, abandons him when "All is [not] neat."

As the poem progresses, the Christian describes God's dwelling (as he imagines it), in which live discipline, order, beauty, harmony, obedience, and joys. It is almost idle to inquire whether he describes a preconceived ideal or what happens to his own heart even as he describes it. In the process, he forgets his immediate past, remarking that griefs are in God's dwelling as often as joys—though they are strangely silent:

> This is thy house, with these it doth abound:
> > And where these are not found,
> Perhaps thou com'st sometimes, and for a day;
> > But not to make a constant stay.
>
> (21–24)

The downcast speaker wants constant perfection within to secure God's perpetual residence. Obviously, he does not understand several things: he cannot *merit* the indwelling presence; his wishes are unattainable in this life; and God does not desert him though his thoughts and fears are loud. He has yet to approach the insights of "Bitter-sweet," in which he tells his "deare angrie Lord," "I will complain, yet praise; / I will bewail, approve."

Though mistaken in his conclusions, the Christian assumes that his emotions enlighten him about his standing with God. Self-observation enables him to seek help and thereby to control immediately the distress that causes him yet more distress. Even in the first stanza, in which the noisy thoughts just then unsettle the heart, the rhymed couplets contradict claims of serious disorder. Like "Longing," "The Familie" suggests an unacknowledged order at work. As Joseph Summers remarks in another context, a paradox underlies "all the poems concerning grief and disorder and the sense of God's absence: if the experience were absolute, poetry would be impossible; so long as the poet can create a poem, he remembers or imagines or believes in or anticipates or is inspired by an order and value which reflect the divine."[3]

Self-analysis can also alert the Christian to hidden problems in his relationship with the Divine. "The Size" demonstrates how his preconceived idea of what is proper for the faithful compels him to monitor his emotions. It represents self-analysis in the sense that he confronts and contends with discontent about his status, but along the way he reveals an underlying resentment against God:

> Content thee, greedie heart.
> Modest and moderate joyes to those, that have
> Title to more hereafter when thy part,
>                         Are passing brave.
>         Let th' upper springs into the low
>         Descend and fall, and thou dost flow.
>
>         What though some have a fraught
> Of cloves and nutmegs, and in cinamon sail;
> If thou hast wherewithall to spice a draught,
>                         When griefs prevail;
>         And for the future time art heir
>         To th' Isle of spices, is't not fair?
>
>                                   (1–12)

At Cambridge University in the seventeenth century, a *size* was a specific serving portion of ale or bread.[4] The Christian wants more joy but almost manages to hide his dissatisfaction by lecturing his heart as if it were a self-indulgent child asking for yet more sweets. The problem he airs is serious: the justification for a life that is more grief than joy. Though he knows the answer already, faith in his blissful future does not satisfy as he reasons patiently with his present appetite for more joy. His envious glance at others' portions and the question of fairness reveal a buried complaint; the underlying conflict is with God's seemingly unjust management.

3. Summers, "From 'Josephs coat,' " p. 4.
4. For the interpretation of *size* as a Cambridge portion, I am indebted to Amy M. Charles (see *OED* 1.7). In the context of the poem, this denotation is more appropriate and precise than Hutchinson's gloss: "a modest status" (*Works*, p. 525).

From the first, the poem does not really progress. Each stanza seems self-sufficient, stating the problem and supplying its appropriate resolution. Yet the Christian goes on, with each restatement enabling us to gauge the depth of his dissatisfaction. To deal with the question of God's seeming unfairness, he reminds himself in the third stanza that the Son "was hungrie here," but the first reminder does not suffice. The fifth stanza finds him declaring, "Thy Saviour sentenc'd joy, / And in the flesh condemn'd it as unfit, / At least in lump." The controlling metaphor of supplemental foodstuffs (spices, cake, and sweet lumps) underlines his knowledge that joy is nourishing only in moderation, classifies his desire for it as an appetite that, like others, requires control, and more than grants it its delicious appeal.

The second stanza, given above, referred enviously to "some" as vessels laden with a fragrant cargo of present delights, and the final stanza returns to that strand of imagery:

> Then close again the seam,
> Which thou hast open'd: do not spread thy robe
> In hope of great things. Call to minde thy dream,
> An earthly globe,
> On whose meridian was engraven,
> *These seas are tears, and heav'n the haven.*

Striving still to reconcile himself to "A Christians state and case," the speaker assures himself that the vessel is more important than its cargo and that his eventual arrival at the port can be expedited not by the joy he craves but by the grief he disdains. Altogether, he accomplishes self-reprimand and a measure of reassurance, but not resolution of his problem. His heart's desire for a full portion of joy must be frustrated so long as he sails toward his haven. Nevertheless, observation and analysis of his inward self enable him to uncover and dissipate his anger toward God's supposed unfairness by reminding himself of the example he should emulate. Finally, the balance of "content and care" is less a restrictive formula than a pattern of spiritual health against which to examine and adjust his own condition.

The emotions merit observation for other reasons as well. Despondency can interfere with the steadfastness of faith or with the worship of God. In the two linked pairs that follow, though the Christian is unhappy about his changeable feelings, he assumes that his emotions can be useful to him and that God often commands them. If God sometimes intervenes or participates in the Christian's life by commanding his feelings, it follows that they reveal his intentions. Though often significant, however, the shifting feelings are still troublesome and unsettling. They are as capable of misleading the careless man as of disclosing divine intentions or yielding personal insights. Consequently, the poems also consider the question of mastering the emotions.

It is a commonplace that Herbert's poems complement one another, that the explication of one poem often depends on the reading of another, and that one poem may function as a corrective to another. In other words, insights or conclusions drawn from some poems in *The Temple* may by themselves be incomplete or inaccurate. Only when these poems are linked with others and read together do their full meanings emerge. The relatedness of two or more poems is sometimes suggested by their titles, the importance of which Herbert characteristically stresses. For example, "Mans medley," inaccurate and incomplete in itself, and "Josephs coat," its complement by correction and completion, are related in the first place by their titles. *Medley* means "a cloth woven with wools of different colours or shades" as well as "a combination, mixture" (*OED*), so one correspondence between the two poems is evident.[5] This link alone might be insignificant, but both also deal with the extremities of joy and grief. The image of a multicolored fabric refers to other subjects in each, but to man's variable emotions in both poems. A reading of the two suggests that the poet uses designedly flawed poems to present most cogently the distressing state of the Christian who is not in

5. This correspondence is confirmed also by Mary Ellen Rickey's suggestion that "Josephs coat" "denotes not only the parti-colored nature of life, and the Old Testament type of Christ's body torn to give joy, but also the motley of the fool" ("Herbert's Fool for Christ's Sake: A Note on 'Josephs coat,' " p. 58). The *OED* lists *motley* as one meaning of *medley*.

harmony with God, who has yet to achieve the more adequate understanding that the linked, rectifying poems reflect.[6]

"Mans medley" is an impersonal review of the Christian Everyman's dual nature and extreme emotions. The speaker, pondering the problem of a consistent reference to God in spite of potentially disruptive feelings, speaks with a disanimated resignation even when he refers to present and future joys. The sobering thought of death depreciates what the world can offer and makes it impossible for him to rise to cheerfulness even when his meditation leads him to a colossal image of man, "with th' one hand touching heav'n, with th' other earth." His perspective simply does not allow for an appealing particularization of earthly joy:

> Not that he may not here
> Taste of the cheer,
> But as birds drink, and straight lift up their head,
> So he must sip and think
> Of better drink
> He may attain to, after he is dead.

> (19–24)

The sprightly image of birds' heads bobbing quickly after minuscule sips of water is at odds with the Christian's somber tone. Earthly "cheer" he sees as a potential trap unless it serves as an opportunity for spiritual improvement. Man should control dangerous joy by using it to aid in imagining the superior joy he hopes to attain.

The speaker's expressive power improves when he turns to grief. With conviction, he describes man's outer and inner winters, the latter blowing thoughts so frosty they sting his lip to numbness. Fearing two deaths, the Everyman is plagued by griefs and pains. But the trouble the Christian describes *is*

6. See Stanley Fish, *The Living Temple: George Herbert and Catechizing*. Fish there refers to individual poems that draw "from the reader a completing, or correcting, or, in some cases, a mistaken, response. That response is given not simply at the end of the poem but at every moment in it" (p. 27). My argument is that entire poems sometimes require "completing or correcting," that Herbert himself undertakes the task in subsequent poems, and that he marks his objective with some correspondence between the "flawed" and the correcting poems.

double, and his frigid seasons are only half of it. The final
stanza reveals the more serious trouble:

> Yet ev'n the greatest griefs
> May be reliefs,
> Could he but take them right, and in their wayes.
> Happie is he, whose heart
> Hath found the art
> To turn his double pains to double praise.

Uncontrolled spiritual troubles prevent praise by creating a
turmoil that rivets the Christian's attention on himself. Caused
by grief in the first place, "the inability to praise is [itself] a
source of grief because praise is the only mandated sacrifice"
under the New Covenant.[7] Wistfully, the Christian suggests
that sorrow might be given purpose and pressed into God's
service. Theoretically, properly understood griefs should be a
relief because they indicate the griever's concern for his soul.
Pains should occasion praise since God is the source of all
curative (and hence desirable) feelings. No wonder the Christian is dispirited—what he suggests is well-nigh impossible.
Surely, it is an incredible feat of emotional repression or mental
contortion to feel relief in the experience of grief and to respond to pain not naturally, with groans, but with praise. The
reader can only agree that the man who achieves that para-
doxical art is fortunate indeed.

The speaker of "Josephs coat" is that happy man. Here are
the intense emotions of "Mans medley" and the same idea of
their utility, but with a difference:

> Wounded I sing, tormented I indite,
> Thrown down I fall into a bed, and rest:
> Sorrow hath chang'd its note: such is his will,
> Who changeth all things, as him pleaseth best.
>    For well he knows, if but one grief and smart
> Among my many had his full career,
> Sure it would carrie with it ev'n my heart,
> And both would runne untill they found a biere
>    To fetch the bodie; both being due to grief.

---

7. John R. Mulder, "George Herbert's *The Temple:* Design and Methodology," p. 38.

But he hath spoil'd the race; and giv'n to anguish
One of Joyes coats, ticing it with relief
To linger in me, and together languish.
　　I live to shew his power, who once did bring
　　My *joyes* to *weep,* and now my *griefs* to *sing.*

The Christian's initial disbelief and subsequent wonder—as he
describes the paradoxes of conflicting emotions in coexistence
and of responses happily inappropriate to their stimuli—are
perfectly understandable. He experiences relief in grief and
expresses pain as praise, the unlikely conjunctions mentioned
at the conclusion of "Mans medley." But such a feat is not a
matter of ignoring feelings or transforming them, somehow,
into their opposites. It is *God's* art to combine contradictory
feelings so that they coexist and yet paradoxically retain their
particular character. He—not the speaker—uses joy to relieve
but not to eradicate anguish, so that the anguish lingers, purging but not destroying his child. Believing this, the suffering
speaker gratefully praises the Father's evident love, part of
which he experiences as the agony of chastisement, part as the
joy of relief. The title of the poem, then, refers to the Christian's diverse emotions; it alludes to God's fatherly love, which
motivates him to curb potentially destructive emotions with
the gift of joy.

Especially toward the end of the sonnet, the speaker's fervent gladness may cause the reader to underestimate his
wounds and torments. Herbert provides, with characteristic
subtlety, evidence of distress in the first quatrain of the sonnet:
with its *abc* endwords, it graphically illustrates the inditer's
weakness. With his awareness of God's mercy, he achieves
rhyme (*abcb*), which becomes regular (*abab*) in the succeeding
quatrains and final couplet. Moreover, the reality of sorrow is
emphasized by its light personification: the discordant groaner
becomes a harmonious singer. Before its conversion to song,
sorrow was a brawny racer hastening its burden of body and
soul (with the help of the willing heart) to the grave. The
transformative agent between its two identities is the God-
given coat, for God is no less active in the poem than sorrow.
He "changes," "knows," "spoils," "gives," "tices," "brings,"

and, most of all, seizes from the grasp of killing grief the Christian speaker who lives "to shew his power."

Herbert links the two poems to emphasize the threat to the heart from uncontrolled joy or grief that usurps the place of spiritual concerns. The emotions are mastered by referring them to God, who sends and uses them for his creature's welfare. Every joy and sorrow has its purpose. Man's part, Herbert suggests, is to understand that purpose as best he can and to praise the love and will thus revealed. These insights may be inferred from both poems, but each conveys them in a significantly different fashion. The first posits a difficult ideal, which depends finally on a paradox ("Happie is he, whose heart / Hath found the art / To turn his double pains to double praise"); the second shows the experiential validity of the paradox and demonstrates the effortless attainment of the ideal—with God's grace. In retrospect, then, "Mans medley" is shown to be inaccurate and incomplete, "Josephs coat" to complement it by correction and completion. The dejection of the first poem is due to the speaker's incomplete perspective. His observations refer only to what the Christian should do; they do not refer to what God might do, so they seem impossible to achieve, and his outlook is correspondingly dismal. Vis-à-vis "Josephs coat," the central purpose of "Mans medley" is to dramatize human deficiencies, which are fearful before the stringent requirements of Christianity. Only in the context of these deficiencies can God's all-sufficient love and power be fully apprehended.

Another pair of poems with an analogous relationship is "The Glimpse" and "The Glance," which refer respectively to the speaker's short look at delight and to God's brief glance that results in recurring delight. *Glimpse* also means "a momentary shining," while *glance* can mean "a flash or gleam of light" (*OED*); thus, delight is the ray of light relieving the speaker's dark grief in both poems. Though their titles suggest that the poems focus on transitory delight, they attend as carefully to the consequences of sin. The two describe the inconstant joy, define its particular purposefulness, and offer the Christian consolation for the brevity of delight amid a fairly persistent sorrow. As he did in "Mans medley" and "Josephs coat," Herbert uses these poems not only to expand on the same subjects, but also to dramatize a problem in the first and to present its solution by God's grace in the second. This development is expressed as a growth of the speaker's understanding. "The Glimpse" articulates his powerlessness, but "The Glance" describes his awareness of the divine power that acts to protect him.

The success of "The Glimpse" is due to the nuances of the speaker's polite conversational tone as he states his rueful case, or, rather, his heart's case. There are three distinct characters here, the speaking "I," his heart, and the departing delight. The latter is addressed with elaborate courtesy, though the Christian chides it, pointing out the unfairness and unseemliness of its brief visit:

> Whither away delight?
> Thou cam'st but now; wilt thou so soon depart,
>  And give me up to night?
> For many weeks of lingring pain and smart
> But one half houre of comfort to my heart?
>
>  Me thinks delight should have
> More skill in musick, and keep better time.
>  Wert thou a winde or wave,
> They quickly go and come with lesser crime:
> Flowers look about, and die not in their prime.
>
> (1–10)

His manners do not fail the surprised and affronted host. Nevertheless, he is shaken: after his plaintive reference to "me," the speaker attributes his fears and needs to his heart, as if he were merely the spokesman for this less articulate friend. The voice is so gentle as it mildly teases the intractable delight that the reader may minimize the situation. Trying hard to stay happy even as he feels the mood leaving him, the Christian reasons with himself that his lengthy pain deserves a more extended delight. Beneath the courtly accents, he accuses delight as an ungraciously hurrying guest, an incompetent timekeeper, and (consequently) an unskilled musician; moreover, it has unnatural, irregular, and foolish habits.

Subsequently, the delinquent is told that it is an antidote that soon worsens the condition it was meant to alleviate. Such cruelty to a heart so loyal that it has lived on crumbs of hope seems callous, though the reader understands delight has comforted and given hope. The heart is pitiful because it is more trusting than the pessimistic speaker, who "foretold this" turn of events. "A slender thread a gentle guest will tie," responds the heart, whose proverbial naivete gains him nothing:

> Yet if the heart that wept
> Must let thee go, return when it doth knock.
>     Although thy heap be kept
> For future times, the droppings of the stock
> May oft break forth, and never break the lock.
>                    (21–25)

The Christian's gentle, persuasive charm gives way to accommodation. Delight is asked to come again often when the heart seeks it and to allow an occasional tidbit to escape from its locked trunk, whose contents are reserved for the future. The final stanza reveals that the speaker's resignation is laced with apprehension about the "lingring" guests who threaten to arrive in the wake of joy's departure. Pains, weeping, grief, and the sin that summons them "disturb the work" of the speaker, no longer hiding wittily behind his ironically treated "heart." The image of the spinning wheel suggests that the turmoils he anticipates endanger his life—and also the life of his heart. Powerlessness is the lot of the host who must receive guests who come or go at will. He can control neither the sustaining delight nor its threatening opposites. Intensely conscious of an essential need, the Christian can only plead, "O make me not their sport, / Who by thy coming may be made a court!"

When we turn to "The Glance," we see that the Christian generalizes about what past experiences (like the one recorded in "The Glimpse") have enabled him to understand. The poem explains why his hope for relief is justified. His recurring need for nourishing portions of joy has been satisfied ever since God looked on him, he remembers, and potentially perilous situations have actually revealed God's power and love:

> When first thy sweet and gracious eye

Vouchsaf'd ev'n in the midst of youth and night
To look upon me, who before did lie
        Weltring in sinne;
   I felt a sugred strange delight,
Passing all cordials made by any art,
Bedew, embalme, and overrunne my heart,
        And take it in.

   Since that time many a bitter storm
My soul hath felt, ev'n able to destroy,
Had the malicious and ill-meaning harm
        His swing and sway:
   But still thy sweet originall joy,
Sprung from thine eye, did work within my soul,
And surging griefs, when they grew bold, controll,
        And got the day.

   If thy first glance so powerfull be,
A mirth but open'd and seal'd up again;
What wonders shall we feel, when we shall see
        Thy full-ey'd love!
   When thou shalt look us out of pain,
And one aspect of thine spend in delight
More then a thousand sunnes disburse in light,
        In heav'n above.

For all its help, delight might have come fortuitously in "The Glimpse," but in grateful and wondering retrospection, the speaker asserts that joy's timely appearance is due not to chance but to God's protective love. Herbert pictures sinful griefs and God's loving delight in liquid images that stress a tremendous power condensed to compactness. God's restorative delight is a cordial "sprung from thine eye"—Herbert distinguishes between the true *Lachryma Christi* and that mentioned in Thomas Coryate's 1611 *Crudities* (see *OED*). The drops of sweet red wine are potent: they overrun and take in (rather than being taken in by) the Christian's heart; they calm the surging seas of grief and sin. Most remarkably, the permanent gift of joy continues to work though time has elapsed since it was given. As if it were magic, it works when it is needed, for this is not unbroken delight but a foretaste of what will be "in heav'n above." Though the speaker has still felt dark storms, he looks forward to the day of a thousand suns. The Christian, defenseless against the consequences of his own shortcomings, is not defenseless at all. He gratefully acknowledges that he is protected by God's love and power.

Herbert uses these title-related poems to present a grim situation in its most acceptable form and to reveal the opera- tion of God's love where it might be difficult to see. Both poems depict the Christian's life as primarily pain and sorrow, relieved only by momentary delight, yet justify this state of affairs and offer a consolation for it. Sin causes the speaker's unhappiness. With its disturbing consequences, it could dev- astate the soul, so powerless is the Christian to govern his emotions. If he can survive the assaults of sin and pain, he believes his future holds the heavenly "heap" of delight. For the present, his heart lives only because he manages to catch a few glimpses of delight. This much can be learned from "The Glimpse." "The Glance" is its complement because it stresses the same ideas and because Herbert stretches the Christian's (and the reader's) understanding, enabling him to discover the love and mercy tempering justice. The source of the fleeting delight that unfailingly protects the helpless Christian from a justified destruction is God. Unable himself to attain the res- torative and sustaining joy, he is protected by God's power. Seen in this light, the joy whose evanescence has been cause for sadness in "The Glimpse" is made mighty and significant: what seemed an accidental and meager respite from sorrow is proof of God's great love for the undeserving man.

Once again, the first poem of the linked pair characterizes the powerlessness of the Christian to obtain what he needs. The second corrects that characterization by showing that grace, the protective power of God, acts on his behalf. In both of the linked pairs, the second poems rectify but do not sup- plant or invalidate the earlier ones, in which Herbert gives his reader an accurate depiction of the human condition as it is before the full meaning of its relation to God is realized.

As a thematic group, the six poems above offer a coherent interpretation of joy and sorrow. There are two kinds of grief. The first is salutary, the inevitable "care" the Christian experiences because he is like "a pretender, not a bride"—because his great object of reaching heaven is not certain. The second, the sorrow resulting from the Christian's sin, can be dangerous because it can prevent praise (as "Mans medley" points out) and because it can actually destroy the heart it visits. "Josephs coat," "The Glimpse," and "The Glance" all refer to the destruction wrought by powerful feeling when it is not controlled. But the Christian can try to control grief and, even more, to make its power beneficent by understanding its cause and source. If he can achieve this, repentant sorrow will occasion praise of God. It is God, of course, who uses and controls the emotion within man for his own purposes: sorrow's function is to purge the heart. God controls its potential devastation simply by sending joy to relieve the troubled spirit. Herbert's Christian speaker reads these meanings in his intermittent experiences of grief.

He interprets joy or delight according to the same twofold classification that he uses for grief. The world's joy is sometimes innocent, but even then, the Christian states in "The Size" and "Mans medley," its attraction can be dangerous. He wishes to use earthly joy as an impetus to imagine and hope for the real bliss attainable only in heaven. Rather than worldly joy, however, Herbert's poems refer more often to the joy whose only source is God. The transience of this joy grieves the Christian, who would like to feel constant delight, but this fleeting emotion is God's occasional gift to relieve the just suffering of the imperfect man. He understands that God uses it to comfort him for past anguish, to keep his heart from destruction, and to give him hope. There are love and significance even in its brevity: "a bit [of joy] Doth tice us on to hopes of more." In these poems, as in "The Bunch of Grapes," the Christian knows that fleeting joy will become perfect and eternal in the next life. He interprets present joy as the means by which God reveals himself and carries out his loving purpose.

What Herbert suggests about joy and grief is not original, and his preoccupation with them is not unusual. Seventeenth-century preachers continually emphasized the divine origin and purposes of happiness and affliction.[8] No modern-day analysand was ever more convinced of the life-or-death importance of his self-scrutiny than the Christian who believed that his emotions were not random or inexplicable, but directed by God to test or punish, to relieve or sustain. The six poems discussed above are only a few of many portrayals in *The Temple* of a man trying to control his potentially destructive emotions or to interpret the meaning of the feelings that come and go, with the conviction that what he seeks is ultimately God's meaning.

Each of the poems cited above—indeed, most of the poems in *The Temple*—contributes to an understanding of one person or the other in the human-divine relationship. Unfairly but inevitably, poems such as "Sepulchre" and "Ungratefulnesse" suggest and emphasize the obvious contrasts between God and man. The immediacy with which God acts in response to the Christian's petitions and needs characterizes him as accessible and lovingly responsive. That he acts at all after the speaker's whining prayer in "Longing" shows a mighty forbearance. In the group of poems that feature the Christian's self-scrutiny, God's power is emphasized. He achieves what is impossible for his human partner: control of the curative or destructive emotions. A stern but protective deity, he is intent on the preservation and improvement of his creature.

Fresh evidence continually reminds Herbert's reader of how undeserving man is, despite his best efforts, of divine love. Certainly, "The Sinner" and "Assurance" reveal some of the traits that make the Christian less than a desirable lover. Though he cares about his alliance with God, he jeopardizes it by sin. After he incurs divine displeasure and suffers the fears created by his own actions, he expects God to rush to his aid. When divine assistance does not come immediately, the impatient Christian often lapses into injured complaints and, worse, into doubts that God keeps his promises. In "Longing," he throws a self-pitying tantrum to make the lover he

8. See Charles H. and Katherine George, *The Protestant Mind of the English Reformation, 1570–1640*, pp. 109–10.

accuses of indifference feel guilty. Inconstant and distrustful himself, he expects constant love—and gets it.

The poems treated in this chapter highlight the Christian's helpless and dependent condition. He cannot control his feelings though they interfere with his pious duties or his heavenly goal. He yearns for more joy than God gives him and, very naturally, wishes he could avoid sorrow, however beneficial. Self-observation is vital to the Christian, who must beware of his own dangerous nature and inclinations. Understood as manifestations of his spiritual condition, his emotions alert him to submerged problems. Self-analysis is imperative because it keeps the Christian in touch with himself as it keeps him in touch with God. Further discussion of the human and the divine natures, and of the character of the love between God and the Christian, will follow a reading of the "constant creation" sequence of poems, which is relevant to these topics.

\*     \*     \*

Anyone who reads "The Altar," "The Sacrifice," "The Thanksgiving," and "The Reprisall" understands that Herbert encourages the reader to ascribe meaning not only to individual poems but also to their relationship with one another. "Longing" and "The Bag" are linked, like those initial poems, by a position relative to one another that proves significant because the second poem is a continuation of, or a development that follows from, the first. This continuation or development, rather than mere juxtaposition, designates a significant poetic relationship in *The Temple*. Following "The Bag," for example, is "The Jews," a poem unrelated to its predecessor.

The relevance of some lines from "The H. Scriptures" (II) to Herbert's organization of his own volume has long been acknowledged: "This verse marks that, and both do make a motion / Unto a third, that ten leaves off doth lie." Louis Martz singled out these lines to suggest, "It is the method of the *Temple*, where one poem marks another, and both make a motion toward a third, which may lie some ten or twenty leaves away: but the reader strikes a chord, and understands the destiny thus offered." Poems mark near or distant others,

Amy M. Charles suggests, by virtue of "related imagery, re
lated forms, [or] related themes."[9] As Fredson Bowers remarks, Herbert "planned large sections of *The Temple* for a
cumulative effect that could be gained only by reading a sequence in order and understanding its larger theme." Such
sequences are responsible for the reader's sense of "a flow of
time, an ordered chronology" beneath the surface of *The Temple*. Whether or not he is aware of them, they "supply the sense
of change and development necessary to a narrative or a
drama." But these insights about the relatedness of separate
poems have not brought about a thorough examination of this
aspect of the poet's art. Sidney Gottlieb concludes a recent
article by suggesting, "Readers of Herbert will more and more
find an important key to the meaning of Herbert's poems by
understanding that this meaning is embedded not only in the
individual poems but in the ways poems interact."[10] Because a
poem can participate with another or several others to unfold a
pattern of meaning larger than that it can disclose alone, Herbert frequently organizes the dispersed sequence as an
ordered unit of instruction for the reader who traces the development of the speaker or of a theme from poem to poem.

The goal of Herbert's poetry, Stanley Fish suggests, "is the
involvement of the reader in his own edification . . . [The
poetry] functions as questions function, by drawing from the
reader a completing, or correcting, or, in some cases, a mistaken, response. That response is given not simply at the end
of the poem, but at every moment in it; it is a developing
response."[11] These comments can be applied profitably to a
related group of poems. A sequence has the obvious advantage over a single poem of a greater space in which to explore a
complex subject and its various implications; the reader's response is capable, consequently, of a more refined and com-

9. Louis L. Martz, *The Poetry of Meditation*, p. 296; Amy M. Charles, "The
Williams Manuscript and *The Temple*," in *Renaissance Papers 1971*, ed. Dennis
G. Donovan and A. Leigh Deneef, p. 67.

10. Fredson Bowers, "Herbert's Sequential Imagery: 'The Temper,' " p.
202; Stambler, "The Unity of Herbert's 'Temple,' " pp. 256, 261; Sidney
Gottlieb, "How Shall We Read Herbert? A Look at 'Prayer' (I)," p. 37.

11. Fish, *The Living Temple*, p. 27.

plex development. Later poems also serve as a safeguard for the reader whose Christian education is not sufficiently advanced to allow him to complete partial insights or to correct errors in earlier ones. In spite of himself, such a reader is led to more mature perspectives. A sequence can include poems (such as "Mattens," "Giddinesse," and "The Pulley") that do not require a completing or correcting response from the reader, and yet involve him in his own edification by their own completing or correcting of the other poems.

A sequence, in other words, provides the reader accruing information that forms the basis for poetical strategies in addition to those that Fish mentions. One poem may test what the reader has learned from an earlier one; another may contain a generalization proved correct by his achieved context or enlivened by dramatic presentation elsewhere within that context. Herbert's method in the dispersed poetical sequence often consists of informing or preparing his reader on some subject and subsequently giving him an opportunity to learn yet more by using or testing his knowledge. One short group of poems, consisting of "Nature," "The Temper" (II), "Mattens," "Man," "Giddinesse," "The Pulley," and "The Priesthood," illustrates Herbert's sequential and instructive methods. The poems are linked by the image of God as Creator or artist. They have other themes in common, notably that of constant creation, though three of them approach this subject from the perspective of the first Creation. As a whole, this sequence is about man's unworthy nature, its perfectibility, and the divine role in the process.

God is the "workman" of the heart and soul in "Nature." Because he made them, the self-critical speaker insists on his responsibility for their welfare:

> Full of rebellion, I would die,
> Or fight, or travell, or denie
> That thou hast ought to do with me.
>                 O tame my heart;
>                 It is thy highest art
> To captivate strong holds to thee.
>
> If thou shalt let this venome lurk,

And in suggestions fume and work,
My soul will turn to bubbles straight,
                    And thence by kinde
                    Vanish into a winde,
Making thy workmanship deceit.

O smooth my rugged heart, and there
Engrave thy rev'rend Law and fear;
Or make a new one, since the old
                    Is saplesse grown,
                    And a much fitter stone
To hide my dust, then thee to hold.

The Christian's strident description in the first stanza seems to flaunt his rebellion, but after the vigorous rush of the first three lines, he pauses and his plea ("O tame my heart") breaks the rhythm with quiet distress. Actually, he is "full of rebellion" against himself—against the restive heart he cannot control. He is more submissive than his self-characterization makes him out to be: not wanting to be separated from God by his faults, he begs God's power to subdue them.

But admission of a childlike helplessness provokes a childish strategy. In a sharp tone, he threatens and challenges God to remind him of his responsibility: if *you* allow the soul's rebellious evaporation, its immortality is a deceit. This sly appeal to God's artistic pride, made in a querulous tone, is an index to the rebel's fear. If the soul cannot actually "vanish into a winde," unrepented sin can consign it to eternal destruction. The speaker's fear somewhat mitigates the reader's judgment of his transparent childishness; but, while that explains, it does not justify the genuine rebellion against God's direction: the speaker doubts that his Creator will preserve him from his own flawed nature. Perhaps hearing his inappropriate challenge causes the speaker to change his tactics in the final stanza. Beseeching God to rid his heart of rebellion, he reasserts his faith and submission. God is the only sculptor who can plane and chisel the stony heart—painfully—into righteousness. The Christian is also a sculptor, but an untalented one with no control over his work. The rebellious "I" shapes his heart into a fortress and then a sepulchre, though the faithful "I" wishes to create a dwelling for God. Because of his ineptitude, the rebel-sculptor gives God the alternative of forgetting the old "rugged" heart altogether and making a new one.

The speaker's assumption in "Nature" is that God's creative activity was not a one-time event but is a continual possibility reflecting incessant care for his creatures. However, this faithful insight is where the Christian ends after learning (by watching his own imperfect "Nature" in submission, rebellion, and submission) that God's handiwork is liable to dangerous self-modification. The title of the poem refers as well to God's power and love, the attributes of the divine nature that were in question in the second stanza. With the final prayer, they are reasserted; fresh awareness of these divine characteristics enables the petitioner finally to trust God as continual Creator.

From the Christian's perspective, the poem is an emotional prayer that asks God to make him a submissive heart to preserve his soul. From the reader's perspective, the poem is also an arresting dramatization of the frailty of human nature. Against his wish and better judgment, the speaker is divided against himself. He alternates between his devout and mutinous selves with a disheartening facility. The images of fort and sepulchre suggest enclosure, the power of the rebellious heart to imprison sometimes its devout double. Subject to real fear, the Christian is yet incapable of self-control. That incapacity ultimately makes the poem so affecting: its depiction of a self entirely out of control, of a paralyzed helplessness in the face of a fully apprehended danger, is the stuff of nightmares. Only the speaker's faith in God's re-creative power promises relief.

The reason for hope in "Nature" is reason for complaint in "The Temper" (II):

> It cannot be. Where is that mightie joy,
>     Which just now took up all my heart?
>     Lord, if thou must needs use thy dart,
> Save that, and me; or sin for both destroy.
>
>                             (1–4)

The Christian's first words convey disbelief and a mild exasperation, such as might result from misplacing some household whatnot. His saucy advice about the proper and improper use of God's displeasure confirms his annoyance. In the implied image, the heart is something like a leather balloon just pierced and deflated before the Christian's exclamation. Irritably, he goes on to contrast the permanent "grosser world" with the transient "world of grace," which God suddenly raises and razes, becoming "ev'ry day a new Creatour." The speaker thinks God's unceasing creative activity depends on unceasing destruction (like dismantling one building-block structure to make another) and consequently has its disadvantages for one who desires stability. The Lord who wounds his adherents but not sin, who destroys the "diviner" but not the "grosser" world, seems to have confused priorities.

But the reader's sympathy cools with his awareness that the speaker's lecture springs from a naive wish to live in uninterrupted "mightie joy." Moreover, the speaker's complaints are based on errors: the disgruntled Christian equates his joy with the entire "world of grace"; he forgets that, for all its apparent permanence, the visible world is ephemeral compared to the eternal spiritual world. Because he does not understand the tempering he undergoes and its attendant difficulties, he implies that God's daily creation is inconsiderate and careless. He does not doubt the Creator's power; indeed, he thinks he has evidence of it. In his temper, however, the Christian doubts the adequacy and love of God's constant execution.

But the prayer asking God to stop being "ev'ry day a new Creatour" ends with the speaker restored to good sense: "O fix thy chair of grace, that all my powers / May also fix their reverence." The image of God's portable throne reverenced by the lesser eminences of the speaker's heart only when that throne is actually present predicts turmoil. Since the minor powers take over the Lord's place in his absence, God is advised to deal severely with them:

> Scatter, or binde them all to bend to thee:
>> Though elements change, and heaven move,
>> Let not thy higher Court remove,
> But keep a standing Majestie in me.

> (13–16)

The Christian is a military strategist against his own familiar princes for the King he prefers to serve; the unruly upstarts must be separated to dispel their joint strength and mischief or bound to obeisance. The little world can be secured only by occupation.

The Christian's petition incorporates but neutralizes his earlier criticism. Rather than reproaching God, he explains why he needs the deflated world. Once again, he describes his weaker, rebellious self critically and chafes against it. Once again, he acknowledges his dependence on God's grace and prays for an immediate (but, in this life, impossible) solution to his changeability. His prayer for the uninterrupted presence of God within is understandable ardor; his desire for unflagging joy is a wish for heaven on earth. The entire poem gradually defines the "world of grace" whose seeming instability first annoys and then saddens the speaker. The phrase is personal shorthand for the state of joy and harmony that the Christian experiences when God is with him. When awareness of the divine presence commands the concentration of all his faculties, he feels whole, and wholly at peace. Though the reader may conclude that the speaker is unrealistic, yet he cannot fault him for wishing for permanent bliss. As is typical in Herbert's poems in which the speaker is in error or in which his reasoning is partly wrong, he nevertheless concludes irreproachably: "Let not thy higher Court remove, / But keep a standing Majestie in me." Obviously, his tempering is not an entirely happy experience. Perhaps his ignorance accounts for the poem's lukewarm effect. His retreat from criticism and exasperation does not follow from any new awareness on his part of what is happening to him, and his annoyed complaints are the liveliest and most engaging part of the poem.

Still concentrating primarily on the spiritual creation, the speaker of "Mattens" does not complain or make helpful suggestions to the "workman" whose artistry awes him:

> I cannot ope mine eyes,
> But thou art ready there to catch
> My morning-soul and sacrifice:
> Then we must needs for that day make a match.

> My God, what is a heart?
> Silver, or gold, or precious stone,
> Or starre, or rainbow, or a part
> Of all these things, or all of them in one?
>
> My God, what is a heart,
> That thou shouldst it so eye, and wooe,
> Powring upon it all thy art,
> As if that thou hadst nothing els to do?
>
> (1–12)

The Christian's amazement that God anticipates him daily and lavishes such artistry on a single heart leads him to weigh its worth. The first time he considers it, he compiles images of earthly value or beauty; the second time, he corrects himself with the realization that its value and beauty are a function of the attention God gives it. God's ardent courting of the sweetheart prompts its possessor to consider the Wooer. Here is an artist, the speaker suggests, whose talent and generosity are equally divine: he falls in love with his own creation and foregoes his just claims, preferring to win it through courtship and persuasion.

When the speaker realizes God's lavish attentions to the heart, he sees that properly it should be the other way around:

> Indeed mans whole estate
> Amounts (and richly) to serve thee:
> He did not heav'n and earth create,
> Yet studies them, not him by whom they be.
>
> (13–16)

God should be wooed assiduously, not man, who "did not heav'n and earth create." But God is so accomplished a Maker that his servants mistake their vocation and become students of his creation. Studying his elaborate work disinclines them to look beyond to the artist and his motives. The Christian prays to avoid such myopic tribute by seeing "both the work and workman." The poem itself, of course, with its stress on the jeweled or iridescent but hidden heart and on its attentive and loving but invisible Maker, suggests that the prayer indicates the Christian's zeal rather than a spiritual problem. Even the dawn, which coincides with (and is) his illumination, consists of shimmering ladders that ascend to God—daily, God re-creates a way to himself for the man who will perceive and use it. The wonder, humility, and rich imagination of the speaker make him the reader's guide in the just, simultaneous appreciation of work and workman.[12]

Having suggested in "Mattens" that contemplation of the creation alone is an error, Herbert lets the reader catch the speaker of "Man" on the verge of making that shortsighted mistake:

> My God, I heard this day,
> That none doth build a stately habitation,
> But he that means to dwell therein.
> What house more stately hath there been,
> Or can be, then is Man? to whose creation
> All things are in decay.
>
> (1–6)

The image of man as edifice is Biblical. Paul tells the Corinthians, "Ye are God's building" (I Cor. 3:9), and the Ephesians that they are "built upon the foundation of the apostles and prophets, Jesus Christ himself being the chief corner stone; In whom all the building fitly framed together groweth unto an holy temple in the Lord: In whom ye also are builded together for an habitation of God through the Spirit" (2:20–22). Here, the architect is informed that, since man is a "house more stately" than any other, he ought to "dwell therein." The Christian seems unaware of his boastfulness. He uses "stately" twice to characterize man as imposing and dignified, but his repetition, together with his reasoning, immediately alerts the reader to other meanings of the word—"arrogant" and "showing a sense of superiority" (*OED*).

A good part of the lengthy poem consists of praise for man, but thinking of the whole universe that serves this mighty microcosm eventually leads the extoller in a more useful direction. Evident pride marks such lines as "Nothing hath got so farre, / But Man hath caught and kept it, as his prey." How-

12. Noel Kinnamon points out that the poem alludes to Psalm 51 and especially 95: "'Mattens' is a personal response to the Psalmist's invitation to praise" ("Notes on the Psalms in Herbert's *The Temple*," p. 17).

ever, the many "servants [that] wait on Man" and so attest to
his preeminence are finally seen to have a beauty of their own:

> Each thing is full of dutie:
> Waters united are our navigation;
>            Distinguished, our habitation;
>            Below, our drink; above, our meat;
> Both are our cleanlinesse. Hath one such beautie?
>            Then how are all things neat?
>
>                                              (37–42)

Initially, the world is conjured up to add the dignity of servants
to masterful man. But the realization that the natural world's
service is its beauty and that it evinces great care for mankind
makes the speaker remember the architect in a humbler frame
of mind:

> Oh mightie love! Man is one world, and hath
>            Another to attend him.
>
> Since then, my God, thou hast
> So brave a Palace built; O dwell in it,
>            That it may dwell with thee at last!
>            Till then, afford us so much wit;
> That, as the world serves us, we may serve thee,
>            And both thy servants be.
>
>                                              (47–54)

Study of the world yields a valuable insight that causes at least
one "stately habitation" to pray with humility for "so much
wit" as the trees, beasts, and herbs exhibit by serving. Looking
back over the poem for some indication of man's service to
God, the reader finds only the incongruous possibility of a
human service to parrots:

> Reason and speech we onely bring.
> Parrats may thank us, if they are not mute,
>            They go upon the score.
>
>                                          (10–12)

The speaker's humility is appropriate; he needs the wit God is
asked to give.

"Mattens" prepares the reader to recognize the speaker's
potential error. Eventually, the speaker overcomes it in "Man"

and demonstrates how it may be avoided. If man is not dazzled by God's greatest creation and considers the world in its serving role, he will discover the Maker and his love. The boastful attempt to persuade God to dwell in the stately habitation turns into a perception of duty and an experience of humility by suggesting, finally, a retrospective contrast between superior man and the nonrational world. This contrast moves the Christian, whose praise for world and man has been unqualified, to ask God to improve his human creation. By sprinkling wit wizardlike on his brave but inattentive Palace, God can transform it into a good servant.[13]

Whereas "Man" is filled almost entirely with self-satisfied praise, "Giddinesse" presents a harsh and unflattering view of mankind, delivered by a dispirited critic. God's most glorious creature is unstable and fickle: "He is some twentie sev'rall men at least / Each sev'rall houre." This is the first poem in the sequence that is overtly didactic. It is purely descriptive, though the speaker's somber tone suggests that he generalizes to distance a painful experience of "our" contrarieties. Man is volatile: a thought can "creep" in and change him; a passing mood or a different frame of mind can make a different person of him.

God was the architect in "Man," but man is the builder in the present poem:

> He builds a house, which quickly down must go,
> >    As if a whirlwinde blew
> And crusht the building: and it's partly true,
> >    His minde is so.
>
> O what a sight were Man, if his attires
> >    Did alter with his minde;
> And like a Dolphins skinne, his clothes combin'd
> >    With his desires!
>
> Surely if each one saw anothers heart,
> >    There would be no commerce,

13. For a different perspective on "Man" as "the most important humanist document in *The Temple*," see Richard Strier, "Ironic Humanism in *The Temple*," in *"Too Rich to Clothe the Sunne": Essays on George Herbert*, ed. Claude J. Summers and Ted-Larry Pebworth, p. 34.

> No sale or bargain passe: all would disperse,
>     And live apart.
>
> (13–24)

It is man's nature to remake himself constantly by his thoughts, moods, or circumstances, but never has that commonplace received a more colorful treatment. Just as the Christian revealed himself to be an inept sculptor in "Nature," he now discloses that he is a builder of extravagant energy and wastefulness. Having within himself a whirlwind, man is helpless to preserve his creation. The speaker's giddy imagination then suggests man's absurdity with the implied image of a man all day in his closet busily trying to outfit himself to reflect his mind—or helplessly realizing that his complexion is changing like a telltale litmus paper. But the Christian's mood changes again, and his next premise, "if each one saw anothers heart," is chosen to make the invisible re-creation seem shameful, even repulsive. Man's remaking of self is disheartening because it is uncontrollable and destructive. Since man is constantly (and dangerously) remaking himself anyway, the Christian ends with a prayer requesting God to take over the job. His tone suggests that he is moved by personal insight:

> Lord, mend or rather make us: one creation
>     Will not suffice our turn:
> Except thou make us dayly, we shall spurn
>     Our own salvation.
>
> (25–28)

The Christian's immediate self-correction is a pathetic indication of his awareness of the gross human imperfection he shares in and even exemplifies. "Turn" harks back to the various inner revolutions he described. Constant creation is man's only hope—if it is undertaken by the Maker who can build sound, blameless structures and control the whirlwind as the human architect cannot.

The reader who follows this short sequence of poems has specific evidence to add to the speaker's examples of "Giddinesse." The radical shift in the assessment of humanity from "Man" to the present poem has already been mentioned. Both poems tell the truth about man: he is God's preeminently superior creation, but he is also giddy and foolish. Another clear instance of changeability is his attitude toward constant creation. In "The Temper" (II) he complained that God was "ev'ry day a new Creatour," but the final stanza of "Giddinesse" shows an entirely different attitude. He knows that man ruins himself because alone he cannot be steadfast. A serene perception of the "diviner world of grace" depends not only on God's "tempering" and his unfathomable will; it depends as well on man's unreliable and imperfect nature. Because this is so, God must daily re-form to save his creature.

Herbert's treatment of God and man as Creator and creature instructs the reader subtly, but it also leads him to a problem. On the one hand, each of the five poems insists on God's incomparable power and artistry as Creator; on the other, each poem states (or reveals indirectly, through the very natural speaker) that man, God's most impressive creation, is flawed. "Oh, what a thing is man! how farre from power, / From setled peace and rest," the speaker laments in "Giddinesse." Herbert does not ignore this seeming inconsistency, and "The Pulley" is his resolution. The Christian (like the reader) is aware of the paradox of perfect Creator/imperfect creation. He uses what is evident from observation and experience (the sequence gives the reader his own experience) and what he believes (that God is power and love) to invent a tremendous dramatic scene that explains everything. In the first line of the poem, the speaker takes the reader back to "when God at first made man" so that he can see and hear God in the act of creation. Blessings lie like rich and colorful gems in a beaker beside him as the Maker speaks: "Let us (said he) poure on him all we can." This divine and powerful generosity contracts "into a span" the riches dispersed in the world, instilling into the microcosm strength, beauty, wisdom, honor, and pleasure. We witness not the physical but the moral creation of man.

But God stops before the "glasse of blessings" is empty, seeing that "alone of all his treasure / Rest in the bottome lay." And he muses, explaining his pause and his retention of the blessing, rest:

> For if I should (said he)
> Bestow this jewell also on my creature,
> He would adore my gifts in stead of me,
> And rest in Nature, not the God of Nature:
> So both should losers be.
>
> Yet let him keep the rest,
> But keep them with repining restlesnesse:
> Let him be rich and wearie, that at least,
> If goodnesse leade him not, yet wearinesse
> May tosse him to my breast.
>
> (11–20)

If man rested in the created universe and adored the world inferior to its Maker (the dangerous inclination mentioned in "Mattens"), he would lose the close relationship with him that God wants. So much is obvious. God's matter-of-fact assertion that he too would be a "loser" is arresting. He would lose man and his adoration; he needs neither, but as a loving God he desires both.

The familiarity of some ideas in "The Pulley" is a clue to its synoptic quality in terms of the Creator-artist theme. Tremendous love characterizes God, a love that motivates him from the beginning of human existence. Man is created for love, and God's plan is that he live that love, whether he is led to it by goodness or by the alternate way of weariness of the world. Either way will do; the important thing is that man come, finally, to God. God's generosity is evident in his provision of alternative motivations for man and in all the blessings he *does* give. The poem echoes "Mattens" and "Man" in its emphasis on God's love and generosity. The poem also underlines God's power, as did "Nature" and "The Temper" (II), and adds omniscience to his attributes. This addition is crucial because it helps to explain in part the problem of the perfect Creator and his imperfect human creation. From the first, God is concerned with the danger to free and rational man from his own nature. As a conscious artist with total knowledge of the design, God foresees that, given rest along with everything else, man would subvert the divine plan of mutual love. And so God acts. He withholds rest, leaving man incomplete, imperfect, so that he might desire and achieve the higher perfection of union with his Maker. What might seem imperfection in his creature is paradoxically supreme evidence of God's artistry and love: restlessness is "The Pulley" that draws man to God.

The essentially splendid but flawed creature described in "The Pulley" corresponds to the image of "man" progressively drawn and detailed by the Christian in the sequence. He has wonderful attributes, such as the imagination revealed in "Mattens" and in "The Pulley." But "Nature," "The Temper" (II), and "Man" confirm that he is also weak and liable to error. He is as likely, and as welcome, to turn to God from weariness ("Giddinesse") as from goodness ("Mattens"). "Man" asserts that the riches of the world are his birthright. But they do not satisfy because they were intended not to do so; the wealthy creature yearns for, and needs, yet one more boon: the indwelling presence of his Creator. Because he is not perfect or complete, God must be called upon constantly to complete or remake his creature. The sequence demonstrates what "The Pulley" suggests: man's flaws and emotional complexities are so many reasons for him to turn to God. If he is rebellious, joyless, proud, or sick of his own giddiness, there is one foreordained remedy. God desires everyone to come to him, and only he will give rest.

Perhaps to suggest that it is not only the refractory or restless spirit who benefits from God's creative love, Herbert placed "The Priesthood" after "The Pulley." The speaker's character is the new aspect of this declaration of faith in the continual creation by which God re-forms his people. A summary of the poem will suffice, since it and "Man" will be discussed below in a different context. Far from rebellion or restlessness, the speaker considers himself a militant Christian, but hopes to be made a priest. His humility is evident: the priesthood is "sacred and hallow'd fire," he is earth and clay. The theme of artistry is introduced in the third stanza:

> Yet have I often seen, by cunning hand
> And force of fire, what curious things are made
> Of wretched earth.

> (13–15)

The speaker knows how little the condition of the lowly clay matters to the potter, who makes beautiful things from earth on which he himself might have "scorn'd to stand." So, although the speaker feels unworthy of the priesthood, he believes he can rely on God. At God's feet, where earth properly belongs, he rests in his submission and in his faith that the artist's ability and love will transform him.

*       *       *

After "The Priesthood," the Creator-artist theme disappears from *The Temple*, save for a few brief references such as the allusion to God's "quickning" power in "The Flower," or the troubled question in "The Search": "Lord dost thou some new fabrick mould[?]" But the seven poems constitute a review of some Christian tenets about God and man that is palatable chiefly because its acquisition depends on the reader's exercising his inferential and critical powers. The exceptional art with which Herbert guides in self-instruction secures the reader's interest. Whether he has the pleasure of detecting the speaker of the poems in an error, of applying an insight from an earlier to a subsequent poem, of realizing that two apparently contradictory poems complement each other, or of formulating the conclusions implicit in the order of the poems, the reader "participates in his own edification."

There is nothing extraordinary (in regard to the Christian tradition) to be gathered from the Creator-artist poems. They indirectly characterize God, for example, as powerful, generous, omniscient, and especially loving. Through constant creation, he persists in patiently remaking man to rid him of his faults, which is to say, to bring him closer to himself. Herbert underlines God's willingness to remove human imperfection as many times as necessary. The loving God wants man to be saved; constant creation is his way of helping his creature achieve that goal. The idea of constant creation was a "traditional . . . basic concept"[14] in Herbert's time. Although it may strike some readers today as novel, others will recall the prayer

14. C. A. Patrides, "A Crown of Praise: The Poetry of George Herbert," in *The English Poems of George Herbert*, p. 17.

in Psalm 51:10, "Create in me a clean heart, O God," or Paul's assertion that "if any man be in Christ, he is a new creature" (2 Corinthians 5:57). For this poet, as Fish remarks, "Success is marked not by the [reader's] acquiring of new knowledge (that is, of information), but by the more conscious apprehension of knowledge that was always, in some sense, available."[15] The Christian's strengths and flaws give human urgency and credibility to the items of faith that Herbert conveys in the sequence; his dramatic speeches and situations enliven abstractions so unexceptionable they might otherwise elicit impatient nods. Besides, the reader is less likely to forget or to dismiss what he gathers for himself.

Herbert's sequential arrangement impels the reader to live out the Christian's experience in dramatic, comprehensible units of progressively maturing thought. In the Creator-artist poems, for instance, the speaker's different experiences, changing attitudes, and deepening understanding lead the reader from a consideration of the particular Christian to reflections on mankind; from doubts about the advantageousness of constant creation to certainty that it is an absolute necessity; from perplexity regarding the perfect Creator and his imperfect creatures to insight into the highest perfection; from probable misapprehension that only the weak or doubtful need constant creation to realization that no one is beyond improvement by God's regenerative love. Patterns of meaning such as these require several poems; the individual poem contributes its unique share to a significance greater than it alone could provide.

The technique Herbert uses to treat a subject more or less comprehensively centers on the speaker, using his reflections and upheavals to explore Christian commonplaces from different perspectives. The Creator-artist poems are not abstract meditations on God's constant creation; they are personal and emotional responses to a daily option given the Christian by his attentive and heavenly lover. When it is as real a negotiable subject as any mundane transaction between two intimates, the traditional idea achieves life and substance. Whether the

15. Fish, *The Living Temple*, p. 43.

Christian disputes the worth of constant creation or begs for it, it is relevant to him in his present moment—the doctrine means and matters personally. Such vitalizing of religious truth is Herbert's aim.

*       *       *

From the speaker's habitual self-analysis and his frequent colloquies with God, the reader gains a vivid sense of the two protagonists of *The Temple* and of the nature of the love between them. One of the peculiarities of their relationship is that the Christian (or mankind) is characterized by the poems as an undesirable or inconstant lover. Poems such as "Nature" or "The Temper" (II) show that human frailty and error sometimes make him doubt, despair, rebel, or distrust, though it is what he least wishes to do. Sometimes he goes so far as to neglect God altogether, as "Giddinesse" remarks; but even when he ardently desires to approach him, the Christian is deficient. He is in error sometimes, as when he complains about God's re-creation of himself. Within a poem, or in the larger context of a sequence, there is time for the unworthy lover to change his mind (as he often does), and his mistake will not be held against him. The critical and grumbling man cannot be steadfast in trust and loyalty. As "Mattens" and "Man" suggest, he is sometimes inclined to regard his lover's property with more interest than he accords the lover himself. Unstable and self-destructive, he is still proud.

Though his faults are impressive, the Christian is often dissatisfied with himself and prays for amendment. This is his only recourse because, as poems such as "The Glimpse" or "The Familie" show, he is powerless to preserve himself from his own nature. This Christian's prayers are heard and answered. God foreknew his failings, loved him, and committed himself to redeem his creature from his own error. Unworthy though he undoubtedly is, the Christian is God's beloved.

In contrast to the unfit lover, the divine partner in the relationship is endlessly solicitous. He overlooks complaints and slights; he persists in giving tokens of his love meant to elicit a like response; he sometimes even schemes to obtain love, as

"The Pulley" suggests. Whether it is with a stormy-weather hint, with an eloquent affliction or grief, or with an invitingly beautiful dawn, he always uses his power to attract the inattentive man and to mend the man's deficiencies so that he can approach. Over and over again, poems such as "Josephs coat" and "The Glance" suggest, God uses his unfathomable power to protect the Christian from his own fallen nature. In spite of these sterling qualities, however, God is sometimes a misunderstood or unappreciated lover.

The course of religious love runs no more smoothly than that of the mundane variety, but the Christian is the unstable or undependable figure in the relationship. When he is estranged from God, it is by his own limitations or lapses rather than by any disdain or indifference on God's part. He wishes he could be irreproachable because he loves his Lord, but he is incapable of perfection. As we saw in "The Size," the Christian knows that the Savior is the pattern of perfection whom it behooves him to emulate, but imitation is difficult. Turmoil is inevitable because the inferior lover, who depends on the all-powerful, invisible, and inscrutable Deity, is weak and self-defeating. The inescapable differences between the human and the divine natures as well as the indirection by which God communicates his will make it vital for the Christian to be analytic and self-aware. They also make it inevitable that, limited and uncomprehending, he will experience and express conflict. Ultimately, this conflict is inappropriate, but it makes an immense contribution to Herbert's depiction of an empirically active relationship.

A word is in order about the speaker's habit of verbally separating himself from his greedy or naive heart, his despair, his whole family of disruptive thoughts, his past and present selves, or his present and future selves. Though such self-fragmentation is a dramatic boon for the poet and the reader, it may seem peculiar to some readers—as remarkable as the divided heart so often imaged in Herbert's poems as a dwelling with various rooms or spaces, a box, a closet, or other enclosures capable of subdivision. Though certainly this poetic strategy usually reflects the speaker's discomfort or dissatisfaction—his mental or spiritual condition—it also reflects the

state of affairs taken for granted by Christianity about imperfect human nature. The distinction between the weak flesh
and the willing spirit and phrases like the "Old Adam" or the
"New Man" assume the dual identity of the whole individual.
One of Paul's formulations of the unresolved dichotomy within is in Romans 7:22–25: "For I delight in the law of God after
the inward man: But I see another law in my members, warring
against the law of my mind, and bringing me into captivity to
the law of sins which is in my members . . . So then with the
mind I myself serve the law of God; but with the flesh the law
of sin." For the wayfaring Christian, there are at least two
selves—the imperfect reality and the perfect ideal, the unregenerate and the regenerate "I," or the past sinner and the
present sanctified self (or vice versa)—in a continual struggle
until he reaches his destination. Herbert capitalizes on the
traditional concept.[16]

After all, there is no place in *The Temple* for persuasions to
love or for laments of unrequited love—the Christian loves and
knows he is loved in return. Because of his failings, however,
such lyrics are replaced by poems seeking reconciliation as
they grieve over God's coolness, anger, or absence. Though
the Christian sometimes sorrows and pleads with God because
he feels ignored or abandoned, his reconciliatory poems differ
from those of the ordinary lover. God's chastising anger and
withdrawal are ultimately recognized as expressions of divine
love. The Christian speaker must feel concern and grief, he
must experience the frustration and dissatisfaction of unfulfill-
ment, because he can be only "Like a pretender, not a bride."
His great desire, the perfect joy of God's "full-ey'd love," is not
to be attained in this life.

16. For other examples of the divided heart, see "The Sinner," "Good
Friday," "Sepulchre," "The H. Communion," "Deniall," "Ungratefulnesse,"
"Decay," "Conscience," and "Confession."

# 4

# "All Things Are Busie"

This chapter and the two that follow concentrate on the Christian speaker's search for vocation. The subject of the poetic sequence through which his story unfolds is employment; underlying it are the greater themes of grace and charity. The perimeters of *The Temple*'s world of grace have been indicated in preceding chapters, as have some of the aspects of the love between God and the Christian. The employment sequence offers the reader a more comprehensive exposition of these topics. When Herbert poses for the speaker of the sequence the problem of responding to divine love, the difficulties of obeying the first commandment surface. The Christian's desire to return love for love brings with it the related problems of achieving an adequate understanding of the nature of God and his love, of coming to a realistic understanding of his own nature, of finding the relation in which he can stand to God, and of discovering a satisfactory, particular mode of expressing his love. The "questions regarding the possibility and the nature of 'love' between beings as disproportionate as are man and God" arise naturally as the Christian explores personally the possibility of man's "'utility' to God."[1] Herbert's sequential technique affords these complex topics the extended treatment they require. The speaker's experience gives concreteness and lucidity to problems such as finding God's grace in the texture of daily experience and distinguishing between the divine will and one's own.

The sequence begins with the Christian struggling to find an active mode of expressing his love of God; it ends with the Christian, who has identified himself as a poet and finally

1. Rosemond Tuve, "Herbert and Caritas," in her *Essays by Rosemond Tuve,* pp. 168, 194. In my discussion of Herbert's treatment of love between God and man, I am indebted to Tuve's essay.

becomes a priest, declaring that to sweep a room for God's sake is a fine endeavor. Obviously, a poet who struggles to identify a vocation and eventually chooses the priesthood resembles George Herbert in some important respects. Indeed, of the twenty-three poems that comprise the employment sequence, at least eight have been described as autobiographical or as more or less "personal" poems.[2] Of course, we cannot know how accurately these poems reflect Herbert's experience; we do know that the poet wished his readers to be instructed by them and so "make a gain" ("The Dedication"). We also know that the speaker of the *Temple* poems is sometimes naive or in error regarding doctrinal matters, thus forbidding an easy identification of poet and speaker. In "The Thanksgiving," for instance, the speaker wants to repay Christ for his sacrifice. We might guess that Herbert is describing himself in the past, before he fully understood the matter, and that self-examination has revealed that, although he knows better, repayment has been an underlying motive of his efforts. But it is far simpler to accept the poet's stated intention of enriching the reader by spiritual instruction and to honor the distance that often separates speaker and poet. The speaker's error in "The Thanksgiving" is not Herbert's humble self-revelation; it is his device to instruct or to remind the reader about the futility of attempts to repay God. Though there are vital resemblances between the two, Herbert is not the speaker of the employment sequence. As biographical material, the poems can at best give us some insight into the complexities inherent in the choice of vocation for a man like Herbert. The poet offers his reader a spiritual autobiography designed and

2. Amy Charles suggests that "Affliction" (I), "Employment" (I) and (II), "The Priesthood," and "The Crosse" directly relate to Herbert's life (see *A Life*, pp. 84–85, 81–82, 140–41, 127–29). On "Affliction" (I) as autobiographical, see also Larry Brunner, "Herbert's 'Affliction' (I) and 'The Flower': Studies in the Theme of Christian Refinement," pp. 18–28; Anne C. Fowler, " 'With Care and Courage': Herbert's 'Affliction' Poems," in *"Too Rich to Clothe the Sunne": Essays on George Herbert*, ed. Claude J. Summers and Ted-Larry Pebworth, pp. 129–45. Helen Vendler thinks "The Starre" illumines Herbert's employment problems (*The Poetry of George Herbert*, pp. 253–54). Joseph H. Summers suggests by quotation that "Submission" was based on personal experience and characterizes "The Crosse" and "The Answer" as "more personal than most of Herbert's poems" (*George Herbert: His Religion and Art*, pp. 48, 183).

depersonalized by the values and demands of his instructive art.[3]

Apart from its personal relevance, Herbert's treatment of one of his age's favorite subjects is not surprising. "English divines were obsessed" with the doctrine of the calling, the belief that God directs and enables each man to employ himself in some useful occupation. Preachers strove to make their congregations see a calling "as almost the whole embodiment of a Christian's worldly, as distinct from his directly religious duty. The religious duty and the duty of the calling were seen to be, in fact, inextricably intertwined. The calling thus becomes a kind, and an absolutely essential kind, of Christian worship."[4] In "The Country Parson," Herbert states that the priest "represents to every body the necessity of a vocation. The reason of this assertion is taken from the nature of man, wherein God hath placed two great Instruments, Reason in the soul, and a hand in the Body, as ingagements of working: So that even in Paradise man had a calling" (*Works*, p. 274). Herbert goes on to mention the individual gifts each Christian must use and improve "to our Masters Advantage." The response to a calling was a response to the will of God; that was evident in his equipping man with the "instruments" of abilities and talents. Herbert's employment sequence treats a theme of universal relevance: the problem of vocation that each Christian was supposed to decide for himself.[5]

3. The term *depersonalized* is Leon Edel's: "When a novel is subjective, it is in some form or other, autobiographical. It is autobiography depersonalized. And if the life behind it is, from one point of view, irrelevant for the study of the creative imagination, it has also a singular relevance" (*The Modern Psychological Novel*, p. 157). In addition to Summers's cautionary statement about Herbert's view of the relation between language and experience, quoted in Chapter 2 above, Paul Delaney's comment about a seventeenth-century Presbyterian autobiographer is pertinent: "Religious introspection, though it doubtless sprang from a greater awareness of individual personality, was in its expression often governed by utilitarian and communal purposes" (*British Autobiography in the Seventeenth Century*, p. 56).
4. Charles H. and Katherine George, *The Protestant Mind of the English Reformation*, pp. 126, 129.
5. Though I use the word *vocation* in the sense that it commonly retains today, it had two meanings in the seventeenth century: "the mark of our eternal destiny" and "the particular occupation or place in society to which each of us is assigned by God for the course of our earthly life" (Robert B. Shaw, *The Call of God: The Theme of Vocation in the Poetry of Donne and Herbert*, p. 1). Shaw's study is highly recommended to anyone interested in the subject.

*      *      *

We may trace in *The Temple* a narrative sequence of twenty-three poems that is George Herbert's partial and depersonalized autobiography, the only record he left of the experience and resolution of the vocation problem that troubled him for many years:

| | |
|---|---|
| The Thanksgiving | Obedience |
| Affliction (I) | Dialogue |
| Employment (I) | Providence |
| Grace | The Method |
| Praise (I) | Praise (III) |
| Even-song | The Priesthood |
| Content | The Crosse |
| The Starre | The Answer |
| Employment (II) | Aaron |
| Man | The Invitation |
| Life | The Elixir |
| Submission | |

The preeminence of God's grace is stressed by an introduction to the sequence, the importance of his love by an epilogue: the employment sequence is set in motion by "The Sacrifice" and set in its proper perspective by "Love" (III). The twenty-three poems are linked by their shared reference to the theme of employment. This recurring concern with practical activity, productivity, or usefulness appears in different guises. The preoccupation might, for instance, be expressed in individual poems as a problem under consideration by the speaker; as a reason for his general dejection; as a basis for speculation about different possibilities; as a problem solved; or, subsequently, as a glimpse of the Christian engaged in the employment he has undertaken at last. Read together, the separate poems outline a story within which the theme of employment expands to explore the two greater themes of grace and charity.

Sequences such as the one described here and in the preceding chapter contribute to our apprehension of *The Temple* as an organic whole rather than as a collection of poems. They are the underlying structures that create the sense of "growth and development" the reader experiences as he progresses through "The Church."[6] The unspecified time frame implied by the spatial arrangement of the relevant poems in a dispersed sequence lends credence to the developments in the Christian's understanding, while the poems that intervene between related ones add psychological realism to the volume by recording other preoccupations. A succession of varied concerns and emotional states corresponds to the complexity of experience; Herbert's awareness of this is reflected in his careful arrangement of the poems in *The Temple*.

The identification of the poems that compose the employment sequence is arbitrary, inasmuch as Herbert ordered but did not separate the poems, give them all identical titles, or otherwise than by a common theme indicate that they might be read as a group. Identifying a dispersed sequence is unquestionably an act of extraction and exclusion, undertaken for the sake of focusing on a manageable field of vision. The reader temporarily extracts a poem from its immediate context and places it in a different one—a context more obviously (or differently) significant than the apparent one given it by the poet. (Of course, the order in which the related poems appear in *The Temple* is the order they retain in a sequence, relative to each other.) Necessarily, the process is one of exclusion: the Creator-artist sequence treated in the last chapter does not include, for example, poems like "Love" (I) and (II), though the first refers to the "authour of this great frame" and the second to "him who did make and mend our eies," for those poems do not concern themselves primarily, or even very much, with God as Creator.

A sequential reading of separated poems may seem to posit a precise rigidity of design that does not correspond to the character of *The Temple*. However, removing one by one as many separate sequences as it would take to incorporate every poem in the volume would not thereby exhaust the meanings of the poems or of the total collection. When the reader commits himself to tracing one of these patterns, he commits

6. Helen C. White, *The Metaphysical Poets: A Study in Religious Experience*, p. 165.

himself to reading a multifaceted and multireferential poem in a somewhat restricted way. And the poem will not stay still after he has placed it in a specific relationship with others; it retains its individuality and its right to join other poems or groups formed by different criteria. Each poem in the Creator-artist sequence is related to the others by its images and subject, but it is related also, on other grounds, to yet other poems. It is obvious, for example, that "The Temper" (II) has a fellow that was left behind in our consideration of constant creation. "Man" and "The Priesthood," which are a part of that sequence, will claim our attention once again in the employment sequence, and here they will reflect a different emphasis. The context in which we read the poems, then, creates and directs our response. We cannot follow many paths simultaneously, but Herbert's poetry itself compels us to acknowledge several avenues of interpretation.

Because there are so many avenues, tracing a sequence through *The Temple* gives the reader a frame of reference, temporary but nevertheless useful. Reading contextually equips him with a gradually unfolding guidebook to areas of meaning and with an accretion of subjective detail that intensifies the experience of successive poems. We have seen, for example, that an "impersonal" poem like "Giddinesse" is more striking after demonstrations of the Christian's own volatile nature. Even a poem like "The Pulley," arresting on its own, acquires an added dimension from the affective residue of the preceding poems. Reading a sequence modifies our response to successive poems, which benefit by the accumulation of the details of the speaker's history and concerns. This is especially important in the employment sequence; more than any other, it is responsible for the reader's impression that he witnesses the Christian speaker's "cumulative drama over a whole volume."[7]

The Christian is not the only actor in the drama; he is started

7. Elizabeth Stambler, "The Unity of Herbert's 'Temple,' " p. 252. Stambler traces stone and sun imagery in some of Herbert's poems to demonstrate that "through their image linkages [the poems] supply the sense of change and development necessary to a narrative or a drama" (p. 261).

on the path that leads eventually to his vocation not by himself but by "The Sacrifice." This poem is spoken by Christ as the events leading up to the Crucifixion unfold. Rosemond Tuve's placement of the poem in the tradition of the *Improperia*, the complaints of Christ on the Cross, is essential to the understanding of this strange poem. Line after line details the indignities and pains inflicted on Christ, who is very conscious of the nature of those he dies for and of the ironies inherent in his situation. We hardly know what to expect of the Son as he describes these events, but it is a surprise to hear his complaints against mankind contrasted with his own virtues:

> *Oh all ye, who passe by,* whose eyes and minde
> To worldly things are sharp, but to me blinde;
> To me, who took eyes that I might you finde:
> > Was ever grief like mine?
>
> The Princes of my people make a head
> Against their Maker: they do wish me dead,
> Who cannot wish, except I give them bread:
> > Was ever grief like mine?
> > > (1–8)

Christ's love is apparent in what he has done and continues to do. But man's guilt, his damnable nature, is also apparent, and it is difficult to reconcile Christ's love with his deliberate enumeration of man's faults or sins. Louis Martz remarks, "The central strength of Herbert's poem resides in its ability to keep constantly before the mind both the immensity of God's omnipotence and the immensity of God's love, the companion-powers of punishment and mercy."[8] But the divine attributes can be presented only successively, and hence create the effect of clashing opposites. Mankind can only refer to or try to understand God in terms of opposing attributes that the mind can never hold in perfect stasis. This is the problem confronted by the reader in "The Sacrifice": Christ is mercy and love, but he is also judgment and punishment. To read the poem is to experience a persistent discordance.

8. Rosemond Tuve, *A Reading of George Herbert*, pp. 19–99; Louis L. Martz, *The Poetry of Meditation*, p. 95.

Ultimately, Christ's suffering results in the end of all woe for believers. Most notably at the end of the poem, he speaks several times of this benefit:

> *Now heal thy self, Physician; now come down.*
> Alas! I did so, when I left my crown
> And fathers smile for you, to feel his frown:
> > Was ever grief like mine?
>
> In healing not my self, there doth consist
> All that salvation, which ye now resist;
> Your safetie in my sicknesse doth subsist:
> > Was ever grief [like mine?]
>
> Betwixt two theeves I spend my utmost breath,
> As he that for some robberie suffereth.
> Alas! what have I stollen from you? Death.
> > Was ever grief [like mine?]
>
> . . . . . . . . . . . . . . . . . . . . . . . . . . . . . . . . . . . . . . . . . . . . . . . .
>
> But now I die; now all is finished.
> My wo, man's weal: and now I bow my head.
> Onely let others say, when I am dead,
> > Never was grief like mine.
> > > (221–32, 249–52)

Despite its love-judgment tension, "The Sacrifice" finally emphasizes divine love because Christ's terrible judgment, his hints of power restrained and of possible retribution, are made throughout in the context of the supreme act of love. Christ's bitter words in stanzas like these seem at variance with his voluntary suffering—but they are not. All the while he is complaining and pointing out the faults of men, he is undergoing the ordeal that is justly theirs. A major source of his suffering is his awareness that man rejects his love. Through Christ's vivid knowledge of the guilt and unworthiness of the people for whom he suffers and dies, Herbert stresses that God's love is entirely undeserved by man, but remarkably that love is there, and it is tremendous. Because Christ sees that no one deserves it, the poem shows "The Sacrifice" as a free and awesome proof of divine love.

The lengthy poem intends to move the reader by showing

human guilt and divine love in their clearest connection. "Lo,
here I hang," Christ says,

>                 charg'd with a world of sinne,
>     The greater world o'th'two; for that came in
>     By words, but this by sorrow I must win:
>                         Was ever grief [like mine?]
>
>     Such sorrow as, if sinfull man could feel,
>     Or feel his part, he would not cease to kneel,
>     Till all were melted, though he were all steel:
>                         Was ever grief [like mine?]
>                             (205–12)

The entire poem defines the sorrow Christ feels. The wish that
"sinfull man could feel, / Or feel his part" of the sorrow
springs from the conviction that a true understanding of the
Son's sorrow would make the sinner kneel in contrition and
gratitude until he "melted," overwhelmed by grief and love.
This conviction underlies the entire poem as it details the
humiliations and afflictions of the taunted, dying Savior: Herbert wants the reader to feel Christ's sorrow as keenly as
possible. In proportion to this empathy, the reader will understand the nature of the love personified by Christ when he took
man's burden in spite of the creature's ingratitude and unworthiness.

Herbert did more than hope that the reader would respond
to Christ's particularized account of his sorrow and love. He
made sure that Christ's appeal was not in vain, that the Son
had one appreciative, responsive listener in *The Temple*—the
speaker of the employment sequence. In this story of the
Christian who hears, "The Sacrifice" is particularly important
because it is Herbert's representation of prevenient grace. It is
poetic proof that God initiates, that he moves the Christian to
love, good desires, and subsequent achievement. However,
we shall postpone discussion of "The Sacrifice" as a means of
demonstrating prevenient grace until after a reading of "The
Thanksgiving," the poem that follows immediately, beginning
the employment sequence.

A person who has been reading "The Sacrifice" over the

reader's shoulder startles him by suddenly speaking up in
response to Christ—such is the impression created by the first
few lines of "The Thanksgiving." The first poem ends with
Christ's "Never was grief like mine"; the second begins with
the Christian's assent to his claim:

> Oh King of grief! (a title strange, yet true,
> > To thee of all kings onely due)
> O King of wounds! how shall I grieve for thee,
> > Who in all grief preventest me?
> Shall I weep bloud? why, thou hast wept such store
> > That all thy body was one doore.
> Shall I be scourged, flouted, boxed, sold?
> > 'Tis but to tell the tale is told.
> *My God, my God, why dost thou part from me?*
> > Was such a grief as cannot be.

The Christian responds to the Passion as it has just been
described in the preceding poem.[9] The insistence there on the
supremacy of Christ's grief explains the speaker's initial emphasis. The Savior's attitude about grief is complex: "Weep not,
deare friends, since I for both have wept" (line 149) would
seem to prohibit its expression. But "Such sorrow as, if sinfull
man could feel, / Or feel his part, he would not cease to kneel"
(lines 209–10) suggests that apprehension of even a portion of
Christ's sorrow is an impetus to repentance or piety. The
speaker feels his part, but acknowledging the King of Grief's
unsurpassable experience poses the problem of an adequate
response for the man who believes he is both the cause of the
sacrifice and the recipient of its benefits. The extravagant questions the speaker asks about what he might do seem strange
and presumptuous (as if he *could* weep blood), but they are a
simple device to emphasize the impossibility of responding
adequately to the sacrifice. The Christian knows that "it was

9. There are other links to "The Sacrifice" in "The Thanksgiving." The
speaker asks how he can grieve if Christ has anticipated him, or if he should
weep blood. Christ asks his friends not to weep "since I for both have
wept / When all my tears were blood" ("The Sacrifice," 149–50). Christ described how he was "scourged, flouted, boxed, sold" in the preceding poem.
He also asked, "But O my God, my God! why leav'st thou me," a question that
the speaker changes slightly in line 9 of "The Thanksgiving."

such a grief as cannot be" when Christ felt abandoned by the Father.

To respond to matchless grief with a necessarily less intense manifestation of the emotion seems inadequate to the speaker, who considers another possibility:

> Shall I then sing, skipping thy dolefull storie,
>     And side with thy triumphant glorie?
> Shall thy strokes be my stroking? thorns, my flower?
>     Thy rod, my posie? crosse, my bower?
> But how then shall I imitate thee, and
>     Copie thy fair, though bloudie hand?
>
> (11–16)

Singing would mean omitting altogether the dismal tale of the Crucifixion to emphasize Christ's "triumphant glorie"—a phrase that leads the reader to anticipate the Resurrection. When the Christian goes on with the "strokes" and "thorns," we realize at once that the speaker cannot put the sacrifice out of his mind and that Christ's grief *is* his triumph. Far from being "a strange story of the past" whose "painful details" he can omit,[10] the Passion unfits the Christian, at least temporarily, for singing. His manifest dissatisfaction with the possibility of song is understandable because his initial desire to grieve is now a desire to imitate Christ, and Christ is preeminently a figure whose significance lies in his suffering. In itself, the desire to "copie thy fair, though bloudie hand" cannot be considered eccentric or unusual, because the Scriptures encourage it. After the miracle of the loaves and the fishes, for example, Christ tells the disciples, "If any man will come after me, let him deny himself, and take up his cross daily, and follow me" (Luke 9:23). In 1 Peter 2:21, the Christian is advised that "Christ . . . suffered for us, leaving us an example, that ye should follow his steps." Indeed, "The Sacrifice" includes the reminder that the Cross is "The decreed burden of each mortall

10. Ilona Bell, " 'Setting Foot Into Divinity': George Herbert and the English Reformation," in *Essential Articles for the Study of George Herbert's Poetry*, ed. John R. Roberts, p. 74.

Saint" (line 199). What is unusual is this Christian's apparent
determination to imitate Christ's affliction. Rather than simply
feeling a regenerative grief, he wishes to imitate the "bloudie
hand"—to experience a like affliction. His zeal is commendable but ignorant and misdirected.

Since his first two ideas for responding to the Savior's grief
are unsatisfactory, he considers responding to his love:

> Surely I will revenge me on thy love,
>> And trie who shall victorious prove.
> If thou dost give me wealth, I will restore
>> All back unto thee by the poore.
> If thou dost give me honour, men shall see,
>> The honour doth belong to thee.
> I will not marry; or, if she be mine,
>> She and her children shall be thine.
> My bosome friend, if he blaspheme thy Name,
>> I will tear thence his love and fame.
> One half of me being gone, the rest I give
>> Unto some Chappell, die or live.
> As for thy passion—But of that anon,
>> When with the other I have done.
>
> (17–30)

"Revenge" defines his motive: he wants to make recompense
for Christ's love and test whether he or Christ loves more. He
is wrong to think he can repay the Savior, doubly wrong to
think he can surpass him. From the beginning of the poem, the
speaker's tremendous feeling of obligation to respond to the
sacrifice has been clear; now it is clear that the obligation is
perceived uneasily as indebtedness. The Christian is a debtor
determined to repay his creditor with abundant interest.
Obviously, he does not fully appreciate the nature of the
divine love of which he is the object. Considering the competition he sets up, the reader is bound to judge him to be presumptuous and foolish.

As the speaker's plans to repay Christ's love (with a surplus)
tumble out confidently, he has no sense of their inadequacy.
Only the thought of the Passion makes him falter momentarily
before he resumes his inventive schemes. The intrepid Christian will repay and match God's predestation with his own

predetermined plan to build a "spittle" or to "mend common wayes"—put roads in good repair or mend public faults. Such is the predestination of which he is capable. His failure to measure up to God is both obvious and amusing: his ability to predestine his actions first depends on whether he lives for three years. If he does, he will do one of the two things he mentions, but he is not sure which it will be. The pun on "mend common wayes" underscores the speaker's inability to predetermine anything, but he seems unconscious of any incongruity in his words as he asserts that he will mend his own ways immediately. He also plans a monastic withdrawal from the unimportant world to praise the divine attributes with harmonious music.

It is an ambitious program the Christian outlines, but he is not finished:

> Nay, I will read thy book, and never move
>     Till I have found therein thy love,
> Thy art of love, which I'le turn back on thee:
>     O my deare Saviour, Victorie!
>
>                 (45–48)

When he has read the Bible incessantly and there learned divine love, he will return this love to Christ. Now, exuberantly, the speaker believes he has achieved "Victorie!" He will win, compensating Christ's love and overpaying when he can love as the Savior did. It never occurs to this impetuous speaker that he might not be able to achieve perfect love. But he cannot forget that he intended to deal with Christ's Passion, and his tone goes swiftly from confidence to uncertainty to quiet perplexity as he says, "Then for thy passion—I will do for that— / Alas, my God, I know not what."

George Herbert Palmer's comment on the poem that "the mode of thanksgiving appropriate to the Christian is to vie with his Master, and still to acknowledge himself surpassed" might be more helpful did the speaker's last words not seem such an involuntary, amazed admission of helplessness. But, surely, that is Herbert's point: the best thanksgiving for the enormous gift of the sacrifice is to acknowledge that it is literally impossible to thank God adequately. To make this point forcefully, the speaker must be so naive that he proposes everything he can think of to repay divine love before he comes finally to an impasse. Helen Vendler suggests that the speaker of the poem is proud, guilty of "a somewhat frantic attempt to establish a footing of equality with God."[11] Though charging him with spiritual pride is just, he seems more ignorant than sinful. Facing a love unlike any other, he finds it difficult to accept that he is loved for no reason, for nothing in himself, for nothing he can do. His first impulse is to try to make an equal exchange, a fair reciprocity, to make himself retroactively worthy of the love of the Cross. To his credit, he wants to be deserving, but such worthiness can never be.

The discomfort of being the recipient of unmotivated love explains the Christian's feverish intensity. To read the poem is to be involved in the movement of his thought, a complex set of responses to the experience of divine love. First he sees Christ as the King of Grief and himself as a witness who wants to grieve. Then he sees Christ as a model and himself as a would-be imitator. He turns to love and sees the Savior as creditor and himself as debtor determined to repay, but also as a competitor determined to surpass the one to whom he is indebted. His successive stances toward Christ are efforts to cope with the obligation he feels. His error in wanting to overpay and overlove Christ notwithstanding, he is responsive and eager. His rapid listing of possible projects to alleviate his discomfort indicates his understanding that his love, like Christ's, must be expressed through activity. "What can I do?," he is asking beneath his grandiose plans.

"The Sacrifice" is a necessary preface to "The Thanksgiving." It enables the reader to share with the Christian speaker the awareness of God's gift that makes him a nervous debtor; it is also related to the second poem by the principle of cause and effect. "The Sacrifice" precipitates the thoughts, words, and feelings the speaker expresses in "The Thanksgiving." More precisely, as the speaker of "The Sacrifice," the Son creates or initiates the speaker's response, and in this sense Christ's

11. *The English Works of George Herbert*, 2:286; Vendler, *Poetry of George Herbert*, p. 232.

poem is a representation of prevenient grace. The Savior awakens the Christian to the great debt of love he owes; he inspires him to imitate the divine example by giving him a vivid consciousness of the Passion. Herbert wished to depict the action of grace: the only possible way to show that grace is a force from without, the influence of God, was to show Christ speaking and initiating, with the man responding to an impetus not his own. The Christian loves God because God first loved him.

The superior-subordinate relationship between God and man finally implied by "The Thanksgiving" is the basis of "Affliction" (I), a long complaint addressed to God. The Christian who contended against God in the first poem now accuses God of contending with him. The poem is an expression of frustration, confusion, and contained resentment as the speaker describes his feelings of betrayal, entrapment, and paralysis. As if to neutralize his explosive feelings, he speaks as a courtier-servant addressing his king-master, but the gist of his remarks shows the two more truly as hapless victim and cruel victimizer. The poem is as remarkable for its strong language as for its portrayal of God. The speaker has no doubt about who causes his afflictions.

The poem starts quietly enough as the courtier reviews the history of their relationship for the king he serves. Some time has elapsed since it began. A hint of accusation colors even the first sentence: "When first thou didst entice to thee my heart, / I thought the service brave." The impressionable youth was "enticed" to the king by visions of joy, by a dazzled appreciation for the king's "glorious household-stuffe" (which he felt would, in a sense, be his), and by expectations of pleasure:

> What pleasures could I want, whose King I served,
> > Where joyes my fellows were?
> Thus argu'd into hopes, my thoughts reserved
> > No place for grief or fear.
> Therefore my sudden soul caught at the place,
> And made her youth and fiercenesse seek thy face.
> > (13–18)

The servant pleads youthful inexperience and eagerness as his reason for accepting the place in the master's service. The foolish belief that incessant joy and pleasure would follow decided the impetuous soul and mind—not, obviously, the mature and regretful "I"—to seek the master's face. Ignorantly but wholeheartedly, the Christian misled himself into his present dismal situation. In "The Thanksgiving," he remarked on the impossibility of grieving for Christ, "Who in all grief preventest me." Evidently, he surmised along the way that grief or fear would have no place in his experience.

The servant got his own "wish and way" of happiness for a while but soon found himself suffering. Illness and the death of friends left him feeling "thinne and lean without a fence [means of defense] or friend." To make matters worse, he discovers that he dislikes the employment given him by the master.

> Whereas my birth and spirit rather took
> > The way that takes the town;
> Thou didst betray me to a lingring book,
> > And wrap me in a gown.
> I was entangled in the world of strife,
> Before I had the power to change my life.
>
> (37–42)

Inevitably, the eagerness of the speaker's vow in "The Thanksgiving" comes to mind: "I will read thy book, and never move / Till I have found therein thy love." Now he complains sullenly about a slowly paced book (possibly the Bible) or about the slow pace of his studies. In either case, his master set the task whose progress seems elephantine to one naturally disinclined toward it. Ironically, he "never moves" because he is entangled in a scholar's gown. "The way that takes the town," a less retired, more spirited employment, would have been more congenial, he informs the master, who is apparently insensitive to his servants' aptitudes or preferences. It is not difficult to understand why the quietest of occupations has bred loud feelings of powerlessness, entanglement, and strife. The responsibility is the master's.

Internal strife has frequently led the Christian to threaten "the siege to raise," but the master has cleverly dissipated his impulse to rebel. Using the simple expedient of giving the speaker the "sweetned pill" of praise for his endeavors, the crafty master has succeeded in paralyzing him to the point that "I could not go away, nor persevere." This praise is potent medicine, melting and dissolving rage but causing eventual paralysis. The image of the sugar-coated pill is very suggestive. It implies a curative action so harsh it must be made palatable by the addition of a nonessential ingredient. The pill-dispensing master apparently means to bend his servant's will to the employment that currently repels him. For the rebellious speaker, the pill's sweetener is most important, but he must also swallow the medicine that keeps him in a degree of health, faintly obedient. It keeps him, though unhappily, where his master wants him. Obviously, the master intends some undisclosed purpose; just as obviously, the Christian chafes against it even while he values the master's praise for the work he dislikes. However sullenly and unwillingly he stays, he cannot go away from his prescribed task. But because of his feeling that it is unsuited to him, he cannot persevere in it either.

The bitterness of the servant against his malevolent superior is strongly expressed as he accuses the master of using his great power to thwart him: "Turning my purge to food, thou throwest me / Into more sicknesses." Illness disables the man so that he can neither pursue the disagreeable occupation into which God has thrust him nor follow his own inclinations. Feeling victimized and paralyzed, he turns to the future:

> Now I am here, what thou wilt do with me
>           None of my books will show:
> I reade, and sigh, and wish I were a tree;
>           For sure then I should grow
> To fruit or shade: at least some bird would trust
> Her houshold to me, and I should be just.

>                    (55–60)

The servant speaks with a graceless pseudoresignation, the product of his exasperation. Since he is no longer under his own power, has no control over his own affairs, he can only wonder impatiently what his master intends to do with him. The wish that he were a tree is related to his past and present afflictions. The tree is useful: it gives fruit, shade, and shelter

to nesting birds, and does this simply by being its leafy self.
Undoubtedly, he mentions it and its natural "duties" primarily as a simple contrast to himself in his unsuitable (as he sees
it) occupation, but he also reveals his ignorance. As Asals
suggests, he has yet to learn that "*he is the tree* ('a tree planted
by the water-side, that bringeth forth his fruit in due season'—
Psalm 1:3).''[12] Of course, it does not occur to the speaker that
the tree does not debate the precise mode and season of its
fruitfulness with the husbandman. The tree has yet other
advantages—the speaker is no stoic, but one especially apt to
appreciate the benefits of a wooden existence: trees do not
suffer, nor do they employ will.

The jealous thought of the fortunate tree seems too much for
the servant, who explodes in a bitter complaint:

> Yet, though thou troublest me, I must be meek;
> > In weaknesse must be stout.
> Well, I will change the service, and go seek
> > Some other master out.
> Ah my deare God! though I am clean forgot,
> Let me not love thee, if I love thee not.
>
> (61–66)

The metaphor the Christian has been using to blunt his angry
dissatisfaction finally betrays him; simultaneously, it brings
him to his senses by disclosing the enormity of his rebellion.
Shocked, he drops the metaphor that has facilitated his rash
and dangerous threat, gives his master his proper name, and
reaffirms his commitment to God. The severest punishment
the speaker can imagine is not to be allowed to love the master
whom, despite all his complaints, he loves.

The final declaration of love may seem rather a brief counter-
weight to the many grievances the poem voices, but its brevity
is eloquent. The reader is meant to be impressed by the swift-
ness with which the force of love invalidates the speaker's
rebellion. In spite of love's effective power, however, the

___

12. Heather Asals, *Equivocal Predication: George Herbert's Way to God*, p. 45.

poem concentrates on the struggle between the Christian's "right to himself (the real essence of sin) and God's superior right to [him] by virtue of the sacrificial death of Jesus."[13] Though we are impressed by love, we are uneasy because the conflict is not resolved but disowned by the speaker, and we anticipate its recurrence. Irresolution notwithstanding, "Affliction" (I) is remarkable as the depiction of a helplessly beseiged man. His long address to God has the air of troubles long building, laid out in a list of grievances prepared in advance that gets out of hand in the recounting. The Christian was drawn to the suffering and loving God of the Passion, but now finds himself the entrapped subordinate of a stern and seemingly cruel master. His relationship with a God who strikes so harshly forces him to sound as if *he* were the king of griefs, and his circumstances remind us of his previously expressed desire to imitate Christ. There is still another sense in which the speaker (very unwillingly) imitates Christ: his lament in "Affliction" (I) that he is "clean forgot" parallels Christ's agonized feeling of abandonment in "The Sacrifice": "But, *O my God, my God!* why leav'st thou me." The speaker who so blithely mentioned the possibility of being scourged and flouted seems to have lost his fearlessness; the experience of pain and misfortune shows him to be very humanly disinclined to suffer.

The speaker's shortcomings as unwitting imitator of Christ are made clear in many ways, but in the employment sequence the reader is especially interested in his attitude toward his God-given occupation. The speaker thinks it suits neither his good station in life nor his sociable inclinations. Besides, he does not think it a useful occupation—stolid trees outdistance him in service. He is eager to serve and acknowledges his need of God's direction, but he is a grumbling servant with his own ideas about what activity best suits him. Such a servant could hardly expect a long tenure in most households, but he is unable to perceive that his own figurative language accuses him. Still, though he fails to live up to the superhuman self-image he projected in "The Thanksgiving," he is more meek

13. Larry Brunner, "Herbert's 'Affliction' (I) and 'The Flower,' " p. 19.

and stout than he knows when he reaffirms his trusting commitment to the God who afflicts him.[14]

The speaker's fantastic wish that he might be a tree is transformed into a more reasonable request to be made useful since,
wherever he looks, he sees a purposeful world. Natural productivity is the focal point of "Employment" (I):

> If as a flowre doth spread and die,
>  Thou wouldst extend me to some good,
> Before I were by frosts extremitie
>                     Nipt in the bud;
>
> The sweetnesse and the praise were thine;
>  But the extension and the room,
> Which in thy garland I should fill, were mine
>                     At thy great doom.
>                           (1–8)

The speaker's identity as a bud fearful of death before fulfilling
its destiny conveys very well his despondent frame of mind. It
is significant that he who wished to be a tree in the last poem
would be content now to be a much smaller flower. The blos-

14. For a detailed interpretation of this poem from a different perspective,
see Barbara Leah Harman, *Costly Monuments: Representations of the Self in George
Herbert's Poetry*. I disagree with Harman's suggestion that the "giving over of
the heart is not, and never was, a matter of choice" (p. 91) because the speaker
say he was "enticed" to enter service voluntarily. Moreover, I do not see
"Affliction" (I) as a "collapsing poem" according to Harman's definition. A
characteristic feature of collapsing poems, she writes, is a speaker who "offers
a fully articulated, intact account of a significant set of events in his life, only to
remind us that the account is retrospective and that there is a major discrepan-
cy between his current feelings and those he has just described. He indicates
that he has no faith in his account, that it no longer represents him . . . The
narrating speaker discovers nothing in the course of the narrative. He knows
what he knows *from* the start, even when he does not disclose what he knows
*at* the start. Instead, he waits until the narrative's end to reveal a change that
took place before the narrative began" (p. 64). In the poem's "present," the
speaker addresses God to give his retrospective account summarizing their
relationship as a reproach, a history of his ill treatment. The retrospective
account culminates in, and is the basis of, his present feelings, and the
suffering it describes continues into the present moment: "thou throwest
me / Into more sicknesses" The speaker does not know at the start that the
expression of his feelings will lead him to utter rebellion; he discovers that,
notwithstanding his past and present "mistreatment" or his present feelings,
he still wants to continue his relationship with his master.

som, traditional symbol of life's brevity and transience, retains its significance in these lines but not its typical pathos. Herbert's image accepts the natural state of affairs so far as it includes death, but not so far as it may include a premature end. Desiring an expansion of self into usefulness, the Christian feels contracted into vulnerability. The implied metaphor by which the righteous are God's colorful and fragrant garland is set against a background of fearful violence. The perfect flowery circle seems incongruous on Doomsday, but such is the difference between the two destinies that God promises man. Since the speaker naturally prefers a place in God's crown, he bargains. A mutually beneficial arrangement is what the bud offers the husbandman, pointing out the benefits the latter would reap from its blossoming.

The following two stanzas emphasize the Christian's dependence on God and repeat his petition, supporting it with another image of vulnerable contraction: what he does not want is "A life as barren to thy praise, / As is the dust, to which that life doth tend." Again, his sense of purposelessness is made acute by his awareness of the natural world:

> All things are busie; onely I
> Neither bring hony with the bees,
> Nor flowres to make that, nor the husbandrie
>       To water these.
>
> I am no link of thy great chain,
> But all my companie is a weed.
> Lord place me in thy consort; give one strain
>       To my poore reed.
>             (17–24)

The controlling metaphor plainly indicates the scheme of interrelated, universal productivity instituted by the Creator. But the "great chain" functions without the Christian. With the ideal flower at the center of his description, his self-characterization as a weed conveys again his humility and fear. Not only is a weed useless to the particular business the Christian describes, it is also entirely out of place, even taking up space that could be more productively employed. The lack of a purposeful place is not perceived simply as a personal problem, then; it is seen as a disharmony with the order and purpose God implemented in the world. The speaker's final words drop the strand of imagery that he has used most consistently—he wants God to transform him, take him into the universal harmony of utility, under any terms.

Though it depresses him, the book of nature helps the Christian to begin defining his purpose: he wants to do some unspecified "good" in praise of God. He does not think in terms of repayment or compensation when he considers activity. What urgency he feels arises from his recognition of death's inevitability. In order to make his petition more attractive, he explains precisely how his being employed would benefit God, but the speaker is aware of his dependence. God must "extend" and place him. God must "impart . . . grace" if the Christian is to achieve his purpose. Powerlessness adds to his dejection. The would-be flower is an unwilling and unhappy weed, understandably anxious for a metamorphosis before the shears come. But only God is a powerful-enough gardener to turn the weed into a blossom. The simple natural imagery the speaker uses is well chosen to convey his conviction that "Employment" in God's scheme is the fundamental object of life.

The Christian's homely imagery and his awareness that he must depend on God continue in "Grace." He does not try to bargain with God; four of the six stanzas conclude with a petition that grace "drop from above":

> My stock lies dead, and no increase
> Doth my dull husbandrie improve:
> O let thy graces without cease
>                     Drop from above!
>
> If still the sunne should hide his face,
> Thy house would but a dungeon prove,
> Thy works nights captives: O let grace
>                     Drop from above!
>
> The dew doth ev'ry morning fall;
> And shall the dew out-strip thy Dove?

> The dew, for which grasse cannot call,
> > Drop from above.
>
> Death is still working like a mole,
> And digs my grave at each remove:
> Let grace work too, and on my soul
> > Drop from above.
>
> > (1–16)

As Hutchinson notes, the text underlying the poem is Job 14:7–9: "For there is hope of a tree, if it be cut down, that it will sprout again, and that the tender branch thereof will not cease. Though the root thereof wax old in the earth, and the stock thereof die in the ground; Yet through the scent of water it will bud, and bring forth boughs like a plant." The plant metaphor is a commonplace used by moralists to depict man's "obligation to grow upwards." Ryley reads "stock" as the speaker's natural "Capacitys . . . Capable of being Improved, to good advantage" but left undeveloped by his dull tending.[15] The speaker-husbandman's distress flourishes because his "stock" is entirely dependent on factors beyond his control, sunshine and rain. His address to God is composed of complaints, petitions, and expressions of fear. Though he takes the responsibility for his dullness, he knows that grace only can animate his efforts. An occasional note of exasperation breaks through his urgency as he tries to persuade God to dispense the life-giving drops that will end this dark, unproductive interlude: what justice is there if the mute grass every day gets its dew while he languishes despite his eloquence? The frustrated husbandman's reproach stems from his fear that the mole works more energetically than the Dove.

The Christian's address to God ends with yet another reproach:

> Sinne is still hammering my heart
> Unto a hardnesse, void of love:

15. Elizabeth Mackensie, "The Growth of Plants: A Seventeenth-Century Metaphor," in *English Renaissance Studies Presented to Dame Helen Gardner in Honour of Her Seventieth Birthday*, ed. John Carey, p. 195. Mackensie refers (p. 194) to the same quotation from Job that Hutchinson suggests as central. John M. Heissler, ed., *Mr Herbert's Temple & Church Militant Explained and Improved . . .*, 1:160.

> Let suppling grace, to crosse his art,
> > Drop from above.
>
> O come! for thou dost know the way:
> Or if to me thou wilt not move,
> Remove me, where I need not say,
> > *Drop from above.*
> >              (17–24)

The speaker's change to a different metaphor at the end is like that noticed for "Employment" (I). Herbert uses this device to depict the agitated mind casting about for the best way to express its trouble or, when addressing God, for the most persuasive terms to present its condition. The blacksmith sin goes about his business regardless of the horror of the heart's possessor; only grace can soften his iron handiwork. The forging image stresses the power of "suppling grace," but the Christian's faith in its immediate advent wavers, and he ends with a reproach that is wonderfully sly. By sounding resigned, more than accommodating and reasonable, in the last stanza, he manages indirectly to suggest that God is stubborn and uncooperative. It is a clever effort to manipulate God. Either of the alternatives the speaker proposes would remove him from all the problems he faces. Either way, given grace here and now or transplanted to another world, the Christian demands relief from his misery.

Apparently simple poems like "Grace" often give us insight into the complexities of the Christian's relationship with God. It is impossible for him to avoid self-pity when he feels unjustifiably ignored, difficult for him to avoid resentment toward the only one who can help but will not. Yet these feelings, inappropriate though they may be and controlled though they certainly are, underlie his prayer. When faith and a sense of decorum do not allow him to give them full or direct expression, their sharp undertones yet produce a rich tension and depth.

Immediately following and complementing "Grace," whose stanzas end with the request that grace "Drop from above," is "Praise" (I), which stresses the ascending power (figurative, for the time being) that is the Christian's gain. Grace descends to man, enabling him to rise, to move closer to the celestial source of all power and love. But the Christian still needs divine aid and pleads urgently again that God might do more so that he (who deserves more) might have more praise. Each of the five stanzas ends with "more," three with "do more." This repetition emphasizes the speaker's distressing valuation of the "less-ness" of his praise at the same time that it emphasizes the "more," the "much much more" that is God's due.

Though the Christian is not idle, that is small consolation as he pauses to reflect:

> To write a verse or two is all the praise,
>> That I can raise:
> Mend my estate in any wayes,
>> Thou shalt have more.
>
> I go to Church; help me to wings, and I
>> Will thither flie;
> Or, if I mount unto the skie,
>> I will do more.
>
> (1–8)

The speaker is a poet whose meager productivity strikes him as insufficient praise. His writing of more verses depends on God's improvement of his situation. It is the same with his lack of enthusiasm in worship. With God-given wings, he would fly to church, or better yet to the sky, where he imagines the perfect praise he could offer. The Christian's tone is so matter-of-fact that the reader can almost overlook his equal readiness to die or to praise more zealously on earth. Wings to speed him to church or wings to confirm his heavenly citizenship seem to have an equal appeal. He asks for help because he *acts* his devotion, but with a sense of its inadequacy. His dependence on God is total. According to what the Deity gives so he receives, because the poet's zealous desire to praise cannot soar into accomplishment without grace. The Christian is like a child asking his father for money with which to buy him a present, an insistent child asking for a considerable sum to supplement what he has already been given so that he can buy a really generous gift.

Convinced that he could "flie," "mount," if God gave the grace he requests, he is instead earthbound and frustrated. It does not help much to realize that his incapacity is shared by all men. He continues glumly:

> Man is all weaknesse; there is no such thing
> > As Prince or King:
> > His arm is short; yet with a sling
> > He may do more.
>
> An herb distill'd, and drunk, may dwell next doore,
> > On the same floore,
> > To a brave soul: exalt the poore,
> > They can do more.
>
> (9–16)

Just in case God has forgotten, the Christian reminds him that David's sling, with which, in spite of his relative weakness, he overcame Goliath, represents the remedy. Even physiological details show forth the simple principle he wants God to effect: when one drinks a humble medicinal potion, it ascends to the brain, and thus mere herbs acquire a rich neighbor (the soul was believed to reside in the head). If God exalts the poor (the context suggests that Herbert means all men, since all are poor in abilities without God's help), they can outdo the herbs and "dwell near God."[16] Though they may be unnecessary lessons when addressed to God, the Christian's examples are calculated to persuade; at the least, they persuade the reader that the small may achieve mighty goals—with assistance.

Having stated and restated his and Everyman's weakness and dependence on God, outlined the possibilities for improvement with grace, and implied that all ought to praise more than they do, the dissatisfied poet comes back to himself and ends with yet one more plea:

> O raise me then! Poore bees, that work all day,
> > Sting my delay,
> > Who have a work, as well as they,
> > And much, much more.
>
> (17–20)

Here again are the bees of "Employment" (I), but these sym-

---

16. Hutchinson provides this reading by H. F. B. Brett-Smith of the difficult lines (*Works*, p. 497).

bols of incessant industry irritate the Christian's frustration: he feels the sting of the comparison between himself and the winged insects. He is pained that his work, much more important than theirs, does not progress with the same energy and consistency. If things are to change, if he is to do more than what fails to satisfy him, God must do more for him—mend his estate, help him to wings, provide him with a sling, exalt or raise him. Of course, this poem in which the poet-speaker laments the insufficiency of his praise is praise indeed. His intense dissatisfaction with the results of his striving indicates his estimation of what God is due.[17]

There is muted frustration for the same reason in "Evensong," but it fades into the Christian's stronger experience of contentment and wonder. He wants to do his utmost because he believes that God's love is incessant; this belief, rather than his disappointing inability to reciprocate adequately, is uppermost in his mind. The poem shows two contrasting perspectives on employment, the speaker's and God's. It is a sign of a growing understanding of divine love that he can imagine a perspective so different from his own. This emerging maturity is evident as well in his understanding that God's different attributes are summed up in love. "Even-song" moves quickly from a grateful enumeration of God's gifts to a witty confession of guilt, followed swiftly by a relieved statement of faith. Indirectly, the Christian's words also yield a characterization of God:

> Blest be the God of love,
> Who gave me eyes, and light, and power this day,
> Both to be busie, and to play.
> But much more blest be God above,
> Who gave me sight alone,
> Which to himself he did denie:

17. For a different perspective on "Praise" (I), see Sharon Cadman Seelig, *The Shadow of Eternity: Belief and Structure in Herbert, Vaughan, and Traherne*, p. 19: "As the persona goes through the motions of faith and praise, the lines make us feel the lack of fervor and conviction." I suggest that the "lack of fervor" is dejection caused by the Christian's inability to praise as he would like to do.

> For when he sees my waies, I dy:
> But I have got his sonne, and he hath none.
>
> (1–8)

He seems to be praying to two Gods, "the 'God of Love,' and that more powerful and more to be thanked 'God above,' the God, presumably, of the higher region."[18] However, the distinction is based not on degrees of power, but on contrasting attributes. The first God is the loving giver of all, who even enables his creatures to play; the "God above" is the wrathful, just God who must be blind, because he would otherwise have struck down the man guilty of unspecified offensive "waies." The distinction quickly proves to be superficial. Herbert plays with the tradition of blind Justice: God is blind for the sake not of impartiality but of partiality to man. The "God above" is also a giving, loving God whose mercy is evident in the gift of his Son and in his forbearance toward sinful man.

The speaker's awareness of the breakdown of his initial distinction is evident when he immediately asks:

> What have I brought thee home
> For this thy love? have I discharg'd the debt,
> Which this dayes favour did beget?
> I ranne; but all I brought, was fome.
> Thy diet, care, and cost
> Do end in bubbles, balls of winde;
> Of winde to thee whom I have crost,
> But balls of wilde-fire to my troubled minde.
>
> (9–16)

His anxiety is aroused as he considers the futility of his efforts to discharge his debt of gratitude. He tried to make a return for the most basic of gifts—for the God-given room and board that allowed him to live another day—but brought only foam. The image is pathetic because it depicts the appearance of substance gradually contracting into nothingness. It suggests that the Christian imagined he had achieved something and only subsequently realized he had achieved nothing. At present, he is not concerned about the little he does or his lack of fervor, as

18. Stanley Fish, *Self-Consuming Artifacts: The Experience of Seventeenth-Century Literature*, p. 163.

he was in "Praise" (I). He tried hard—and his efforts came to nothing. The "bubbles, balls of winde" to the "crost" God (opposed and crucified by the speaker's sin) are the "balls of wilde-fire" fueling the Christian's anxiety. The painfulness and the potentially destructive capacity of his self-evaluation are conveyed vividly by the image of the fireballs searing the mind as they roll uncontrollably about.

Thus far, this is the familiar self-scrutinizing and dissatisfied Christian, but he continues:

> Yet still thou goest on,
> And now with darknesse closest wearie eyes,
> Saying to man, *It doth suffice:*
> *Henceforth repose; your work is done.*
> Thus in thy ebony box
> Thou dost inclose us, till the day
> Put our amendment in our way,
> And give new wheels to our disorder'd clocks.
>
> (17–24)

Anxiety turns to wonder as he envisions a loving Father reassuring his tired child at the end of the day. The foam "doth suffice"; the bubbles are classified and accepted as "work." Incredibly, God takes into account the Christian's efforts rather than their result. This insight seems to come from out of the blue until we remember that this is "Even-song." The speaker finds significance in the cycle of day and night, activity and repose. That God himself stops with night the day's "running" must mean that he judges what is done as sufficient. Besides, after the "ebony box," a new day will provide the reassured man with a fresh opportunity for amendment.

The final stanza of the poem shows the speaker's contented recognition that he has every reason to continue in his efforts but no reason to despair:

> I muse, which shows more love,
> The day or night: that is the gale, this th' harbour;
> That is the walk, and this the arbour;
> Or that the garden, this the grove.
> My God, thou art all love.
> Not one poore minute scapes thy breast,
> But brings a favour from above;

And in this love, more then in bed, I rest.
(25–32)

"Gale" and "harbour," "walk" and "arbour," "garden" and "grove" are paired metaphors for day and night that begin as opposites but progress to similarity, so that day and night combine to prove the conclusion implicit in the first stanza of the poem: God is "all love." Every minute is caught or enfolded in the loving divine breast and is evidence of the never-ceasing love in which the Christian's spirit finds repose. The foam of ineffectual efforts does not alter the tireless love of God.

Earlier we noted the Christian's difficulty in accepting an unmotivated love not based on his character, his ability to reciprocate, or some other value in himself. "Even-song" shows him not merely accepting divine love (after an interval of the usual self-criticism) but also finding relief in the knowledge that it does not at all depend on his efforts. From the love he sees in all he receives, he concludes that the divine, ongoing love is proof that God is not as critical as the speaker thinks he deserves. The Christian will always be "behinde" in love, but the thought, if seen as an assurance that divine love is constant despite his inability to merit it, is a comfort.

*       *       *

Looking back on the speaker's restlessness because of his inability to find a satisfactory employment, the reader may now expect that he can relax. After all, once the Christian accepts that divine love does not depend on his efforts, that God accepts the imperfect human return of affection, what could possibly trouble him? But the speaker cannot now stop thinking in terms of activity: it is no longer simply a matter of his inner need to act his love as well as he can, although that need persists—it is a matter of doing God's will as it is evident in the world. Having seen nature's busyness and concluded that it enacts God's plan, he must continue to contemplate employment, even when he is not himself striving.

The development of the Christian within these poems is evident when we recall that the contented debtor started as an eager challenger of Christ's supremacy. By degrees, through the different roles the speaker assigns himself and God, Herbert shows him defining and redefining himself according to a growing understanding of God and divine love. These attempts to define the two participants gradually elucidate their relationship. The speaker begins as a contestant, confident in his ability to repay, imitate, and surpass divine love. He surrenders his flattering self-image when he is tried in "Affliction" (I). There he first depicts himself as a servant-victim, but as an unwitting imitator of Christ's grief he eventually reaffirms his love and trust with a full consciousness of the difficulties of his commitment. With "Employment" (I), he begins to present himself as an unprofitable creature with a desire to do practical good in praise of God. Dependent on his master, he stands before him as a suppliant for grace and proceeds along a course of humbling self-discovery. His expanding outlook intensifies the pain caused by his shrinking self-conception as he is forced to acknowledge his dependence on God's grace for his capacities. Around him is a world carrying out a divine plan of activity, but unhappily he takes no part in it though his thoughts are constantly on employment.

God figures in these poems successively as a prodigious giver who inspires, burdens, and challenges the speaker with a debt of love; as a cruel, inscrutable, but beloved master; and finally as a powerful, essential God, the source of order, direction, ability, and love, the source of vital grace. The Christian's successive characterizations of God depend on the experience he undergoes, but in each poem, his acquaintance with the Deity deepens. Nevertheless, he has problems responding to God in spite of the grace he receives. He attempts to act at first as he might in response to an ordinary human love. But the rules that apply in human relationships have little relevance to the relationship with God. It is difficult to know how to deal with a debt that can be neither discharged nor forgotten. Then there is the mystery of the divine nature: how is the Christian to understand the hardships God inflicts? Physical illness, dejection, and tragedy are strange wages for a loyal servant, and Herbert dramatizes the Christian's justifiable confusion and its only possible dissolution in submissive love. Moreover, trusting the inscrutable God is difficult when actualities run counter to expectations and the future is uncertain. Even a proved commitment does not solve all the problems of love when the speaker experiences feelings of uselessness and alienation in a productive, busy world.

Regardless of what the Christian sometimes thinks, he is not "without a fence or friend." As a recipient of grace, he has Christ, the Bible, and God's other book, the natural world, for guidance. Though Christ's example proves troublesome because the speaker thinks in terms of afflictive imitation, he does learn that love is expressed in practical action. He seems to be able to take no more than this from the divine paradigm. Aligning the lessons learned from his "lingring book" with the example of the natural world helps the Christian to start defining the "useful" expression he wants his love to take. In this regard, he is unlike the typical fashionable youth. In "The Country Parson," George Herbert casts a severe eye at "the Gallant, who is witty enough to abuse both others, and himself, and who is ready to ask, if he shall mend shoos, or what he shall do? Therfore the Parson unmoved, sheweth, that *ingenuous and fit* imployment is never wanting to those that seek it" (*Works*, p. 275). The first six poems of the employment sequence show that seeking it can be disheartening and frustrating, even for a willing Christian as eager to do his duty as Herbert must have been.

# 5

# The "Blest Order"

Until fairly recently, most critics regarded George Herbert as John Donne's disciple and inferior. Joan Bennett's remarks on the poets' literary relationship and relative merits, originally set forth in 1934, went generally unchallenged: "The influence of the elder poet on the younger was strong and permanent . . . But, for various reasons, [Herbert's] poetry is simpler than Donne's . . . Herbert's narrower experience not only limits his choice of subject-matter, but simplifies the texture of his poems." Today, Helen Vendler's assessment that Herbert deserves to be ranked "higher than Donne" might be disputed, but few would deny that the author of *The Temple* is one of the major poets of the seventeenth century.[1]

Though he uses some of the devices associated with the elder poet, Herbert is not an anemic Donne. He does not always aim for the mercurial excitement that is a characteristic of Donne's poetic voice, though he can certainly achieve it. Some of his poetry, like Donne's, presents a dramatic confrontation or a highly charged situation and then, as "Affliction" (I) shows, Herbert can convey a splendidly feverish agitation. But when the Christian's primary auditor is God, emotions like bitterness, resentment, or anger, if expressed, must be rejected finally as inappropriate. So long as his faith holds in the loving Deity whose purpose toward him is essentially beneficent (if often incomprehensible), such emotions can be only temporary. Implicitly or explicitly, his eventual rejection of them confesses and classifies them, in retrospect, as distrustful outbursts that violate his relationship with God. This divine-human relationship is central in "The Church"; consequently, many of Herbert's poems end in a quiet dissolu-

1. Bennett, *Five Metaphysical Poets: Donne, Herbert, Vaughan, Crashaw, Marvell*, p. 49; Vendler, *The Poetry of George Herbert*, p. 5.

tion of the problem or conflict they depict. Donne's religious sonnets, which usually focus on their speaker's doubts and fears, typically end with his unrest and turmoil unaltered. Herbert's Christian speaker does not deny or escape the negative emotions, but his sense of their impropriety qualifies their expression. Often, the feelings whose full articulation he judges indecorous or inappropriate find muted or indirect expression. Consequently, in these poems we often see relatively subtle emotional expression. There will be further opportunities to observe these as we progress through the employment sequence, because the speaker's ambition continues to be frustrated.

\*       \*       \*

The speaker of the sequence has identified himself thus far as a student of good family, a poet, and a candidate for employment. This self-characterization suggests that he is fairly young, and yet "Employment" (I), "Grace," "Praise" (I), and the "ebony box" coffin image for night in "Even-song" reveal that death is never far from his mind either as *desideratum* or disquieting threat. The Christian's illness mentioned in "Affliction" (I), his keen awareness of life's brevity, and his despondency about employment explain this preoccupation. Once illness shows his vulnerability, he fears death before he attains useful service because service is praise, and praise (as we remarked earlier) is the only sacrifice mandated under the New Covenant. His preoccupations with death, praise, nature, and unemployment continue in the middle section of the sequence. Dissatisfied with himself as student and poet, impatient with what he sees as personal uselessness, he suspects that his ambition is a mistake. Despairing of finding an acceptable avenue of service, he muses first about an unstriving serenity and then about a painless translation to the heavens, where he imagines service to be an uncomplicated expression of self.

Beneath the quiet reflection of "Content" is a welter of self-accusation and fear. In "Affliction" (I), the speaker argues that his "birth and spirit" should direct him to "the way that takes the town"—to a prominent employment. In "Content," he tries to talk himself out of his ambitious urges:

> Peace mutt'ring thoughts, and do not grudge to keep
> > Within the walls of your own breast:
> Who cannot on his own bed sweetly sleep,
> > Can on anothers hardly rest.
>
> Gad not abroad at ev'ry quest and call
> > Of an untrained hope or passion.
> To court each place or fortune that doth fall,
> > Is wantonnesse in contemplation.
>
> Mark how the fire in flints doth quiet lie,
> > Content and warm t' it self alone:
> But when it would appeare to others eye,
> > Without a knock it never shone.
>
> > > > (1–12)

Here is the wiser "I," whom we have met before, lecturing the unruly thoughts, whom we have also met before. The thoughts are personified as men who gad about restlessly, refusing to stay quietly in their breast-home. Motivated by ambition, they no sooner hear the trumpets of hope or enthusiasm than they are aroused into wandering. The Christian chides his thoughts because they put themselves forward foolishly, without justification, pursuing offices for which his training or experience does not qualify him. Patiently, he counsels them with the example of the more dignified and reclusive fire. Retiring and contented, fire dwells in its flint, not showing its face unless a knock calls it to its door. The metaphor of men with contrasting attitudes toward their dwellings is precise: the speaker, who admires a quiet detachment, is concerned about the inner self, whose ill-defined ambition is a wish to advance "out of doors," in the public world. Still, the image insists that the flint must be struck if the sparks of fire are to be usable. The "knock" signals a legitimate call to action and suggests that even the Christian's proper ambitions cannot be fulfilled without external assistance—whether such help comes from men or from grace. Without the summoning knock, the frantically scurrying thoughts can accomplish nothing. They would do well to learn patience.

Not aspiration but its attendant unrest troubles the speaker.

He desires an equanimity impervious to his worldly status, a mind that can aim at "a crown, and yet with pleasure / Take up within a cloisters gate." His ideal is both a soul that arches tentlike over the world as its serene domain and the mind that dwells in such a soul, knowing no unsettling effort or enterprise. But the ideal is not the actual, so he continues his exercise to control his restless thoughts:

> The brags of life are but a nine dayes wonder;
> > And after death the fumes that spring
> From private bodies, make as big a thunder,
> > As those which rise from a huge King.
>
> Onely thy Chronicle is lost; and yet
> > Better by worms be all once spent,
> Then to have hellish moths still gnaw and fret
> > Thy name in books, which may not rent.
>
> > > > (21–28)

The speaker's lecture to his thoughts grows severe. Fame does not last and death makes all men equal; if history magnifies a few, even posthumous fame depends on the wit and taste of unknown men who will write or read of the dead. By now, it is clear to the reader that the poem is a simultaneous confession and repudiation of ambition for self-regarding reasons. Though the Christian distances self-criticism by addressing his thoughts as if they were independent characters, he knows better.

His indirection cannot hide how avidly he has wished for exalting employment. Fully a third of his sermon to himself denies the value of worldly fame in revealing terms. Stinking corpses, worms feasting in the grave, and hellish moths gnawing endlessly are all clues to the underlying reason for the Christian's rejection of worldly ambition. "The way that takes the town" may well be the way to damnation, he knows, but this fearful insight is reached circuitously and expressed implicitly. He orders his soul to stop its busy thoughts of advancement, to stop importuning itself and others, and to concentrate on itself: "He that by seeking hath himself once found, / Hath ever found a happie fortune." He counsels himself wisely, as he learns to depend on the inward and not on the external world for his contentment.

Once again, the speaker is at a standstill. He learned previously that God accepts all efforts to serve him, and he realizes now that efforts to serve himself produce anxiety and imperil his soul. These two insights might encourage him to abandon his search for employment if inspiration did not come from the heavens in one of Herbert's loveliest poems. When it comes, the Christian, who has just rejected scrambling for position, requests a high place for himself. "The Starre" is a delightful, witty reflection on the possibilities of Christian activity, but the speaker does not, as Vendler suggests, solve problems "concerning employment" in the poem (p. 253). The shooting star fires his imagination, but it cannot do more than inspire him as other parts of the natural world have done. The bright spark's activities, in contrast to the realistic "employments" of the trees, flowers, and bees, are only figuratively possible; the Christian's imagination of them emphasizes his continuing preoccupation with activity:

> Bright spark, shot from a brighter place,
>> Where beams surround my Saviours face,
>>> Canst thou be any where
>>> So well as there?
>
> Yet, if thou wilt from thence depart,
>> Take a bad lodging in my heart;
>>> For thou canst make a debter,
>>> And make it better.
>
> First with thy fire-work burn to dust
>> Folly, and worse then folly, lust:
>>> Then with thy light refine,
>>> And make it shine.
>
> (1–12)

The lines falling from left to right imitate the descent of the star addressed familiarly by the serene Christian. He imagines the spark of light many times multiplied as the glory of heaven, from which the star is "shot." His verb lightly implies a will whose agent is the star, but his attention is riveted on the bright spark itself. The iconographic image of the stars as a blazing corona around Christ's face gratifies the Christian's fancy, but also makes him curious about the star leaving its dwelling. Ever helpful, he invites it to move into a dilapidated

inn needing extensive repair, if not a thorough gutting to
destroy some undesirable architectural features. The speaker
judges his spiritual condition severely, but he volunteers to
undergo the needed repairs in the faith that his heart can
become a star, shining and loving.

There is no clue, in the first four stanzas, of what love the
falling star expresses, unless it be its refining service to its
fellow creature. But there is more to the Christian's request of
the star. It should reverse its flight, taking with it the tyro star
and getting him a place, employment, in the shining corona:

> Get me a standing there, and place
>   Among the beams, which crown the face
>     Of him, who dy'd to part
>     Sinne and my heart.
>                     (21–24)

Since the experienced star was asked to disengage the heart
"from sinne and sicknesse," the Savior who died "to part /
Sinne and my heart" is identified now as the "shooter"
"whose ministers / The starres and all things are" ("Artillerie"). In addition to being his ministers, the stars are wor-
shipers. The imagined flight into the heavens, close to the
Savior, would enable the Christian-turned-star also to adore
him by simply glittering. Since the star might well refuse such
a one-sided arrangement, the Christian explains the entice-
ment implicit in his proposition:

> Sure thou wilt joy, by gaining me
>   To flie home like a laden bee
>     Unto that hive of beams
>     And garland-streams.
>                     (29–32)

Wistfulness turns into a matter-of-fact tone intended to persuade: obviously, the star's gain of another would be its reward and glory. Naturally, the speaker argues, its adoring
function would be well served if it could add another worship-
er to the hive of beams.

Though he is dissatisfied with himself, the Christian expresses serious assumptions fancifully, in a playful spirit. The
star may not really be able to transform and transport him, yet

it serves by enticing him to think of God. The instant the star accomplishes some missionary work by quickening his desire to adore, it doubles its own adoration and becomes productive like the enviable laden bees. Only the speaker's preoccupation with praise and productive employment can explain this odd identification of two flying creatures. His insight into the productive aspect of worship shows him the capacity of one creature to serve another. Service is possible because man and star are seen as fellow-creatures engaged with different degrees of success in the same function of adoring God; this common end of all the creatures has been implied before by the Christian's jealous attention to bees, trees, and flowers. It is stated unequivocally and imaginatively here, but the unhappily passive and self-critical man does not know yet how "The Starre" might help solve his own problems of vocation.

His request that "The Starre" get him a place for adoration is robbed of its dark implications by the play of his imagination. But after the calm of the ideal and the fantastic, reality reasserts itself in "Employment" (II) and plunges the meditating Christian into dejection:

> He that is weary, let him sit.
>             My soul would stirre
> And trade in courtesies and wit,
>             Quitting the furre
> To cold complexions needing it.
>
> Man is no starre, but a quick coal
>             Of mortall fire:
> Who blows it not, nor doth controll
>             A faint desire,
> Lets his own ashes choke his soul.
>                 (1–10)

Who is the cold and sluggish "He" sitting enveloped in fur, so unlike the speaker's active and manly soul, and why is he introduced? The Christian's initial statement, flatly challenging and combative, seems a defiant and contemptuous belittling of the unknown man's fatigue. Given the poem's title, the speaker's unfulfilled aspirations, and his habit of setting one aspect of himself against another, the contrast could be between the self of his eager soul and the self of his unemployed actuality. However, his despondency demands amplification rather than clarity of exposition, and the second stanza hints at the futility of imagined transformations such as that informing "The Starre" and modifies also the positive image of fire in "Content." Though the speaker refers to "Man," the living coal of mortal fire represents a drastic reduction in his self-image. He is discontented, though his diminution is offset by insight: the star's sparkling may have seemed effortless, but the coal (gifted with mouth and breath) must blow on or choke its fiery soul. Initiative, blowing or knocking, is required of all. No figurative language can blunt the threat implicit in the image of a soul choking on ashes.

The logic of the speaker's reflections eludes the reader, but the reason for his gloom begins to emerge when he acknowledges man's responsibility to use his initiative. Immediately, such responsibility becomes evident everywhere:

> When th'elements did for place contest
> > With him, whose will
> Ordain'd the highest to be best;
> > The earth sat still,
> And by the others is opprest.
>
> Life is a businesse, not good cheer;
> > Ever in warres.
> The sunne still shineth there or here,
> > Whereas the starres
> Watch an advantage to appeare.
>
> (11–20)

This zealous soul sees everything glumly in terms of a competition for supremacy, which reminds the reader of the speaker's initial contest with Christ. If God ordained the hierarchy in which fire is superior and earth inferior, the Christian implies, God also ordains the competition within man in which either the body's sluggish earth or the soul's "mortall fire" must gain the ascendancy. No wonder the speaker has a grim definition of life: the hierarchies without inspire the wars within and leave him a joyless, judgmental perspective. His former appreciation of the stars' twinkling adoration fades when he thinks of the sun's greater strength.

Undoubtedly, the Christian wishes to be as constant and strong as the sun, but he names a humbler (and more familiar) fellow creature as his ideal. His tone lightens into enthusiasm briefly:

> Oh that I were an Orenge-tree,
> > That busie plant!
> Then should I ever laden be,
> > And never want
> Some fruit for him that dressed me.
>
> But we are still too young or old;
> > The Man is gone,
> Before we do our wares unfold:
> > So we freeze on,
> Untill the grave increase our cold.
>
> (21–30)

The speaker does not select the orange tree merely as his sentimental favorite. The sun always shines, but the orange tree adds another dimension to the perfection the speaker wishes to attain: it gives fruit, a tangible gain, as acknowledgment and repayment for the cultivator's care. The speaker's life as yet is fruitless. His tone plummets to its lowest register in his capsule description of man's life, reflecting his frustration and at last confirming the identity of the cold and languid "He" in the first stanza. He is the self the speaker rejects but cannot transcend or discard. Life seems brief to one unable to discover his talents; the period for mature employment seems elusive and severely limited to one frozen in unwilling inactivity. The Christian's lack of direction weighs him down with hopelessness and thoughts of death; his intense frustration does not allow him to think, as he did when he confronted similar problems in "Even-song," of God's love and acceptance. Unfulfilled self-expectations and disappointment lead him to perceive God as measuring and demanding on a universal scale. As the ordainer of contests proving "the highest to be best," God cannot be pleased by a creature who ranks, if at all, with the lowest. Besides, the speaker's own standards are high: like the fire, sun, and laden orange tree, he wants to be the best, the highest he can conceive in terms of service.

Herbert does not write of hell and damnation. The devil is

mentioned in "Sinne" (II), but the poem concludes that "devils are our sinnes in perspective." These omissions notwithstanding, fear of eternal consequences is constantly present in the employment sequence. Time and death are the great enemies threatening the speaker, though his attitude toward death varies with his mood and perspective. Death is supposed to hold no fear for Christians, and indeed the serene speaker sees it as restorative sleep, a gift of the loving God, in "Even-song." Death is the flight of "The Starre" into a heaven far above mundane problems, a desired translation enabling endless "Praise," and so resolving the problem of service. But the speaker's "Content" is not unbroken. When he admits his sinful imperfection, death holds the tormenting possibility of worms and hellish moths. Besides, he cannot dismiss the conviction that "Employment" is imperative in *this* life and that death is disastrous for the unextended bud. Death approaches swiftly, terrifying him when "Grace" seems absent, and threatening, as time passes without "Employment," to freeze the cold, human earth eternally. Without resorting to hell, devils, and damnation, Herbert conveys very vividly the awesome fears that haunt the Christian who perceives his failures of piety or service.

Everywhere he turns in "Man," the speaker sees a purposefully serving nature. His perspective includes creation and Creator in a long poem expressing the awe of one who truly sees for the first time. Built by God, man is "A stately habitation" unlike anything else:

> For Man is ev'ry thing,
> And more: He is a tree, yet bears no fruit;
> A beast, yet is, or should be more:
> Reason and speech we onely bring.
> Parrats may thank us, if they are not mute,
> They go upon the score.
>
> (7–12)[2]

2. There is some uncertainty about line 8 of "Man," "He is a tree yet bears more fruit." Following the Williams manuscript, Hutchinson gives the phrase "bears more fruit," but Patrides chooses "bears no fruit" in accordance with the Bodleian manuscript and the 1633 edition of *The Temple*. Because of the implied characterization of the Christian as a fruitless tree in "Affliction" (I)

Intending praise of mankind, the Christian is unaware that his grand claim is immediately rendered absurd by his own qualifications: man is a tree, but fruitless; he is a beast who might be more, if he would. Only he has reason and speech, which he may use to oblige parrots by teaching them to speak. The squawk the speaker evokes is an ironic comment on man's sole contribution to the busy, interdependent universe.

Man is "all symmetrie," the unperturbed speaker continues. He is "in little all the sphere" and is waited upon by the entire universe. Medicinal herbs serve him gladly because they "finde their acquaintance" in the elements of his flesh. Like the herbs, the wind, earth, heavens, and fountains exist for man's benefit. The list of services man receives culminates in an example:

> Each thing is full of dutie:
> Waters united are our navigation;
> Distinguished, our habitation;
> Below, our drink; above, our meat;
> Both are our cleanlinesse. Hath one such beautie?
> Then how are all things neat?
>
> (37–42)

Water exemplifies the evident duty even of inanimate things. Rivers and seas serve for navigation; "distinguished" water, dry land, makes man's dwelling place. It is drink; it is the rain essential to the production of food; it is used for cleanliness. Considered as a versatile servant performing its duty in many ways, water is beautiful. One of the multitude of servants that "wait on Man," it is visible evidence of God's love, but it is also a mute but visible reproach to the indolent "Man."

Keenly alert to the beauty and love of God's creation, the speaker ends by talking his way to an insight in prayer:

> Since then, my God, thou hast
> So brave a Palace built; O dwell in it,
> That it may dwell with thee at last!
> Till then, afford us so much wit;

---

and "Employment" (II), the latter reading is more likely to be the correct one. See *Works*, p. 91, and C. A. Patrides, ed., *The English Poems of George Herbert*, p. 106.

> That, as the world serves us, we may serve thee,
> And both thy servants be.
>
> (49–54)

The Christian finally grasps the meaning of his own examples.
God's evident design is that his nonrational creatures should
serve him (and express his love) by serving mankind. Therefore, the reasonable speaker concludes, man should heed that
design and emulate the pattern in his own efforts. Once service emerges as its true subject, what the poem lacks is any
indication of how man serves the other creatures. The reader
can forget the few talking parrots because the speaker forgets
them, probably for shame. Appropriately, he asks God for the
wit to serve him as well as the world serves mankind. For all
his stateliness, man—the speaker has all of "us" utter the final
prayer—is as woefully behind in service as he is in love.

The Christian begins "Man" with confidence in the preeminence and dignity of mankind, but ends with a retreat into
humility. His own observation of the commonplace and ordinary leads to the radical diminishment of an uncritical pride in
his order. It seems to be his fate to acknowledge continually a
shrinking of his justifications for self-satisfaction. Even when
he thinks safely about all men, he is unable to keep intact the
comfortable idea of the superior and mighty microcosm; it
does not survive the test of service. The Christian's concentration on employment makes for an uncomfortable perspective.
There is no more consolation in regarding himself as a part of
mankind than in standing on his own accomplishment. But
one of the positive aspects of "Man" is the calmness of his
petition for help when he has just realized—yet again—that in
usefulness he is lower than the lowly.

As though he were intent on driving home the pattern of
service in the larger world, the speaker focuses on a small
bouquet of flowers in "Life." In a moving little story, he tells of
having made a posy that soon withered in his hand. The
simplicity of the development of the bouquet into emblem is
incomparable, as is the meditative, sweet quality of the Christian's tone. He meant the posy, as Vendler suggests, "to stand
only for the form he would have his life take" (p. 129)—but
even a harmony of extended flowers must respond to Time's

beckoning. As it makes the flowers wither, the gentlemanly
Time makes the speaker think of his own death, though Time
considerately sugars the thought with the sweet odor of the
dying blossoms. Finally, the Christian addresses the withered
posy in his hand:

> Farewell deare flowers, sweetly your time ye spent,
> Fit, while ye liv'd, for smell or ornament,
>                    And after death for cures.
> I follow straight without complaints or grief,
> Since if my sent be good, I care not if
>                    It be as short as yours.
>
>                                        (13–18)

Affectionately, the speaker compliments the flowers for what
they do during their proverbially brief lives. Even in death,
they extend their service, and he is just the man to appreciate
this capacity. Could he attain to usefulness like theirs, he tells
them peacefully, he would not regret a similarly brief life: "It's
not of so much moment *how long,* as *how well* we live. they y^t
Live usefully, will dye Sweetly; & y^e Sooner the Better."[3] The
enthusiastic thought comes rather too soon for the Christian,
however; he has not yet found his mode of usefulness in a
world busy with creatures of every variety loving and praising
God by service. Living and dying, the posy serves the speaker
well.

Indeed, the whole of nature serves him well. By now, the
Christian's reference to the natural world seems characteristic.
Herbert's natural images place the speaker in a universe where
he seems to be the sole idle creature. Their very ordinariness
reinforces his ambition, exacerbates his frustration, and continually goads or inspires him. Especially because the poems
refer so rarely to the world of society, of friends or family, his
attention to nature suggests a solitary existence from which
everything extraneous has been removed to allow him to concentrate exclusively on his spiritual situation. His obsession
with employment guarantees, of course, that trees, bees, stars,
and flowers cannot be irrelevant.

3. John M. Heissler, ed., *Mr Herbert's Temple & Church Militant Explained and Improved . . .,* 1:293.

When the speaker thinks of himself again, he cannot continue to feel serene, though he attempts a sham composure in "Submission." He disputes with God, but in the mild, almost agreeable manner of one unwilling to admit he is quarreling:

> But that thou art my wisdome, Lord,
>     And both mine eyes are thine,
> My minde would be extreamly stirr'd
>     For missing my designe.
>
> Were it not better to bestow
>     Some place and power on me?
> Then should thy praises with me grow
>     And share in my degree.
>                                 (1–8)

The speaker lies: he is "extreamly stirr'd" by the suspicion that he missed his "designe." "Blind" because he is dependent on God for wisdom and reason, he fears he has failed to see a plan of action for his employment. In spite of his steady, quiet tone, the metaphor he uses is a powerful indication of the difficulty of submissiveness. We begin to fathom what dependence costs him when we realize that his blindness, though essential, is self-imposed and likely to create stress, as it does here. Stress covers itself, however, with tactfulness; diplomatically, the Christian suggests that a powerful position for himself would yield more praise than God gets from a servant without it. The identification of his achievement with praise for God is not new. In "Employment" (I), after asking to be "extended to some good," he generously added that "the sweetnesse and the praise" of his good would be God's. Now, the speaker is totally unaware of anything incongruous in God's praises sharing in *his* degree.

Before it occurs to the reader to wonder how it is possible or why it is necessary for the blind man to try to direct his guide, it occurs to the speaker, who reconsiders what he has just spoken:

> But when I thus dispute and grieve,
>     I do resume my sight,
> And pilfring what I once did give,
>     Disseize thee of thy right.

> How know I, if thou shouldst me raise,
>   That I should then raise thee?
> Perhaps great places and thy praise
>   Do not so well agree.
>
> (9–16)

The poem deals with the problem of "how a will is supposed to choose—to act and do—when it has made over the eyes of the understanding."[4] The speaker's gift to another of the eyes of wisdom and reason is so vital a part of his person that it is almost impossible not to reclaim it. When he catches himself trying to dictate wisdom to God, he sadly acknowledges his "pilfring": either it is God's right to make the plans in his wisdom, or this is not submission at all. The implied contrast between God's omniscience and the speaker's own limited knowledge produces insight: there may be a reason why God will not give the "great place" he wants. The Christian has enough self-doubt to admit that, raised to a powerful position, he might not praise God; he has enough trust, after his initial doubt, to believe that God's very inaction is wisdom.

His attempt to reason as his Creator might satisfies him. He ends with a request for divine guidance in the matter of employment:

> Wherefore unto my gift I stand;
>   I will no more advise:
> Onely do thou lend me a hand,
>   Since thou hast both mine eyes.
>
> (17–20)

He reasserts his submission with a rueful promise to withhold further advice. Half of his petition, however, seems tight-lipped: "lend me a hand" is an urgent prayer for grace and providential guidance, but the unnecessary reminder that God has his eyes echoes with a stifled impatience.

Like "Submission," "Obedience" includes a request for guidance. One of its attractions is that a request the Christian makes is answered within the poem itself. But before this marvel, there is an impressive gift to consider:

4. Rosemond Tuve, "Herbert and Caritas," in her *Essays by Rosemond Tuve,* p. 193.

> My God, if writings may
> Convey a Lordship any way
> Whither the buyer and the seller please;
> Let it not thee displease,
> If this poore paper do as much as they.
>
> On it my heart doth bleed
> As many lines, as there doth need
> To passe it self and all it hath to thee.
> To which I do agree,
> And here present it as my speciall Deed.
>
> If that hereafter Pleasure
> Cavill, and claim her part and measure,
> As if this passed with a reservation,
> Or some such words in fashion;
> I here exclude the wrangler from thy treasure.
>
>                              (1–15)

One imagines the Christian clearing his throat before he speaks in a self-consciously businesslike tone: the poem is a deed, he and God respectively the giver and the receiver of property. The speaker denies authorship of the legal writings though he assents to their stipulations. They are the work, he says, of his bleeding heart, which gives itself and all its property to its Maker. (The reader is familiar with some of the heart's rooms, inns, and territories.) There are, then, three parties to this transaction: God, the speaker's heart, and his intellect— four when the Christian recognizes yet another aspect of his total self in the recalcitrant "Pleasure." The giver outlines, in advance, the wrangler Pleasure's punishment for contesting his will. His clever references to himself, the heart, and Pleasure stress the deliberate consciousness of his gift of self to God, but they also obscure his description of instability. "I give myself to you with all my heart and with all my mind," he tells God, "but if the time comes that I regret doing so (because Pleasure is important to me), disregard my regret, we will ignore my desire for Pleasure, and I will still be yours." Here is a curious blend of self-knowledge, self-distrust, and foresight to express the self-conscious Christian's wish to belong to God above all—in spite, even, of his own weaknesses or second thoughts on the subject.

His scheme for protection against himself forces him to appreciate his inadequacies. Moved by the description of himself as incapable of abiding by the commitment he most desires, his calm disposal gives way to a fervent petition and some reflection:

> O let thy sacred will
> All thy delight in me fulfill!
> Let me not think an action mine own way,
> But as thy love shall sway,
> Resigning up the rudder to thy skill.
>
> Lord, what is man to thee,
> That thou shouldst minde a rotten tree?
> Yet since thou canst not choose but see my actions;
> So great are thy perfections,
> Thou mayst as well my actions guide, as see.
>
> (16–25)

The Christian requests that God's will be expressed through him and perceives that such conduction is possible if his actions are influenced by divine love. He acknowledges a distinction between his way and love's way of "thinking" an action, but he is eager to be swayed, influenced by God's will, or moved by grace, all of which come to the same thing. "Resigning up the rudder," the speaker resigns the command of a vessel whose crew, if Pleasure is any indication, is sometimes mutinous. But his awareness of imperfection disallows this image, and it is dropped for another corresponding more closely to his humility. His gratitude that God would bother with "a rotten tree" springs from his own fascination with the useful and busy varieties, but in fact unpromising material frequently arouses the divine interest: "And all the trees of the field shall know that I the Lord . . . have made the dry tree to flourish" (Ezekiel 17:24).[5] Once the speaker infers from his

5. I should note that the divine attitude toward unproductive trees is not always beneficent. The fruitful trees to which the Christian refers appear frequently in the Bible as images of service: "I am the vine, ye are the branches: He that abideth in me, and I in him, the same bringeth forth much fruit: for without me ye can do nothing . . . Herein is my Father glorified, that ye bear much fruit" (John 15:5, 8). But in Matthew 21:19 and Luke 13:6–9, the fruitless fig tree is cursed or in danger of being cut down as useless.

own treatment that condescension is one of the divine perfections along with omniscience, he asks for guidance with an
offhand confidence.

He seeks God's direction because the rare love of the divine
sacrifice promises to lead in the way of perfection and goodness. The Christian asserts that the Crucifixion was "no faint
proffer" but a gift that gives the Savior some rights and must
elicit a response. The speaker's first response is to revise the
heart's deed: he realizes that it is not accurate to speak of giving
himself. Christ bought and paid for him with his "death and
bloud," evidence of a "strange love."

But the real surprise for the reader follows the speaker's
revision:

> He that will passe his land,
> As I have mine, may set his hand
> And heart unto this Deed, when he hath read;
> And make the purchase spread
> To both our goods, if he to it will stand.
>
> How happie were my part,
> If some kinde man would thrust his heart
> Into these lines; till in heav'ns Court of Rolls
> They were by winged souls
> Entred for both, farre above their desert!

$$(36–45)$$

The speaker, who has been concerned solely with his relationship to God, suddenly turns from him and offers the use of
his own deed to the reader who is similarly willing to yield his
territory. There seems to be no preparation in the poem for this
concern for others until we realize that the speaker's prayer is
being answered. Thinking in the spirit of Christ, he is swayed
by divine love to attempt the good of any man who "will
stand" to the purchase as he does. Just as Christ's death was
efficacious for others, so the lines of the speaker's deed could
be "entred" for others in "heav'ns Court of Rolls." In a small
way, he imitates the "strange love," and this obedience to the
"sacred will" explains the title of the poem. The love of the
Christian for his fellows—his wish that others might also
"passe their land" is charity—springs from his love of God.
Because he is moved by grace and divine love, the writer of the

deed would be delighted if his words could serve a reader, enabling him to enter into a like relationship with God.

The definition of the speaker's utterance temporarily sets aside the convention that the reader simply overhears the Christian's thoughts and prayers. The reference to the deed as "this poore paper" acknowledges its status as a poem, and the reference to "some kind man" who "hath read" acknowledges at least the potential presence of its reader. Over and over, we have seen the poem as the medium of the poet-speaker's communication with God; now we witness his discovery of it as a medium of indirect communication with an unknown reader, with us. Heretofore, our unobtrusive presence was not recognized in "The Church"; our role was not defined.[6] But what we inferred earlier about the intention of Herbert's poetry here becomes the poet-speaker's inspired discovery: there is an unknown reader whom he might help to approach God. Acknowledging that reader's existence as a potential participant in the poem's dramatic situation, the poet offers this shadowy figure the use of his words. The reader may become the speaker of the first part of the poem, if he wishes, and the poet then renders him an important service as a by-product of his primary objective—to love and praise God. Characterized in "Praise" (I) as insufficient praise, poetry now approaches the status of a bee, a star, or even an orange tree. It seems capable of multiplying its yield in proportion to its accessibility to responsive readers. Herbert's introduction of this insight when the reader is cognizant of the speaker's yearning to serve suggests that poetry such as his springs from the poet's love of God and desire to serve.

"Obedience" finally shows an untroubled speaker who is all willingness, wonder, gratitude, and generosity as he addresses God and then the reader. But this harmonious state is not permanent. "Dialogue" finds him disputing within himself about belonging to God, a matter "Submission" seemed to settle and "Obedience" seemed to anticipate and settle again. His strange inner debate is motivated primarily by feelings of

6. The "Verser" of "The Church-porch" and "Superliminare" addresses the "sweet youth" he instructs, but in "The Church," the Christian speaker concentrates on himself and God.

unworthiness:

> Sweetest Saviour, if my soul
>     Were but worth the having,
> Quickly should I then controll
>     Any thought of waving.
> But when all my care and pains
> Cannot give the name of gains
> To thy wretch so full of stains,
> What delight or hope remains?
>                     (1–8)

The Christian's sweet reasonableness and his undertone of sadness dispose the reader to sympathy. In the context of the employment sequence, we remember his self-diminishing insights and know the heavy weight of the nothingness yielded by his "care and pains." Still, the "waving" he mentions implies that a divine offer precedes his responding "Sweetest Savior." Even if his rejection of a divine proposition does spring from an extreme humility and a touching concern that Christ not be cheated by their bargain, it is suspicious. The referential ambiguity of his last line underscores the hidden doubleness of his concern: he supposes there can be no delight for Christ in acquiring a fruitless soul, and he knows there is no delight for him if he can give his Savior nothing. But Christ has his own thoughts. Grace enables the speaker, once again, to perceive the divine in juxtaposition to his very human point of view:

> *What, Child, is the ballance thine,*
> *    Thine the poise and measure?*
> *If I say, Thou shalt be mine;*
> *    Finger not my treasure.*
> *What the gains in having thee*
> *Do amount to, onely he,*
> *Who for man was sold, can see;*
> *That transferr'd th'accounts to me.*
>                     (9–16)

The imagined Christ seems to raise his eyebrows with a little smile as he answers, but the irony in the gentle rebuke puts the disputant in his place. Though he shares with his creature a grave courtesy, Christ is authoritative and firm. He need not deny the applicability of "gains" when he insists that the Cross made him the only proper reader of the divine scales. The stained, spotty wretch becomes his "treasure" *if* he claims him, he reminds the Christian. With tart economy, he orders his child not to trifle with his valuable property.

The reprimand is as firm as the imperative "Thou shalt be mine," and we expect the argumentative treasure to hush, but we are dealing with a stubborn soul displaying "pride, willfulness, and resistance to the divine will."[7] If he says his soul is not worth having, it is not worth having. Determined to make his point, he repeats his objection to himself and, remarkably, refuses to take part in this incomprehensible scheme:

> But as I can see no merit,
>     Leading to this favor:
> So the way to fit me for it
>     Is beyond my savour.
> As the reason then is thine;
> So the way is none of mine:
> I disclaim the whole designe:
> Sinne disclaims and I resigne.
>                   (17–24)

Until the fifth line, there was never more dulcet or courteous contention. Nothing in the speaker's past merits his belonging to God, and he cannot imagine how he might, in the future, be "fit." It is disheartening to see that he still believes it is necessary to merit God's love; however, in the context of his frustrated quest for useful employment, doubts that he can be loved by the Maker of legions of busy creatures are not incomprehensible. More disheartening is his low-keyed lack of faith that if such fitness matters, he *will* be made fit. His last four lines are truculent. Speaking with the controlled impatience of one who, unaccountably challenged, knows he is right, he seems to shake his head and cross his arms in frustration with Christ's illogical argument. As a sinner, he disclaims the whole scheme and "resignes"—he will have no part in it. Certainly, no sinner deserves to belong to Christ, but it is amazing to hear

---

7. Sharon Cadman Seelig, *The Shadow of Eternity: Belief and Structure in Herbert, Vaughan, and Traherne*, p. 21.

one insist on the right his sins give him to withhold himself
from salvation.

Given the Christian's dogged persistence in clinging to his
stains, Christ's response of patient love is incredible:

> That is all, if that I could
>     Get without repining;
> And my clay, my creature, would
>     Follow my resigning:
> That as I did freely part
> With my glorie and desert,
> Left all joyes to feel all smart—— ——
>     Ah! no more: thou break'st my heart.
>                 (25–32)

Generously (and ingeniously) he interprets the speaker's bel-
ligerent "I resigne" to mean "I surrender, yield myself up to
you." Herbert could not have indicated more clearly than with
Christ's deliberate misinterpretation the lengths to which
Christ will go to save a soul from itself. Not that the Savior
entirely overlooks the speaker's unwillingness: if he could get
such resigning *without* complaints and mutterings, he remarks
meaningfully, it is all that is necessary. He directs his creature
(who has been asking, after all, for guidance) to imitate his
resignation. The reminder of his own voluntary submission to
the will of God "to feel all smart" has an instantaneous effect
on the Christian, whose heart breaks with awareness of his
disobedience to one who "left all joyes" for his benefit.
Perhaps, too, he feels the shame of the implied contrast between himself and the Savior. He is asked to surrender only his
wretched self, while the Son gave up divine glory and joy.
Moreover, Christ gave himself to death freely, while the
speaker complains about giving himself to life. Of all his
words, only his last abashed interruption of Christ, with its
implication of obedience and resignation, is to his credit.

"Submission," "Obedience," and "Dialogue" explore some
of the problems peculiar to the Christian's love for God. These
arise in the first place because he is a human being ready to
love and be loved in the ordinary human way. It is as natural,
for instance, for one to be ambitious on behalf of his beloved, to
wish him to be justly valued, as it is to be ambitious for oneself

in order to reflect creditably on the beloved. When the Christian asks in "Submission" to be given "some place and power," he does not seek his own glory. Unaware of the possibility of underlying pride, he seeks praise for God, who would get more praise for a highly placed servant than for a lowly one. The speaker wishes to praise God through glory of the kind the world prizes, but when he admits finally that "Perhaps great places and thy praise / Do not so well agree," he seems dimly aware that the world's ways and glories are not God's. "Dialogue" also shows ambition of this type in the speaker's dislike of God's democratic insistence on claiming a soul the Christian judges to be worthless. His standards for God are so much more stringent than God's own that we can only wonder at this self-belittling subject more royal than his king, until we recognize his protests as another twist of his old difficulty in accepting a free, unmotivated love.

"Dialogue" also raises the question of man's utility to God, related as it is to the problem of accepting divine love. Concern with utility has been evident in all the poems thus far. "Affliction" (I) includes the complaint that "a blunted knife / Was of more use" than the sickly Christian. The prayer in "Employment" (I) to be "extended to some good," the envy of the orange tree laden for its husbandman in "Employment" (II), the plea for enough wit to serve at the end of "Man," and the appreciation of the "deare flowers" in "Life" express the Christian's desire to be employed in some useful capacity. But even this commendable aim gets complicated by his revelation, in "Dialogue," that by his ineffectual "cares and pains" he has wanted to give God profit. This wish reverts to the earlier attempts at repaying God for his love and to the desire "to give his devotion where it is needed" or "to love what he can benefit," though, certainly, "God needs none."[8]

Another problem peculiar to the love of God has to do with will and self-direction. "Obedience" and "Dialogue" refer to the sacrifice as a purchase giving Christ the right to command and to make his inscrutable judgments. When God is felt to have certain rights by the Creation and the Cross, this means

8. Tuve, *Essays*, pp. 192, 194.

the Christian voluntarily surrenders those rights, as "Submission" indicates. In theory, the idea of God's right to direct the actions of the man who loves him is easy, but frustration and impatience are only human when the eager man stands ready and is kept standing. Already in "Affliction" (I) the disgruntled man complained because none of his books showed what God intended to do with him. The concealment of the divine plan continues to be a large part of his trouble. Phrases like "Extend me to *some* good" and "*Let* me not languish" in "Employment" (I) (emphasis added) express the servant's willingness to be guided as well as his uncertainty about a specific course and the master's power over the whole situation. "Submission" indicates that the Christian does not lack imagination or initiative; he lacks only knowledge of the particular direction God wants his active praise to take. The Christian is a servant who wants to express his love as God wills: the problem is to discover the specifics of that will.

To depend on God is to dismiss all self-directed schemes and schedules and to wait as patiently as possible when no discernible divine alternative offers itself. An unflinching trust is required, trust that what God wills or does not will is best, though it may seem otherwise. Herbert emphasizes the effort it takes to wait in uncertainty and inaction and to put reason aside to trust fully in God. When the Deity's plan for him is not revealed, the speaker is thrown into self-doubts that reveal his unpreparedness for action ("Dialogue"). But his ambition for God and his disguised wish to repay God are fought and apparently defeated by a grace that informs his inner consciousness of the divine point of view.

In these poems, Herbert makes palpable the mysterious influence of grace. Only once before, in "Even-song," has the Christian perceived a glimpse of God's "mind": he judged his accomplishments as "foam," but knew God saw and accepted them as "work." Now he seems more consistently aware of two ways of "thinking an action," and thinking the divine way is evidence of grace and proof of a closer relationship to God. In "Submission" and "Dialogue" the Christian first articulates his view of the situation and then thinks again and thinks better, perceiving and stating an opposing point of view.

These successive perspectives allow the reader to see grace "happening" as the speaker's second thoughts supplant his first. The same effect is created in "Obedience" by his unexpected invitation to the reader to use his deed. These manifestations of being favored and influenced by grace do not wholly satisfy the Christian, but his dissatisfaction does not invalidate their significance.

Herbert dramatizes the Christian's recognition of divine love's requirements and their effects in such detail because it signals his necessary spiritual growth. He must try to think, see, judge, and act as Christ might. When imitation is achieved, however imperfectly or intermittently, it is achieved by the influence of grace. Herbert shows that what God requires, he enables man to accomplish; the poet also shows the difficulty of the process for the natural man, who is accustomed to thinking, acting, and judging in his own fashion. "Follow my resigning," Christ says, "obey God as I did." The Christian and the reader learn of Christ's right to command imitation but also of the difficulties of obedience.

\* \* \*

Herbert is leading speaker and reader beyond "God needs none" toward a resolution of the problems of employment and utility that is already generally discernible. The Christian, after all, did not invent the idea of service, nor did it occur to him out of an egotistical and ignorant wish to recompense God. The natural world has been his book after his unpromising start, and there he sees utility of the type he pursues so ardently. He sees that by serving his fellow creatures, the creature may serve the Creator and attain some usefulness. Because this is God's evident plan for the working of his universe, there is, paradoxically, a sense in which man can be useful to the one who "needs none." As Jeremy Taylor informed his seventeenth-century reader, the ploughman, artisan, merchant, king, priest, prophet, and all engaged in honest and necessary employment are "in their calling the ministers of Divine Providence, and the stewards of the creation, and servants of a great family of God, the world."[9]

9. *The Whole Works of the Right Rev. Jeremy Taylor, D.D.*, 4:14.

The Christian's progress has been of the two-steps-forward, one-step-backward variety. In his role as poet, he made an inspired effort to help others ("Obedience"), but one charitable gesture incapable of yielding a visible response appears not to satisfy him, and the path to his destination continues to be an obstacle course. His progress improves in "Providence," "The Method," "Praise" (III), and "The Priesthood," since God does not condemn him to worry a multifaceted problem to death. Instead of continuing to stumble over his difficulties, he pauses to find his way around them, and the poems take us forward with unaccustomed speed and good spirits. Doubts and anxieties give way to sober cheerfulness as the speaker makes use of God's assistance.

The poems encourage the reader to glance back at the old difficulties as the Christian strides ahead, advancing to maturity by obedience to the resignation exemplified and urged by Christ in "Dialogue." Great burdens disappear when he gives himself over to God. Trust in God's guidance means that merit, fitness, and profitableness are no longer the Christian's personal problems. Trust and acknowledged dependence do not mean, however, that he is a robot. Once in accord with God, he discovers that just as there are two ways of "thinking an action," there are two ways of acting an action: alone or in cooperation with God. The cooperation of the divine and human wills is analyzed in the context of the old but revamped desire to multiply God's praise. Happily for the speaker, this persistent desire becomes the basis for the charitable employment he has pursued. "The Priesthood" is his application to be admitted into the service of God and man. Emphasis on the speaker's consciousness of divine help enables Herbert to continue instructing his reader in the experience of grace.

Several steps before the speaker names the priesthood, however, stands the opportune "Providence." This poem treats old and new concerns and suggests the direction the Christian's future will take. A sequel to "Man," which emphasizes nature's service to humanity, it represents a rethinking of the problems of service under divine love's influence. The reader will remember that in the previous poem, "Man" lagged behind nature in service to his fellow creatures. "Providence" is the answer to the speaker's prayer that God would

> afford us so much wit;
> That as the world serves us, we may serve thee,
> And both thy servants be.
>
> (52–54)

The first stanzas of "Providence" present the Christian's witty inference of providential will:

> O Sacred Providence, who from end to end
> Strongly and sweetly movest, shall I write,
> And not of thee, through whom my fingers bend
> To hold my quill? shall they not do thee right?
>
> Of all the creatures both in sea and land
> Onely to Man thou hast made known thy wayes,
> And put the penne alone into his hand,
> And made him Secretarie of thy praise.

The speaker's wonder at his most basic capacity, simply to flex and wrap his fingers around his quill, expresses a childlike delight in limbs as God-given treasures. With the same image we remarked in "Assurance" of the divine hand clasped over the human here implied, he calls attention to his role as poet to attest the divine power that enables him. Providence, with its twin attributes of power and love, moves in the entirety of its immense universe, but the image of the hand-over-writing-hand encourages the reader to read "end to end" as line-end to line-end. From the distant poles of its creation to the speaker's fingers, Providence moves and bends everything. Given these references to his writing, the Christian's generalization in the second stanza is surprising. His interest is not in the poet's role but in man's distinction as the only creature to whom God has revealed himself. This gift indicates the divine will: the Creator put the pen in man's hand and made him "Secretarie" of praise.

Given man's distinctive capacities, the reciprocal service that he can render the natural world now seems obvious:

> Beasts fain would sing; birds dittie to their notes;
> Trees would be tuning on their native lute
> To thy renown: but all their hands and throats
> Are brought to Man, while they are lame and mute.

Man is the worlds high Priest: he doth present
The sacrifice for all; while they below
Unto the service mutter an assent,
Such as springs use that fall, and windes that blow.

He that to praise and laud thee doth refrain,
Doth not refrain unto himself alone,
But robs a thousand who would praise thee fain,
And doth commit a world of sinne in one.

                                                    (9–20)

"Projection," we might say glibly about the speaker's assumption that nonrational creatures are frustrated singers and musicians. From the beginning, though, he has seen the citizens of the natural world as willing praisers through service. Now he stresses their incapacities: stiff-limbed trees would play their woody lutes, growling or roaring beasts would sing, and birds—whose melodious notes would satisfy the trees or beasts—would put words to their music if they could. He suggests that the other creatures are as concerned with multiple forms of praise as he has been. The capacities and deficiencies of the natural creatures shed light on the speaker's. The creatures render concrete service but cannot articulate praise; the speaker's poems are articulate praise, but they seem not to fulfill his idea of concrete service. This may help to explain why his role as poet does not obviate his search for a vocation that is another form of praise and service. According to God's will, after all, all men are the secretaries of verbal praise. The speaker's understanding that this duty is general and his distinction that praise is manifold remind one of the Bible: "By [Christ] therefore let us offer the sacrifice of praise to God continually, that is, the fruit of our lips giving thanks to his name. But to do good and to communicate forget not: for with such sacrifices God is well pleased" (Hebrews 13:15–16).

In the universal mass, "Man is the worlds high Priest," presenting the sacrifice of praise for the congregation of winds, springs, and other creatures, who mutter assenting responses. This is a considerable contribution, an important reciprocal service, one the Christian understands as a solemn duty. Not to praise God would be to rob all those creatures who would praise him through the human intermediary. Because this

passive robbery amounts to "a world of sinne in one," he
hastens to declare that he will "present / For me and all my
fellows praise to thee." Thus the interdependent creatures are
linked by God's design in a relationship of service to one
another. Beasts and trees nourish the man who is their tongue
and hand to utter or write their praise to the Creator.

After the introductory stanzas, the speaker begins his glori-
fication, starting with the relation of the divine and human
wills. He considered the matter in "Submission," "Obedience," and "Dialogue" and will explore it again in more personal terms in subsequent poems. Here, he praises the freedom that is in God's will:

> We all acknowledge both thy power and love
> To be exact, transcendent, and divine;
> Who dost so strongly and so sweetly move,
> While all things have their will, yet none but thine.
>
> (29–32)

God's will is that all things should have their will, although,
given human nature, such freedom often results in sin. The
Creator's love for man is stressed even in the Christian's subsequent "undogmatic affirmation of the permissive theory of
evil" (lines 33–36): God permits but curbs sin, robbing the thief
of some of his booty.[10] Given the secretary's long-standing
desire to increase the praise flowing in to the God who "dis-
poses," "dresses," and "tunes" everything, the reader may be
surprised to find him asserting, "Thou art in small things
great, not small in any: / Thy even praise can neither rise, nor
fall" (lines 41–42). God's praise is "even" because every created thing, from tempests to flies to herbs and stones, praises
its Creator by its very existence. Nevertheless, the speaker
praises by describing his works at length and in some detail.
He praises in spite of his awareness that God does not need it,
because it is his loving duty and because the working of the
intricate plan evokes admiration for its Maker.

The Creator of the universal scheme merits all admiration.
The poem ends with a final example of his artistry and abundant praise:

10. Patrides, ed., *English Poems*, p. 130.

To show thou art not bound, as if thy lot
Were worse then ours, sometimes thou shiftest hands.
Most things move th'under-jaw; the Crocodile not.
Most things sleep lying; th'Elephant leans or stands.

But who hath praise enough? nay, who hath any?
None can express thy works, but he that knows them:
And none can know thy works, which are so many,
And so complete, but onely he that owes them.

All things that are, though they have sev'rall wayes,
Yet in their being joyn with one advise
To honour thee: and so I give thee praise
In all my other hymnes, but in this twice.

Each thing that is, although in use and name
It go for one, hath many wayes in store
To honour thee; and so each hymne thy fame
Extolleth many wayes, yet this one more.

(137–52)

No one can give adequate praise to the Maker so almightily proficient that he varies his basic (but unexcelled) designs just to show that he can. Besides, to praise as he deserves would require knowledge of all his works, and only he has that. Still, inadequate and unnecessary as it may be, the Christian lauds God in two final stanzas whose similarities make the reader pause. G. H. Palmer thought they were alternates and that "Herbert had not decided which of the two to keep as his ending," but George Ryley suggested that double praise is offered here: once for the works of God the Christian knows, and once more for those he does not know.[11] Praise is also double because he praises once for himself and once as the secretary for others; he alerts the reader to the double praise by ending with the complementary stanzas that seem to repeat one thought. A paraphrase conveys their impression of thoroughness: each and all things, which are one as creatures, are yet different and join to honor God together, but they honor him also individually in many different ways. The inverted

11. Palmer, *The English Works of George Herbert*, 3:94; Heissler, *Mr Herbert's Temple*, 2:393.

terms produce an effect of extravagance. The Christian's point is precisely that extravagant praise is inadequate.

The speaker's understanding of the providential scheme shows he is well attuned to God's way. He discovers a portion of the divine will for himself by considering his gifts, and his underlying conviction that these gifts are to be used in God's service results in his recognition of a duty. This duty is attractive because it allows him to enter with the other creatures into a give-and-take relationship based on the abilities and needs of each. He can serve nature as "Man" showed it served him; best of all, he can serve God by doing so. It is not surprising that he praises God's direction of the world: "Providence" describes a neat, efficient execution of an impressive design. The plan by which he serves nature also furnishes a witty solution to a problem he has encountered before: how is it possible to increase God's praise? When he discovers himself to be a divinely appointed secretary of praise and realizes that the citizens of the natural world down to the last stone would praise intelligibly if they could, he finds the solution to his problem. By serving the other creatures, he achieves his long-standing wish to multiply God's praise.

"The Method" is linked to "Providence" by the repetition of two ideas and the expansion of a third. God is characterized again as Power and Love, the one who does not need man. Most important is the poem's elucidation, in experiential terms, of the freedom of the human will in relation to Power and Love. The title refers to the method of cooperation between man and God. These are serious topics—and Herbert treats them with gentle humor:

> Poore heart, lament.
> For since thy God refuseth still,
> There is some rub, some discontent,
>     Which cools his will.
>
> Thy Father could
> Quickly effect, what thou dost move;
> For his is *Power:* and sure he would;
>     For he is *Love.*

                    (1–8)

Herbert secures dramatic interest for this introspection by
suggesting that we listen to one-half of a dialogue initiated by
the heart. As usual, the speaking "I" assumes the position of a
superior explaining things to the less intelligent "poore heart."
Evidently, the heart has proposed something to the Deity, but
has been refused. The speaker characterizes God—if he is
content—as Power and Love at the heart's disposal. God cools
toward the heart, though, if it causes some "rub." Since God's
power is the capacity and his love is the motive to grant what
his servant proposes, the speaker assumes that divine inaction
can be due only to some fault in the proposing heart.

Once the heart's responsibility has been declared, the speaker turns domineering:

> Go search this thing,
> Tumble thy breast, and turn thy book.
> If thou hadst lost a glove or ring,
>        Wouldst thou not look?
>
> What do I see
> Written above there? *Yesterday*
> *I did behave me carelesly,*
>        *When I did pray.*
>
> And should Gods eare
> To such indifferents chained be,
> Who do not their own motions heare?
>        Is God lesse free?
>                    (9–20)

The speaker is the analytic partner of this couple, a sort of
interrogator who cross-examines his intimate and orders him
about. The heart is a well-outfitted little man with gloves and a
ring whose loss would pain him. He also keeps a diary, and
this the speaker seizes to find an entry admitting a fault. With
ironic severity, he rebukes the guilty heart, reminding him that
his freedom to be inattentive to God is matched by God's
freedom to be inattentive to him.

The speaker's verve declares that he enjoys browbeating the
tongue-tied heart. He gets the opportunity to continue:

> But stay! what's there?
> *Late when I would have something done,*

*I had a motion to forbeare,*
            *Yet I went on.*

        And should Gods eare,
Which needs not man, be ty'd to those
Who heare not him, but quickly heare
            His utter foes?

        Then once more pray:
Down with thy knees, up with thy voice.
Seek pardon first, and God will say,
            *Glad heart rejoyce.*
                    (21–32)

The downcast heart tries, in the moment before the speaker's exclamation, to recover his diary. But he is not quick enough for the sharp-eyed speaker, who spots yet another self-accusing notation in the dairy. The heart is upbraided again. This fault is of the will and points to its freedom. In the second stanza of the poem, we learned that God ignores some motion of the heart's. Now the heart discloses that he had earlier ignored a gracious inner *"motion to forbeare,"* instead doing as he chose. God does not need man; the Christian's freedom has allowed him to act carelessly, as if he did not need God either. But especially because he loves God, he does need him, just as God listens because he loves his creature. The right method involves working together. God will do his part to help the petitioner, but he too must do his share. His duty is to approach God not indifferently, but with reverent attention, and to obey the divine promptings of grace. The guilty heart is ordered to kneel, ask forgiveness, pray again, and then, surely, "God will say, / *Glad heart rejoyce.*"

"The Method" is unusual because of its light approach to disobedience. At most, it shows mild disappointment as the Christian catches sight of his faults and scolds himself. But there is no indication that he is "extreamly stirr'd" even though he has been thwarted (by not being helped) in some undertaking. His self-scoldings are amusing because they are addressed to a heart characterized indirectly as a harassed auditor and because they are expressed simply, in terms appropriate to a child lacking sufficient common sense to understand that he has violated a tit-for-tat arrangement. Diction, tone, and the dramatic situation of the poem combine to suggest that the Christian is annoyed with himself because he has made an elementary error. But his faith in divine power and love enables him to believe, without undue agitation, in its imminent rectification.

"Praise" (III) elaborates on the delineation given in "The Method" of human cooperation with grace in the realm of experience and emphasizes again the speaker's appreciation of divine power and love. Primarily, however, it concentrates on his wish, last expressed in "Providence," to multiply God's praise. The poem marks a tremendous advance for the speaker, for these familiar concerns combine to help him define the charitable employment he has sought for so long. The desire to give God praise and then more, so ingeniously satisfied in "Providence," presents itself now as a matter for the Christian to work out within himself. With earnest determination, he pledges constant praise to God:

> Lord, I will mean and speak thy praise,
>        Thy praise alone.
> My busie heart shall spin it all my dayes:
>        And when it stops for want of store,
> Then will I wring it with a sigh or grone,
>        That thou mayst yet have more.
>
>                     (1–6)

The final "more" of this stanza (and of all the others) underlines this poem's relation to "Praise" (I). That poem asked God to "mend" the Christian's lot so he could praise more. Here, with no conditions attached, he commits himself to praise for his entire life. Come what may, his heart will spin homage always. Praise is shown to be the product of the cooperation between the speaker and the heart. This particular verbal separation of heart and speaker doubles the number of praisers—an important achievement in a poem concerned with the quantity of praise. The Christian is an exacting taskmaster, driving the heart to its maximum ability in his determination to get as much work from it as possible. But, of course, he means that it would sadden him so much to stop praising that the sadness would itself become a form of praise.

After this, he moves to what seems an unrelated matter, God's effect on human action:

> When thou dost favour any action,
>            It runnes, it flies:
> All things concurre to give it a perfection.
>     That which had but two legs before,
> When thou dost blesse, hath twelve: one wheel doth rise
>            To twentie then, or more.
>
> But when thou dost on businesse blow,
>            It hangs, it clogs:
> Not all the teams of Albion in a row
>     Can hale or draw it out of doore.
> Legs are but stumps, and Pharaohs wheels but logs,
>            And struggling hinders more.
>
>                                         (7–18)

These descriptions of actions or "businesse" with and without God's blessing may be the busy heart's homage. The Christian's human and mechanical motor images indicate that, to accomplish its purpose, the divine power uses as agents everyone and everything. Actions that God favors move swiftly and smoothly, their agents magically acquiring the perfection of grace. God's gracious help is certainly praiseworthy, but it is hard to see what praise the speaker intends in his description of God in an uncooperative mood. Using the same motor images, he demonstrates that God's disapproval of an action clouds it with a grand sluggishness impossible to dispel. The speaker's past disappointments and frustrations, perhaps, have taught him that "struggling hinders more." Tentatively, we conclude that his underlying faith in God's love enables him to praise God's cooperation and opposition equally. He trusts that God's goodness and wisdom determine which projects should be sped to fruition and which should struggle to a halt without divine aid.

The following stanza, with its echoes of "Providence," verifies that this is praise for the prime mover's power and love. The Christian refers to the "Thousands of things" depending on God's direction to stress the divine love that listens and responds to one voice: angels, devils, winds, and the sea wait upon God's rule, "and yet when I did call, / Thou heardst my call, and more." The same love works to perfect an action of the Christian's:

> I have not lost one single tear:
> > But when mine eyes
> Did weep to heav'n, they found a bottle there
> > (As we have boxes for the poore)
> Readie to take them in; yet of a size
> > That would contain much more.
>
> But after thou hadst slipt a drop
> > From thy right eye,
> (Which there did hang like streamers neare the top
> > Of some fair church, to show the sore
> And bloudie battell which thou once didst trie)
> > The glasse was full and more.
>
> > > > (25–36)

The speaker's assertion that he has not wasted a single tear is strange. His tear's flight to heaven to drop into a gigantic bottle is fantastic, but it is matched by a divine tear so great it overflows the bottle. The questions of why the divine tear falls, why the bottle is so huge in the first place, and why it is likened to a poor box are answered almost as soon as they arise. The tear is a token of the Son's Crucifixion, the "sore / And bloudie battell." The Christian refers to his own essential contrition when he says that he "did weep to heav'n," but more is required: Christ's charitable sacrifice was necessary to make contrition effective for redemption. Contrition, then, is an action God favors, and to which he gave an eloquent perfection when he gave Christ to die for all sins. We may wish the speaker had given a more mundane example of God's cooperation, but the principle is clear. Besides, for praise of divine power and love, he could not have chosen better.

The busy heart has done very well. Considering the quality of his praise, the Christian's initial emphasis on his inability to laud enough and on his goal of increasing God's praise is difficult to understand. With the final stanza, though, the logic of his address to God becomes clear:

> Wherefore I sing. Yet since my heart,
>  Though press'd, runnes thin;
> O that I might some other hearts convert,
>  And so take up at use good store:
> That to thy chest there might be coming in
>  Both all my praise, and more!
>
>                    (37–42)

It now appears that, praising the power and love that saved him, the speaker has done what he could with a heart already pressed to its utmost exertion. This condition and his goal of "more" lead him to make a request: if God allows him to convert others, he could transcend his natural limitations to multiply God's praise. It is his finest aspiration. The reader of the employment sequence knows that "The desire to convert others is no extraneous wish . . . self-indulgently tacked on to the poem";[12] converting others to praise would be productivity of the highest order, challenging even the fruitfulness of the Christian's old nemesis, the "Orenge-tree, / That busie plant!" Praying that he might thus magnify God's praises, he asks God to favor the action and "give it a perfection." His praise acknowledging the necessity of God's cooperation with human effort is as logical a part of the petition as the first stanza, which established his need and desire. This is a request for the help of divine grace. The reader already knows that God will "bless" and not "blow" on the speaker's project.

Both the speaker's promise of an entire life devoted to praise and the prayer that he might convert others makes "The Priesthood" inevitable as the specific employment he finally identifies. In the past, he responded to man's duty as "the world's high Priest." Now he stands at the gate of what seems his only right destination and asks for admission:

> Blest Order, which in power dost so excell,
> That with th'one hand thou liftest to the sky,
> And with the other throwest down to hell
> In thy just censures; fain would I draw nigh,
> Fain put thee on, exchanging my lay-sword
>  For that of th'holy Word.

12. Heather Asals, *Equivocal Predication: George Herbert's Way to God*, p. 73.

But thou art fire, sacred and hallow'd fire;
And I but earth and clay: should I presume
To wear thy habit, the severe attire
My slender compositions might consume.
I am both foul and brittle; much unfit
      To deal in holy Writ.

Yet have I often seen, by cunning hand
And force of fire, what curious things are made
Of wretched earth. Where once I scorn'd to stand,
That earth is fitted by the fire and trade
Of skilfull artists, for the boards of those
      Who make the bravest shows.

(1–18)

Addressing the "Blest Order," the Christian concentrates on
the awesome power of its "just censures." In the context of the
employment sequence, he has focused so exclusively on his
inward battles and personal relationship with God that his
reference to the sword of power in an embattled world seems a
reference to a different universe. With the second stanza, the
reader is on more familiar ground: how can earth become fire?
The speaker supposes the very vestments of the priesthood
burn with sacred authority—and fears they would burn his
unworthy self. The point is not whether he *is* "foul and brittle"; there is no escaping "earth and clay." He sees the office he
wants as so exalted that he feels abysmally unworthy, "much
unfit." But the same metaphors that describe the vast difference between what he is and what he aspires to be seem
suddenly to suggest the answer: earth refined and crafted
achieves beauty.

Immediately, however, the speaker sees a flaw in his
reasoning:

But since those great ones, be they ne're so great,
Come from the earth, from whence those vessels come;
So that at once both feeder, dish, and meat
Have one beginning and one finall summe:
I do not greatly wonder at the sight,
      If earth in earth delight.

But th'holy men of God such vessels are,
As serve him up, who all the world commands:

> When God vouchsafeth to become our fare,
> Their hands convey him, who conveys their hands.
> O what pure things, most pure must those things be,
>     Who bring my God to me!
>
>                                                    (19–30)

His metaphor breaks down when he realizes that the earthly "meat" (in an earthly dish for an earthly "feeder") cannot be compared to the divine "fare." Such fare, he thinks, can be conveyed only by a dish of utter purity. The Christian's self-evaluation notwithstanding, he seems well suited for the priesthood. His contrast between the worldly feast and the sacrament amounts to a complete rejection of the false values of status and opulence.

The "place and power" he wants now have nothing to do with earthly delight. But the formidable power, office, and character of the priest seem to disqualify him:

> Wherefore I dare not, I, put forth my hand
> To hold the Ark, although it seems to shake
> Through th'old sinnes and new doctrines of our land.
> Onely, since God doth often vessels make
> Of lowly matter for high uses meet,
>     I throw me at his feet.
>
> There will I lie, untill my Maker seek
> For some mean stuffe whereon to show his skill:
> Then is my time. The distance of the meek
> Doth flatter power. Lest good come short of ill
> In praising might, the poore do by submission
>     What pride by opposition.
>
>                                                    (31–42)

Perhaps the speaker thinks of Uzzah struck dead by God when he extended his hand to steady the Ark (I Chronicles 13:9–10), but his "Wherefore" links his hesitation to his sense of non-qualification. This lasts only an instant, however, before his metaphor—whose suitability he doubted—rescues him. In his self-effacing objections to it, he had forgotten the potter and his divine powers. The type of the potter is found in several places in the Bible, such as Isaiah 64:8: "But now, O Lord, thou art our father; we are the clay, and thou our potter; and we all the work of thy hand." But the Christian never uses the word *potter*, and his insight has the flavor of inspiration, of fortuitous discovery. His metaphor also discloses his proper attitude: he must still not "put forth [his] hand." Clay (as Christ named him in "Dialogue") awaits the potter's hand. If he is to be the servant of God, if God is to use him, he must submit and wait for God's pleasure. The instrument does not leap into the Maker's hand. Now, when he has identified the employment he wants, when we might expect an eloquent appeal full of reason to God, there is resignation and trust. He will wait until God is ready; "Then is my time." The unfitness the Christian judges to be his condition is not a problem. When God takes "some mean stuffe whereon to show his skill," who can doubt his success?

*          *          *

In retrospect, "Dialogue" was the turning point it seemed to be for the speaker. There he was urged to follow Christ's resigning, and he has done so. As Herbert portrays it, the major aspect of resignation is trust in God, and the major gain from this trust is serenity. We see in "The Method" that the Christian's errors distress but do not unnerve the old perfectionist who once called himself a wretch full of stains. He must repent and pray, but then, *"Glad heart rejoyce"*—his prayer is heard by a God occupied with the management of the entire universe. Whether God's grace helps or the lack of it hinders the speaker, the Creator is to be praised; resignation is the conviction that God's wisdom can be depended upon with confidence. Belief in God's free, accepting love also wipes out other concerns. If the Christian is unfit, he considers God's power and love as capable and willing to mend his flaws. Being profitable to God is so far from his present state of mind that he twice mentions that "God's ear" does not need man or his praise (in both "Providence" and "The Method"). He is moved by his own love for God and by his need to serve.

Grace enables the speaker to understand his function in the providential scheme of service. The "worlds high Priest," intermediary between the world and its Creator, once grieved, "I am no link of thy great chain." But he discovers God's will for himself by considering his gifts. Whether he decides to do that will is up to him, because Herbert stresses the Christian's human freedom. The speaker sometimes experiences grace as a better second thought, once calling it an inner "motion" to refrain from doing something. When he cooperates with grace, he is conscious of the ease and speed with which his project advances; but when God rejects his "businesse" and grace is absent, nothing works and more effort means more frustration. It is right, then, that on the threshold of his long-desired vocation, the Christian should patiently fold his hands and wait for the descent of transforming grace.

This and the preceding chapter have treated most of the Christian's problems concerning employment; it remains only to follow him on the last stage of his journey. The extended treatment Herbert gives the subject is an indication of its importance to him. His assumptions that the question of vocation is vital and that it is a matter under God's direction were not eccentric. In Sonnet 19, John Milton laments the present uselessness of "that one talent which is death to hide." But Milton states elsewhere that he knew from childhood the talent he was to use, and he refers to the "inward prompting" that confirmed him in his choice of vocation.[13] Herbert's experience was different; the difference accounts for the poems tracing the arduous quest for a vocation pleasing to God.

13. "The Reason of Church Government Urged Against Prelaty," in *John Milton: Complete Poems and Major Prose*, p. 668.

# 6

# The Priest and the Poetry

The employment poems form one of the most important sequences in *The Temple* because of the centrality of the priestly vocation, especially for Herbert, and because of the power of the poems themselves. They portray, in the first place, a divine lover meriting the best possible reciprocation. They depict a busy universe in which all creatures love and praise by serving God and in which, consequently, the frustrated Christian speaker is out of step. And they persuade us that the complexities and problems he encounters in his search for vocation are genuine obstacles that must be overcome if he is to fulfill himself. As we approach the end of the sequence and its epilogue, we can only feel that a considerable length of time has elapsed since the Christian was inspired by grace to do *something* for love. He has made considerable progress, and his goal is now in sight. As we shall see, Herbert gives the reader of *The Temple* the pleasure of hearing the poet-priest bid sinners to "come."

"The Sacrifice" indicates that grace and charity are the underlying themes of the employment sequence; in the specific context of the sequence, "Love" (III) is the definitive statement on Christian service and charity. Certainly, God's intervention in the speaker's life and the development of their relationship have been in evidence throughout the group of poems. The conclusion of the sequence, with its accretion of detail, helps reveal Herbert's comprehensive treatment of his two major themes. Finally, because of the evident similarities between the poet and the speaker of the sequence, we shall consider the relation of the poems to Herbert's struggles with his own vocation. It would be remarkable indeed if he had not written about what was probably the most important decision of his Christian life. The biographical interpretation of what he did write, however, must be approached with caution.

\*     \*     \*

In retrospect, the reader can see that the speaker's choice of the priesthood has been in the making for some time under the guise of his preoccupation with praise. This concern has kept pace with his spiritual growth, evolving from a self-centered endeavor to a charitable employment:

> If as a flowre doth spread and die,
> Thou wouldst extend me to some good,
> Before I were by frosts extremitie
>> Nipt in the bud;
>
> The sweetness and the praise were thine.
>
>> "Employment" (I)

> To write a verse or two is all the praise,
>> That I can raise:
>> Mend my estate in any wayes,
>>> Thou shalt have more.
>
>>> "Praise" (I)

> Were it not better to bestow
>> Some place and power on me?
> Then should thy praises with me grow,
>> And share in my degree.
>
>> "Submission"

The first and third of these quotations exhibit the same approach to praise: "Extend *me*, give *me* place and power, and the praise of what *I* do will be yours." The second assures God that if he betters the Christian's situation, he will get more praise than he does under present conditions. All three propose quid-pro-quo transactions that begin well but prove inappropriate between the Almighty and a creature. In "Submission," however, the Christian thinks further and retracts his proposition: "How know I, if thou shouldst me raise, / That I should then raise thee," he asks. This realization that tribute may not depend on the state of his affairs ends his self-centered thoughts on praise.

But the Christian's desire, expressed in the second and third quotation, to give God *more* praise does not end. His withdrawal from the center of the stage seems to clear his vision: God does not need his praise. God certainly does not need to be praised for the speaker's dubious accomplishments when an entire universe glorifies him by its existence; yet God merits all praise, and the speaker's gifts (one of which is his love for God) indicate that it is his duty to praise for himself as well as for those creatures who cannot do it for themselves. To fulfill this duty is, finally, to give God *more* praise. From here, it is an inspired step to the insight of "Praise" (III): just as he can make up for others' inability to laud God verbally, other converts can make up for his inability to laud enough. "The Priesthood" is a scant half-step away for the man who wishes to praise God without ceasing and to convert others to do the same.

But if we expect the speaker's serenity to continue unbroken, we do not count on God's mysterious ways or on the Christian's explosive temperament. Until its final stanza, "The Crosse" is a complaint full of accusations. We recognize the accents of "Affliction" (I) and marvel at the speaker's command of the language of resentment as he stands, head thrown back, arms akimbo, and glares at God:

> What is this strange and uncouth thing?
> To make me sigh, and seek, and faint, and die,
> Untill I had some place, where I might sing,
>       And serve thee; and not onely I,
> But all my wealth and family might combine
> To set thy honour up, as our designe.
>
> And then when after much delay,
> Much wrastling, many a combate, this deare end,
> So much desir'd, is giv'n, to take away
>       My power to serve thee; to unbend
> All my abilities, my designs confound,
> And lay my threatnings bleeding on the ground.
>                                              (1–12)

The speaker's disbelieving question is an angry protest. He knows exactly what this "thing" is, as his subsequent description indicates. Initially, the title of the poem is ironic, since a "cross" is "a trial or affliction viewed in its Christian aspect, to be borne for Christ's sake with Christian patience" *(OED)*, and the speaker is anything but patient. Especially interesting is his synopsis of his search for employment, which suggests a keen appreciation of the difficulties encountered along the way: he has sighed, sought, fainted, and died. The reader can testify that this "place" where he might serve has been found "after much delay." He has already been through "Much wrastling, many a combate," but the Lord who wrestled with Jacob throws him yet again. The Christian's verbs (*make, take, unbend,* and *confound*) accuse God of the responsibility for the Christian's seeking in the first place, for the pain experienced in the process, and for his present inability. This is God's second appearance as a maddeningly cruel and unreasonable master. Learning the hard lesson that "The Lord giveth and the Lord taketh away," the zealous servant wants only to be allowed to labor with the commendable resources of "wealth and family." His confusion makes him exasperated and blunt: what kind of master makes it impossible for his servant to serve, and why? Forced to be an unprofitable servant, the Christian full of "designes" reacts with angry bewilderment.

By suggesting that the "power to serve" taken from the speaker is his ability to write, Heather Asals calls our attention to the speaker's reference to the desired place as one "where I might sing, / And serve thee." But since he refers to his family's anticipated contribution to his endeavors, it is likely that he refers to his two forms of service. After all, as Robert B. Shaw remarks, they are not dissimilar: "Poetry and the priesthood harmonize precisely in their being sacramental activities, each a means of realizing the presence of God and imparting that presence to others."[1] *All* his abilities, he complains, are "unbent." His grieved tones and words like *faint, die,* and *bleeding* suggest that he compares his suffering with Christ's at Calvary. But let us suspend our judgment a little and consider these stanzas:

> One ague dwelleth in my bones,
> Another in my soul (the memorie
> What I would do for thee, if once my grones
> Could be allow'd for harmonie):
> I am in all a weak disabled thing,

1. Heather Asals, *Equivocal Predication: George Herbert's Way to God*, p. 24; Robert B. Shaw, *The Call of God: The Theme of Vocation in the Poetry of John Donne and George Herbert*, p. 95.

Save in the sight thereof, where strength doth sting.

Besides, things sort not to my will,
Ev'n when my will doth studie thy renown:
Thou turnest th' edge of all things on me still,
Taking me up to throw me down:
So that, ev'n when my hopes seem to be sped,
I am to grief alive, to them as dead.

To have my aim, and yet to be
Further from it then when I bent my bow;
To make my hopes my torture, and the fee
Of all my woes another wo,
Is in the midst of delicates to need,
And ev'n in Paradise to be a weed.

(13–30)

Sending disabling illness seems to the Christian to be God's way of taking back the gift of service. Although his illness provokes sympathy, his self-pity when he calls himself "a weak disabled thing" and his petulance when he complains that "things sort not to [his] will" succeed in reducing it. There is unconscious irony in his implicit comparison of his experience with Christ's. A most unwilling imitator of the Savior, the speaker shows his limitations in his lament. After all, his previous faintings and dyings have not done permanent damage. He is tortured, but only frustrated hopes are lashing him; not he, but his designs lie bleeding. He is dead only in the self-image projected by his hopes. The reader might not minimize this heartfelt pain if the Christian's diction did not encourage the comparison with Christ's agony. The comparison does not flatter the speaker, who takes for granted the indignities of the Passion and the Cross, but is outraged that he is forced to figure in a symbolic reenactment of Christ's suffering.

In addition to the depictions of God as a cruel master and of the speaker as an unwilling imitator of Christ, "The Crosse" has other things in common with "Affliction" (I). In both poems, God sends the illnesses that cause the Christian to feel pain and uselessness. In both poems, the speaker suffers from his inability to understand what God means by seeming to contend with him. "Thus doth thy power crosse-bias me, not

making / Thine own gift good, yet me from my wayes taking,"
he cried in "Affliction" (lines 53–54). The "cross" now appears
to be God's will as it thwarts the Christian's, because a major
part of the present complaint involves "*my* will" and "*my*
aim." The impossibility of carrying out his designs, of doing
his will in his disabled condition, causes a good part of the
speaker's anguish: he wants to serve, but to serve as he wills,
according to his own plan. He regresses in this crisis to his state
of mind when he hinted to God that he was "extreamly stirr'd /
For missing [his] designe" ("Submission"). He is certainly
stirred for that reason here, picturing himself as a hungry
beggar staring at an inaccessible banquet.

But misery, the feeling that he is a weed in a flowered
paradise, makes him seek comfort. The torturing enemy, responsible for a situation so bleak the speaker thinks the reward
of all his past woes is "another wo," is seen differently in the
extremity of distress:

> Ah my deare Father, ease my smart!
> These contrarieties crush me: these crosse actions
> Doe winde a rope about, and cut my heart:
>     And yet since these thy contradictions
> Are properly a crosse felt by thy Sonne,
> With but foure words, my words, *Thy will be done.*
>
>                                          (31–36)

When he reasserts the relationship between himself and God,
the pain does not stop, but he discovers how to deal with it by
remembering an essential aspect of service to God. Rather than
by the grand projects he devised, he will serve as Christ did, by
obeying. "The Crosse" is now identified properly as Christ's,
and service to God is once again defined as it was in "Dialogue," where Christ's example urged an obedient resignation. After his subangelic display of temper, the Christian
regains the right attitude when he makes the Savior's words
his own. As Chana Bloch remarks, "The seeming dispropor-
tion is deliberate: Four words of Scripture, Christ's words, can
more than balance all the stanzas of complaint."[2] Again, as in

2. Chana Bloch, "Spelling the Word: Herbert's Reading of the Bible," in
*"Too Rich to Clothe the Sunne": Essays on George Herbert,* ed. Claude J. Summers
and Ted-Larry Pebworth, p. 29.

"Affliction" (I), there can be no resolution, insofar as the word suggests a yielding of *either* party in the relationship or a working out that removes the cause of the conflict. There can be only dissolution: the reasons for the complaint against God remain, but when the Christian resigns himself to the conditions that caused it in the first place, the conflict with God dissolves.

The ability to serve is a divine favor afforded the Christian. To be deprived of the opportunity thus to reciprocate God's love is to suffer grievously. His resignation continues into "The Answer," but it does not entirely alleviate dejection:

> My comforts drop and melt away like snow:
> I shake my head, and all the thoughts and ends,
> Which my fierce youth did bandie, fall and flow
> Like leaves about me: or like summer friends,
> Flyes of estates and sunne-shine. But to all,
> Who think me eager, hot, and undertaking,
> But in my prosecutions slack and small;
> As a young exhalation, newly waking,
> Scorns his first bed of dirt, and means the sky;
> But cooling by the way, grows pursie and slow,
> And setling to a cloud, doth live and die
> In that dark state of tears: to all, that so
>> Show me, and set me, I have one reply,
>> Which they that know the rest, know more then I.

Two images confront each other in the sonnet: the speaker's own image for himself and the one he imagines others accord him. A wintry state of mind evokes a bleak landscape. The Christian feels like a tree that has been blanketed by snow, but even that cold comfort melts. After a gloomy shake of the head, all the youthful hopes and aims that seemed so vital a part of himself detach themselves like ice-crisped leaves. In the speaker's present state, the numerous ambitions he entertained seem false, like fair-weather friends who desert him in his emotionally impoverished condition.

Uncomfortably, he realizes that losing his wealth of projects may seem like losing a hoard of snow. He is as self-conscious as if he were an actor made by his director to play an embarrassing role. To defend himself, he flashes an intelligent and confidential eye at his audience. He admits that he probably looks like a dreamer, all of whose energy has gone into schemes that never got off the ground. He knows that in retrospect the flight and descent of his aspirations may seem a proud overreaching that sank by degrees to a leaden apathy. For all who see or describe him in these terms, he has an answer; but he does not state it. The reader, to whom has been attributed criticism of the Christian, is placed in the position of defending him. He must atone for his peccadillo by giving for himself the speaker's retort. When the Christian remarks encouragingly that since we know the rest of his story we know his reply better than he does, he implies that it involves something he has had difficulty learning or accepting. His "Answer" to our supposed criticism, then, must be a variation of the last words of "The Crosse": God's will be done. His "slack and small" accomplishment is irreproachable—God wills it so.[3]

It seems inexplicable that the man who was all eagerness and energy when he began his noncareer still should not be allowed to serve. For him to reflect on his previous ambitions, to acknowledge that they led to nothing, and to accept that nothingness as God's will is understandably painful. "The Answer" is very moving because the reader knows how much the Christian surrenders when he admits failure according to his standards and discards them. By different standards, however, he achieves something tremendously important: he accepts the divine will for himself. Even the cloud-of-dust image (from James 4:13–15), while seeming to challenge the tree image, points to the same meaning: "Go to now, ye that say, To day or to morrow we will go into such a city, and continue there a year, and buy and sell and get gain: Whereas ye know not what shall be on the morrow. For what is your life? It is even a vapour, that appeareth for a little time, and then vanisheth away. For that you ought to say, If the Lord

3. C. A. Patrides suggests that the speaker's "Answer" is to be found in "The Rose" (*The English Poems of George Herbert*, p. 175). Amy Charles has pointed out to me that "The Answer" might also be the refrain of "The Quip": "*But thou shalt answer, Lord, for me.*"

will, we shall live, and do this, or that." If the divine will
directs him to be a vapor or a barren tree, so be it.

Paradoxically, the speaker's melancholy acceptance of his
nonachievement makes him acceptable at last, and "Aaron"
shows him being re-created for the office to which he has
aspired:

> Holinesse on the head,
> Light and perfections on the breast,
> Harmonious bells below, raising the dead
> To leade them unto life and rest:
> Thus are true Aarons drest.
>
> Profaneness in my head,
> Defects and darknesse in my breast,
> A noise of passions ringing me for dead
> Unto a place where is no rest:
> Poore priest thus am I drest.

$$(1-10)$$

The "poore priest" knows the ideal perfection of one who
brings the dead in sin back to life, but he is at the other
extreme.[4] His passions proclaim him as one of the dead. Herbert's remarks in "The Church-porch" disclose his realistic
attitude toward the order he eventually embraced. The
"verser" advises the "sweet youth" about priests:

> Do not grudge
> To pick out treasures from an earthen pot.
> The worst speak something good: if all want sense,
> God takes a text, and preacheth patience.
>
> God sent him, whatsoe're he be: O tarry,
> And love him for his Master: his condition,
> Though it be ill, makes him no ill Physician.

$$(429-32, 442-44)$$

Priests may be imperfect, but they are still God's instruments
and should be respected as such. The "poore priest" is still a

4. Aaron is "a type of Christ's priestly role," and his "garments are detailed
in Exodus 28:4 ff. : *on the head*, a mitre with a gold plate engraved 'Holiness to
the Lord'; *on the breast*, a pouch bearing the Urim and Thummim who signify
*Light* and *perfections; and below* (i.e. on the robe's hem), 'pomegranates of blue,
and of purple, and of scarlet . . . ; and *bells* of gold between them round
about' " (Patrides, *English Poems*, p. 179n).

priest, though he makes a self-reproaching distinction between himself and "true Aarons."

But the priest does not dwell on his gross imperfections as he
might have in the past. Immediately after he describes himself
as eminently unfit, he describes the invaluable asset that can-
cels his defects:

> Onely another head
> I have, another heart and breast,
> Another musick, making live not dead,
> Without whom I could have no rest:
> In him I am well drest.
>
> Christ is my onely head,
> My alone onely heart and breast,
> My onely musick, striking me ev'n dead;
> That to the old man I may rest,
> And be in him new drest.
>
> So holy in my head,
> Perfect and light in my deare breast,
> My doctrine tun'd by Christ, (who is not dead,
> But lives in me while I do rest)
> Come people; Aaron's drest.
>                                    (11–25)

He feels no uncertainty about claiming Christ as his own.
Vendler remarks that these stanzas are "attempts to arrive at
the single Pauline paradox: 'I live, yet not I, but Christ liveth in
me' (Gal. 2:20). Paul's gnomic expression is brief; Herbert
needs three stanzas to approach and accommodate it."[5] The
stanzas are all necessary to show the transformation by which
the defective "old man," the old Adam, becomes the holy and
perfect servant. The repetition of the end-rhyme words in each
stanza creates the effect of listening to the step-by-step solution of a problem. After describing, in the second stanza, how
he falls short, the priest begins working toward the perfection
described in the first. He is not only making a point about
Christ's in-dwelling; he is also emphasizing the tangible difference effected by Christ within himself.

In "The Windows," the priesthood is a "glorious and tran-

5. Vendler, *The Poetry of George Herbert,* p. 119.

scendent place," and the speaker remarks that though the preacher is "a brittle crazie glass," yet God's grace makes him "a window." In contrast, however, to these windows admitting light that "shows watrish, bleak, & thin," there are stained glass windows through which "the light and glorie / More rev'rend grows, & more doth win" to God. Such winning beauty is the result when "Doctrine and life, colours and light, in one . . . combine and mingle." Such is the perfection of the true Aaron. The old man is described and dies—as he deserves to do, being profane and full of defects—but the new man comes into being and lives, perfect and holy because (and while) Christ lives in him. Christ does not hesitate to endow him with his perfection, and thus "drest," made capable of serving and imitating the Savior's priestly role, the speaker urges the people with Christ's inviting word.

"Come" is the first word also of five stanzas of "The Invitation." At last, this is not the Christian suffering disabling illness, nor is it the priest preparing to serve; this is the priest fulfilling his office by inviting sinners, the goal toward which the speaker has been moving since "The Thanksgiving." But the echo of a fanfare comes only from the reader's sense that a long-desired prize has been won. The priest's duty is not to call attention to himself, but to call others' attention to God:

> Come ye hither All, whose taste
> >    Is your waste;
> Save your cost, and mend your fare.
> God is here prepar'd and drest,
> >    And the feast,
> God, in whom all dainties are.
>
> Come ye hither All, whom wine
> >    Doth define,
> Naming you not to your good:
> Weep what ye have drunk amisse,
> >    And drink this,
> Which before ye drink is bloud.
>                              (1–12)

The priest invites eaters and drinkers to excess—in language so tactful and witty that it barely registers disapproval. This mild attitude leads a commentator of the poem to remark, "That the minister should call 'all' to God is perfectly 'just and right' in Protestant terms; that he should invite all to the Eucharist is not."[6] But the priest's invitation presupposes repentance, as the words *mend, weep,* and *amisse* imply. Cheerfully, he recommends the substitution of the divine body and blood for lesser food and drink, acknowledging the propensity to sin with very mild censure.

God's forgiveness is offered to all whom repentant pain "Doth arraigne, / Bringing all your sinnes to sight," whether they are guilty of gluttony and drunkenness or ensnared in less obvious (but not less sinful) sins. Men caught in earthly joy and those exalted by a human love are corrected with reminders that such joy is destructive, such love limited. These and other sins, the priest suggests, should not keep God's people away because he can give the true joy, delight, and love that will never die. The persuasive appeal to "come" is made on the basis of what the penitent sinners themselves value, grounded on the conviction that God satisfies every need:

> Lord I have invited all,
>           And I shall
> Still invite, still call to thee:
> For it seems but just and right
>           In my sight,
> Where is All, there All should be.
>                     (31–36)

Praise and a pledge of constant service end the poem with the priest's characterization of his master: God is the All who can fulfill all.

The call to sinners is remarkable chiefly as the climax of the Christian's story. The priest can finally address readers and auditors directly to call them to the God he serves. He speaks very mildly, not so much rebuking as belittling sin. He speaks mildly also when he takes up the subject of service again in a prayer. The calm and simplicity of "The Elixir," after everything that has preceded it, seems almost incongruous:

6. Richard Strier, "Changing the Object: Herbert and Excess," p. 31.

Teach me, my God and King,
In all things thee to see,
And what I do in any thing,
To do it as for thee:

Not rudely, as a beast,
To runne into an action;
But still to make thee prepossest,
And give it his perfection.

A man that looks on glasse,
On it may stay his eye;
Or if he pleaseth, through it passe,
And then the heav'n espie.
(1–12)

With a dazzling humility and simplicity, the Christian prays for the grace to see God in the world and to do everything for him. Beneath his praise and the support for his petition, there are illuminating thoughts. To see God "in all things" and to do all things for him would be to experience and respond to the reality of his constant presence. This altered state of consciousness that the speaker asks God to teach him sounds simple enough: before he acts, the Christian must think and dedicate his every action to God. It sounds simple but it cannot be easy, given the natural impulses to self-direction and self-reference; this the reader knows from his shared experience with the speaker. The divine assistance of grace is essential to the attainment of a mode of consciousness that both diminishes and exalts the world by using it as the "glasse" through which to espy heaven. With the phrase "Or if he pleaseth," the speaker emphasizes the human freedom to choose this perspective.

The last three stanzas of the poem elaborate on the operation and power of the elixir:

All may of thee partake:
Nothing can be so mean,
Which with his tincture (for thy sake)
Will not grow bright and clean.

A servant with this clause
Makes drudgerie divine:

> Who sweeps a room, as for thy laws,
>     Makes that and th' action fine.
>
>     This is the famous stone
>     That turneth all to gold:
> For that which God doth touch and own
>     Cannot for lesse be told.

(13–24)

The philosopher's stone consists of two elements: man's conscious desire "to do [any thing] as for [God's] sake," and God's power and willingness when he "favours any action" ("Praise" [III]) to perfect it. The speaker's request to be taught to provide his share of the elixir is a reminder that grace gives him even the ability to cooperate with it. However inconsequential or humble, all things are material on which the elixir can work its magic to make them "bright and clean." By way of concrete example, the Christian conjures up a servant sweeping a room. If the charm is his, the drudgery of his humble vocation becomes divine, and even the clean room becomes "fine." Whatever belongs to God and is touched by his influence becomes, and cannot be counted as less than, precious gold.

What God's servant does, then, is unimportant: " 'The Elixir' is the poem of Herbert's which most fully develops his view of the grace inhering in all callings, of work becoming sacrament." With the proper motivation, anything at all will do. The parson "holds the Rule, that Nothing is little in God's service: If it once have the honour of that Name, it grows great instantly," Herbert remarks in "The Country Parson" (*Works,* p. 249). In an explanation that would do credit to Herbert's priest, Stanley Fish adds, "The value of our various callings is not to be determined by the service they render to society, but by the service they *would* render to God; and in these terms all callings are equally meritorious or base, depending on whether or not they are entered into 'for thy sake.' "[7] It is ironic that the Christian realizes these simple truths after his own long struggle to find a suitable employment in God's

7. Robert B. Shaw, *The Call of God: The Theme of Vocation in the Poetry of Donne and Herbert,* p. 82; Fish, *Self-Consuming Artifacts: The Experience of Seventeenth-Century Literature,* p. 29.

service is over; but, of course, it was through the struggle that he learned the difference between doing things for himself and doing them for God. He had to go beyond the ideas that he could repay God or give him gains by being a worthy servitor in a worthy position. By the time he overcame these errors to accept God's free and unmerited love, he was well on his way to choosing to serve in the priesthood.

"Love" (III) is the epilogue of the employment sequence. A great deal has been written about this exquisite poem, which "simultaneously represents the reception of the sacrament and the admission of the redeemed to the 'marriage supper' of Revelation"; and which, as "the confirmation of man, with all his failings, as God's beloved," represents "Herbert's characteristic plot." Particularly apt is Vendler's comment that the poem is "like some decorous minuet" in which the characters go through "a pace forward, a hanging back, a slackening, a drawing nearer," and various other steps.[8] Our present interest in the poem is as a final statement on love and service, because it summarizes topics that have concerned us:

> Love bade me welcome: yet my soul drew back,
> > Guiltie of dust and sinne.
> But quick-ey'd Love, observing me grow slack
> > From my first entrance in,
> Drew nearer to me, sweetly questioning,
> > If I lack'd any thing.
>
> A guest, I answer'd, worthy to be here:
> > Love said, You shall be he.
> I the unkinde, ungratefull? Ah my deare,
> > I cannot look on thee.
> Love took my hand, and smiling did reply,
> > Who made the eyes but I?
>
> Truth Lord, but I have marr'd them: let my shame
> > Go where it doth deserve.
> And know you not, sayes Love, who bore the blame?
> > My deare, then I will serve.

8. Louis L. Martz, *The Poetry of Meditation*, p. 319; Chana Bloch, "George Herbert and the Bible: A Reading of 'Love (III),' " p. 336; Helen Vendler, *Poetry of George Herbert*, pp. 275–76.

> You must sit down, sayes Love, and taste my meat:
> So I did sit and eat.

One of the reasons Christ smiles at the end of the second stanza of this poem (which shows how true it is that God answers all needs) is that he thinks ruefully, "Here we go again." George Ryley remembers too: "Upon the whole I cant but observe a beautifull Connexion between this, And *The Dialogue* before. The Speakers are the Same, & yᵉ Subject is the Same . . . This Good man, when he begun the Application of the Redemption; it was with the Exercise of Love. And he shouted *Victory!* (Vid *Thanksgiving.*) And, Now he comes to the Closing of yᵉ Scene, he finds his Saviour's Love Victorious. This Love was yᵉ *Primum Mobile;* the Spring that Set all the wheels, yᵗ wrought our Salvation, in motion." There is no doubt that God's free love is victorious over all questions of the Christian's worthiness: "He is an unworthy servant; the matter is not to come in question," remarks Rosemond Tuve, but "he is fully known for what he is and he is the well-beloved one, he is welcome."[9]

When Love says that he "bore the blame" for sin, he reminds the Christian of his imputed righteousness and of the great service Christ rendered man for all time. In consequence of this great gift and many others, all men are unprofitable servants to God, however they strive. Donne is eloquent on the subject:

> All those things that I have done for Gods glory, shall follow me, shall accompany me, shall be in heaven before me, and meet me with their testimony. That as I did not serve God for nothing, (God gave me his blessings with a large hand, and in overflowing measures) so I did not nothing for the service of God; Though it be as it ought to be, nothing in mine own eyes, nothing in respect of my duty, yet to them who have received any good by it, it must not seeme nothing; for then they are unthankfull to God, who gave it, by whose hand soever.[10]

9. John M. Heissler, ed., *Mr Herbert's Temple & Church Militant Explained and Improved . . .* , 2:647–48; "Herbert and Caritas," in *Essays by Rosemond Tuve*, p. 188.
10. *The Sermons of John Donne*, 7:255.

The Christian is made to sit and be served by his master to underscore the point that he is always behind God in giving. Argument must cease and resignation prevail. It finally does in the simple "So I did sit and eat."

Love humbly serving the speaker brings to mind Christ washing the feet of the astonished disciples at the Last Supper. Afterward, he explains his action: "Know ye what I have done to you? Ye call me Master and Lord: and ye say well; for so I am. If I then, your Lord and Master, have washed your feet; ye also ought to wash one another's feet. For I have given you an example, that ye should do as I have done to you. Verily, verily, I say unto you, The servant is not greater than his lord" (John 13:12–16). In whatever fashion the Christian serves, it is because he was first served by solicitous and patient love. He can do no more for others than to try to imitate the divine example of charity as it is here, or as it is in "The Sacrifice," which started him on his way to service.

*       *       *

The employment poems compose a sequence unique in *The Temple* because of its narrative movement. The search for the best mode of reciprocation of divine love has the familiar beginning, middle, and end, and one of the satisfactions it affords the reader is the following of a plot to its conclusion. The poetic sequence we traced earlier (the "constant creation" group) has a narrative element in the sense that it traces a gradual development in the Christian speaker's understanding. But the drama there was of an interior kind: even when the Christian engaged in colloquy with God or exclaimed over the minutiae of nature, the poems represented interior discourse. That must be the result when the speaker's only acknowledged auditors are himself and a spiritual being who listens silently and responds, when he does, by indirection. Most of the vocation sequence is interior drama, but it is in motion toward an exterior development that asserts the impact of the inner life on the world of men and action.

When the speaker becomes a priest, he has arrived at that identity by an inward journey, but, once arrived, he has a role specifically defined as public and social. The fulfillment of his new identity removes him from his inner world, which the reader has visited as an undetected interloper, and places him in a more roomy and accessible sphere in which he must acknowledge and address all the inhabitants.[11] "Aaron" marks the transition from one plane of consciousness to another; "The Invitation" marks the subsequent change in the Christian's mode of discourse. The latter poem implies an audience and requires one to achieve its purpose. That audience has been there all along, of course, but the speaker, having only just defined the relation in which he stands to it, turns to face it for the first time. The narrative movement toward a conclusion that has a tangible effect and a demonstrable external significance makes the vocation sequence unique in *The Temple*.

The length of the sequence creates the requisite space for the treatment of several related subjects. As Herbert depicts it, the speaker's relationship to God is complex, and only a number of poems can begin to indicate its dimensions or the attributes of the divine lover. In the employment poems, that lover is inviting, wise, witty, immensely patient, generous, tender, responsive, forgiving, comforting, protective, together with a host of other positive attributes. He is also demanding, inscrutable, and terribly severe. He is all-giving, but he gives what and when he wants. He accepts the Christian and perfects him in love, but he also exacts trust, obedience, submission, cooperation, and humility. He is generous to forgive defect and sin, but he also inflicts purging and painful affliction. Whereas one poem can portray or suggest only a few of the divine attributes, the sequence negates a static or unduly limited characterization of God. At the same time, its plot imposes a dramatic coherence on the celestial lover whom the entire *Temple* cannot define. It involves the reader in the continual discovery and rediscovery of some of God's manifold aspects through situations so particularized and interactions so vivid that abstractions become enlivened.

Herbert uses this spacious freedom to render the heavenly protagonist in various guises to advantage, especially in depic-

11. As suggested above, "Obedience" and "The Answer" look forward to this sociable development in the Christian's perspective.

tions of the dour master. It turns out that to be loved by God is not to experience undiluted bliss. The Christian suffers, and his improvement by his trials does not lessen the intensity of his anguish. Being improved by the Maker sometimes feels like being tortured for no apparent reason, if the reader can judge by "Affliction" (I) and "The Crosse." Fortunately, God also expresses his love in other, more comfortable ways. Finally most impressive about him in the entire sequence is his inconceivable caring every second for one man and his constant participation in that man's daily life. A multitude of other matters may require God's attention, but always he watches over and responds to his uneven-tempered servant.

Unlike God's love, the speaker's devotion is motivated by the goodness and mercy of "The Sacrifice." It has, besides, the Son's example after which to model itself, so that responding to perfect love might seem to pose no problem. But the inestimable value of the tokens of love the Christian has received, his real inability to love as he knows he is loved, and especially the omnipresent but distant nature of God create difficulties. Particularly at first, the speaker's tremendous gratitude is felt as an uncomfortable obligation. Trusting God's wisdom and love does not come easily, either, when he must rely on his own imperfect capacity to deduce the divine motives, and this trust must be confirmed constantly in dynamic experience.

The pattern that he enacts most frequently in his relationship with God is one of rebellion followed by submission. A frustrating incomprehension of the divine ways provokes the rebellion that must be quelled by resignation. His frustration is understandable: how is he to know what design God is fulfilling through him? How can he not care? The Christian never doubts God's presence or attention. But the God who can "no more not heare, then [he can] die" chooses to communicate his will by indirect means. The speaker hears the silent voice (and the will it expresses) from several sources, two of which are the historical example of Christ and the example of the natural order. From the beginning, the speaker is aware of Christ's human life as a pattern, a source of enlightenment. This paradigm helps but also hinders the immature man before he learns how he can imitate the spirit of the Redeemer's charity—and learns that he can do so but imperfectly. He does have an early understanding of the active quality of love, and this is vital in shaping his vocational aspirations. Nature as a means of divine communication is less obvious. Initially, it seems to be a nagging source of irritation to him, but eventually the natural world helps him to discover the possibility of creature-to-creature charity and consequently the vocation that God wills for him. As the Christian progresses in his spiritual education, he also discerns the divine voice by analyzing his own experience for clues to God's will. That comes later in his story, when he is more adept at the difficult art of hearing the unspoken word.

Inasmuch as it is necessary for the Christian to see himself as he is in order to understand and accept God's love, his experience is one of self-discovery. He learns that his original self-image was inaccurate, that his posture before God cannot be one of an equal or even of a worthy inferior. His self-scrutiny reveals limitations and imperfections that contribute to his humility and to an even greater gratitude for God's love. This diminution of self-esteem plunges him into the considerable self-deprecation evident most notably in "Dialogue." But that is temporary, and he finds his way to confidence and self-acceptance when he understands that he has the worth that belongs to all who belong to God.

The movement from self-love to self-doubt to a Christian self-acceptance is made easier by the fact that he is not the man he was at first. "The Priesthood" and "Aaron" are concerned specifically with his re-creation, but his evolution to the new man is in process from the beginning. The proud man with unreal self-expectations of "The Thanksgiving" becomes the unprofitable servant of "Aaron" and "Love" (III). The impatient man who feared he might be "nipt in the bud" or die before "unfolding his wares" learns to stop wringing his hands and instead to fold them "until [his] Maker seek / For some mean stuffe" to use. The young man whose "birth and spirit" made him a candidate for worldly "place and power" abandons those false values for the priesthood, his "deare end," the more prized because it was so long delayed.

The Christian's imitations of Christ are another manifestation of his spiritual development. He starts out thinking he can imitate both Christ's suffering and his active love. That physical imitation is out of the question is evident in "Affliction" (I), where painful illness and despondency show that if he imitates in this way, it is quite unwillingly. Like Christ on the Cross, he experiences feelings of abandonment, and these add to his bitter misery. In "Obedience," he imitates Christ's loving spirit by offering to be of use to any "kinde man," and in "Dialogue," he is made to see that he should follow Christ in resignation. From that point on, except for his temporary lapse in "The Crosse," which once again shows how unwilling an imitator he can be, he emulates Christ's obedience and loving spirit creditably. It is particularly in his role as priest, of course, that he best imitates the Savior. There can be no doubt that the experience of God's love and grace changes him.

Grace enables him to grow and to obey the commandments of love. Concerned to demonstrate that God's participation in the Christian's life is real, Herbert does not leave grace disembodied in generalizations; he makes its influence tangible by making Christ the speaker in poems like "The Sacrifice," "The Dialogue," and "Love" (III) to suggest the speaker's consciousness of inspired thoughts from God. When Christ does not speak, Herbert shows the influence of grace by giving the speaker successive points of view. In "Submission," for example, he prays for "place and power," but he goes on to retract his request because he thinks of a reason why God might reject it. Then he alerts the reader to what is happening in "Obedience" when he asks God to help him think not in his own way, but in divine love's way. Thereafter, when he thinks differently and better than at first, the reader is prepared to see that as evidence of God's grace. The petitioner lacks the wit in "Man" to serve the world, but "Providence" supplies him with it.

Herbert was inventive in the ways he made grace seem as real as he undoubtedly believed it to be, but he was also true to the realm of experience. All men experience the inner "motions" to do or not to do something that are defined as manifestations of grace in "The Method." There are, besides, the feelings that a project progresses swiftly or plods laboriously along. These the Christian identifies as indications of the presence or absence of grace. Although the reader might quarrel with the interpretation of these familiar feelings, there is nothing to offend his sense of the real or the psychologically possible.

The grace that Herbert dramatizes is not magic. The reader never feels that the Christian loses his will or the awareness of what he is about in his quest for employment. It is not a direct order from the heavens that leads him to the priesthood. He discovers God's will for himself quite naturally, given his desire to love, his preoccupation with *more* praise, and his observation of the natural world. His ideas come from sources accessible to all. He cooperates with grace to the extent that he is conscious of wanting to do what he thinks God would have him do and that he is responsive to these standards. Persistence is necessary in attaining his goal. Grace does not transform him overnight from an obviously uninformed and brash Christian into an instrument of God, perfected for service. He undergoes a process of transformation complete with setbacks, and he changes, as all men do, as a result of his experience.

If grace in the sequence is not magic, it is a heightened imaginative awareness on the part of the Christian that Herbert would say was given by God. The Christian becomes sensitive, for instance, to the purposeful world of creatures serving each other and equally sensitive to his own comparative purposelessness. We have already remarked that he is constantly and acutely sensitive to what he perceives as God's voice speaking to him in various ways. For readers who do not believe in the existence of grace, the interest in Herbert's presentation of it lies in the subtlety and psychological realism of the experience and emotions he creates for his speaker. But for the Christian reader attempting discernment of the divine presence in his life, to perceive that presence as a configuration of believable components is to admit what Herbert claims for it: God's participation is a real force in human experience. This is what the poet wished his reader to gather from the poems related to employment. If this reader understands that grace is

not a mysterious, overwhelming power but is reflected in his
smallest twinge of conscience, in his slightest impulse to
generosity, or in his dimmest aspiration to service, he knows
he has experienced it. If he believes that grace is an expression
of God's love, he knows he is loved. If he seeks to respond by
serving him, he knows it is possible to do so by the deliberate
dedication of his actions to God.

\*     \*     \*

Some years ago, Joseph Summers cautioned readers, "The
poems represent the life which mattered most to George Herbert and which should matter most to his readers; but after
centuries of biographical interpretation, the most serious reader may find that those poems begin to read like glosses on a
suspect biography."[12] The reading of the employment sequence has noted the evident similarities between Herbert and
the poems' speaker, but has not blurred, I hope, the distinction
between the author and the speaker he created. It is not offered
as biography; if we equate Herbert with the Christian speaker,
still the poems cannot yield the kind of information that is
essential to sound biographical interpretation (dates of composition, for example). But the sequence is probably a fairly
reliable gloss on some of the considerations and problems
pertaining to vocation that Herbert confronted. It is bound, at
least, to be more reliable than those theories constructed upon
a few of its member poems or upon unverifiable assumptions
and unreliable dates. The sequence gives the reader not fact
but insight into what Ferrar called Herbert's "inward enforce-
ments," what Walton categorized as the "many conflicts"
about his vocation.

If we assume that the poems reflect some of the problems
that caused or attended the poet's difficulties about his own
career, we can draw some conclusions. Personal ambition
played an early and relatively unimportant part in Herbert's
struggles. This motive was plainly related to the self-
estimation of a young man fully conscious of his social position
and gifts and of the expectations for his future that they justi-

---

12. Summers, *George Herbert: His Religion and Art*, p. 28.

fied. Along with the unmistakable claim to the perquisites of
"birth and spirit," however, there was deep uncertainty about
a specific course of action. And, very quickly, personal ambition was transmuted into ambition for God. On the most
superficial level, this kind of ambition is irreproachable, and
perhaps it was so in the depths of Herbert's heart. It is a matter
incapable of external analysis, complicated as it must be by the
intertwined strands of love and self-interest. Perhaps it is
incapable of analysis even by an acute self-observer when, by
serving the interests of another, he expects to gain what he
desires and believes to be his due. In relation to the God who
"ordain'd the highest to be best" and deserves the best, it is
understandable that the claims of love and duty might have
seemed identical for a time with the wish for self-advance-
ment.

There were also feelings of unworthiness, but the sequence
shows these to have been not a deterrent to a chosen path, but
the result of failing altogether to see a path. Finally, it is not
ambition of any type that stands out as the most serious or
most persistent impediment in the search for an occupation,
but a frustrating lack of direction. Over and over again, the
poems testify to a paralyzing uncertainty. Though it was the
eminent and powerful who failed to bestow "some place and
power," from Herbert's point of view, based on his belief that
the divine hand moves everything, it was God who withheld
for so long his appointed place. In this respect, Herbert was
not unique. John Milton's Sonnet 7 ("How soon hath Time"),
which describes his life as showing thus far "no bud or blossom," refers to its being directed by the "will of Heaven."[13]
Sonnet 19 expresses the unhappiness of inactivity when the
omnipotent will indicates no particular endeavor. Herbert was
made to "stand and wait" a long time before God called him to
the priesthood. The experience of standing in eager but frustrated readiness predominates in the vocation sequence.

The poetry suggests, then, that the young Herbert neither
postponed the priesthood for the sake of ambition nor ad-

13. Quotations of Milton's sonnets are taken from *John Milton: Complete
Poems and Major Prose,* ed. Merritt Y. Hughes.

vanced toward it as an early and definite goal. He intended to
serve God, whose prerogative it was to specify the nature of
the servant's office. Herbert probably interpreted his early
advancement at Cambridge as God's will that he should pursue a secular career. When there were no more appointments
forthcoming, that was also God's will; it meant that he intended something different. Herbert might have guessed at
that intention, but certainty waited for some external sign.
That came in April 1630, when he was presented the living of
Bemerton. It had been ten years since Herbert's last significant
preferment in the university oratorship and some six years
since his ordination as deacon. Despite his acceptance of the
living of Bemerton in April, something prevented Herbert's
ordination to the priesthood at the first opportunity, on 23 May
1630 at Salisbury. Whether it was illness, unresolved conflicts,
or his wish to preach as canon at Lincoln Cathedral on Whitsunday (16 May), he was not ordained until 19 September
1630.[14] Whatever the cause of this delay, perhaps a four-month
period was not too long to ascertain that this was indeed the
will of the God who had himself moved so slowly.

The similarities between the poet and the Christian speaker
of the employment sequence encourage such conclusions, but
since it is impossible to know how closely the experiences of
the speaker parallel Herbert's own, these interpretations
amount only to a theory. The theory assumes that all the
poems in the vocation sequence share a common status; it does
not classify some as invention, others as "more personal," and
yet others as autobiographical. The insights drawn from such a
source must be tentative and partial. This reservation obtains
even though an author who draws a character and situation so
similar to his own would seem to invite, or at the least con-
sciously risk, a biographical interpretation.

If we insist on the separation of poet and speaker, it is
because the poetry discloses that self-revelation was not Her-

14. See *A Life*, pp. 148–53. Charles suggests the possibilities that Herbert
was ill or that he especially wished to preach at Lincoln Cathedral on 16 May
1630. Though she presents a persuasive argument for the latter, the reason
that Herbert was not ordained until September is not certain.

bert's aim. He may have drawn from the materials of his own experience, but his intention was to instruct his reader on the important subject of vocation and on the relation between man and God. Of necessity, the truth of experience was modified by the explicit or implicit exposition of the Christian tenets Herbert wished to impart, by the organization of those in successive and independent poetic units that outline a pattern, and by the artistic demands of the short lyrics themselves. The poems were depersonalized also by the absence of any particularities of names, dates, or places, by reference to matters and problems common to all Christians, and by Herbert's frequent reminders that the speaker represents mankind: "Man is all weakness"; "The Man is gone / Before we do our wares unfold"; "Onely to Man thou hast made known thy wayes"—the reader is not allowed to forget for long that he is reading about himself.[15] From that perspective, questions about the poet's life are irrelevant. George Herbert hoped the reader of *The Temple* would "make a gain," and he led that reader from one gain to another with considerable grace.

15. "Praise" (I), "Even-song," "Employment" (II), "Man," "Obedience," "Providence," "The Method," and "The Elixir" generalize from the Christian speaker's experience. In "Employment" (I), he refers to "us" and "our" concerns.

# Works Consulted

Asals, Heather. "The Voice of George Herbert's 'The Church.' " *ELH* 36 (1969): 511–28.

———. *Equivocal Predication: George Herbert's Way to God*. Toronto: University of Toronto Press, 1981.

Augustinus, Aurelius. *The Enchiridion on Faith, Hope and Love*. Edited by Henry Paolucci, translated by J. F. Shaw. 1961. Reprint. Chicago: Henry Regnery, 1966.

———. *Concerning the City of God against the Pagans*. Translated by Henry Bettenson. Harmondsworth, Middlesex: Penguin, 1972.

Bennett, Joan. *Five Metaphysical Poets: Donne, Herbert, Vaughan, Crashaw, Marvell*. 3d ed., 1964. Reprint. Cambridge: Cambridge University Press, 1971.

Bicknell, E. J. *A Theological Introduction to the Thirty-Nine Articles of the Church of England*. 3d ed. Revised by H. J. Carpenter. 1919; London: Longmans, Green, 1955.

Bloch, Chana. "George Herbert and the Bible: A Reading of 'Love III.' " *English Literary Renaissance* 8 (1978): 329–40.

Bowers, Fredson. "Herbert's Sequential Imagery: 'The Temper.' " *Modern Philology* 59 (1962): 202–13.

Brunner, Larry. "Herbert's 'Affliction' (I) and 'The Flower': Studies in the Theme of Christian Refinement." *Christianity and Literature* 26, no. 3 (1977): 18–28.

Calvin, John. *Institutes of the Christian Religion*. 8th ed. Translated by John Allen. Grand Rapids: Wm. B. Eerdmans, 1941.

Chandos, John, ed. *In God's Name: Examples of Preaching in England, 1534–1662*. New York: Bobbs-Merrill, 1971.

Charles, Amy M. "The Williams Manuscript and *The Temple*." In *Renaissance Papers 1971*, edited by Dennis G. Donovan and A. Leigh Deneef, pp. 59–77. Published by The Southeastern Renaissance Conference, 1972.

———. "George Herbert, Deacon." *Modern Philology* 71 (1975): 272–76.

———. *A Life of George Herbert*. Ithaca: Cornell University Press, 1977.

Colie, Rosalie L. *Paradoxia Epidemica: The Renaissance Tradition of Paradox*. Princeton: Princeton University Press, 1966.

D'Arcy, Martin C. *The Mind and Heart of Love*. 2d ed. rev. London: Faber and Faber, 1954.

Delaney, Paul. *British Autobiography in the Seventeenth Century*. London: Routledge & Kegan Paul, 1969.

Donne, John. *The Sermons of John Donne*. Edited by George R. Potter and Evelyn M. Simpson. Berkeley: University of California Press, 1953–1962.

Edel, Leon. *The Modern Psychological Novel*. New York: Grosset and Dunlap, 1964.

Elsky, Martin. "History, Liturgy and Point of View in Protestant Meditative Poetry." *Studies in Philology* 77 (Winter 1980): 67–83.

Fish, Stanley. *Self-Consuming Artifacts: The Experience of Seventeenth-Century Literature*. Berkeley: University of California Press, 1974.

———. *The Living Temple: George Herbert and Catechizing*. Berkeley: University of California Press, 1978.

George, Charles H., and Katherine George. *The Protestant Mind of the English Reformation*. Princeton: Princeton University Press, 1961.

Gleason, Robert W. *Grace*. New York: Sheed and Ward, 1962.

Gottlieb, Sidney. "How Shall We Read Herbert? A Look at 'Prayer' (I)." *George Herbert Journal* 1 (Fall 1977): 26–38.

Halewood, William H. *The Poetry of Grace: Reformation Themes and Structures in English Seventeenth-Century Poetry*. New Haven: Yale University Press, 1970.

Hardman, Oscar. *The Christian Doctrine of Grace*. London: Unicorn Press, 1937.

Harman, Barbara Leah. *Costly Monuments: Representations of the Self in George Herbert's Poetry*. Cambridge: Harvard University Press, 1982.

Herbert, George. *The English Works of George Herbert*. Edited by George H. Palmer. New York: Houghton Mifflin, 1905.

———. *The Poems of George Herbert*. Edited by Helen Gardner. London: Oxford University Press, 1961.

———. *The Selected Poetry of George Herbert*. Edited by Joseph H. Summers. New York: New American Library, 1967.

———. *The Works of George Herbert*. Edited by F. E. Hutchinson. 1941. Reprint. Oxford: Clarendon Press, 1972.

———. *The English Poems of George Herbert*. Edited by C. A. Patrides. Totowa, N.J.: Rowman and Littlefield, 1975.

Hooker, Richard. *Of the Laws of Ecclesiastical Polity*. 1907. Reprint. New York: Dutton, 1969.

Hunter, Jeanne Clayton. " 'With Winges of Faith': Herbert's Communion Poems." *The Journal of Religion* 62 (1982): 57–71.

Idol, John L., Jr. "George Herbert and John Ruskin." *George Herbert Journal* 4 (Fall 1980): 11–28.

Kinnamon, Noel. "Notes on the Psalms in Herbert's *The Temple*." *George Herbert Journal* 4 (Spring 1981): 10–29.

Lewalski, Barbara K. *Protestant Poetics and the Seventeenth-Century Religious Lyric*. Princeton: Princeton University Press, 1979.

Lewis, C. S. *The Four Loves*. New York: Harcourt Brace Jovanovich, 1960.

Mackensie, Elizabeth. "The Growth of Plants: A Seventeenth-Century Metaphor." In *English Renaissance Studies Presented to Dame Helen Gardner in Honour of Her Seventieth Birthday*, edited by John Carey, pp. 194–211. New York: Oxford University Press, 1980.

Martz, Louis L. *The Poetry of Meditation*. 1954. Reprint. New Haven: Yale University Press, 1969.

Milton, John. *John Milton: Complete Poems and Major Prose*. Edited by Merritt Y. Hughes. New York: Odyssey Press, 1957.

Moffatt, James. *Love in the New Testament*. New York: R. R. Smith, 1930.

————. *Grace in the New Testament*. New York: Ray Long & Richard R. Smith, 1932.

More, Paul E., and Frank L. Cross, eds. *Anglicanism: The Thought and Practice of the Church of England, Illustrated from the Religious Literature of the Seventeenth Century*. 1935. Reprint. London: SPCK, 1962.

Mulder, John R. "George Herbert's *The Temple:* Design and Methodology." *Seventeenth-Century News* 31 (1973): 37–45.

Novarr, David. *The Making of Walton's Lives*. Ithaca: Cornell University Press, 1958.

Nuttall, A. D. *Overheard by God: Fiction and Prayer in Herbert, Milton, Dante and St. John*. London: Methuen, 1980.

Nygren, Anders. *Agape and Eros: A Study of the Christian Idea of Love*. Translated by Philip S. Watson. Philadelphia: Westminster Press, 1953.

Oman, John. *Grace and Personality*. New York: Macmillan, 1925.

Pennel, Charles A., and William P. Williams. "The Unity of *The Temple*." *Xavier University Studies* 5 (March 1966): 37–45.

Rickey, Mary Ellen. "Herbert's Fool for Christ's Sake: A Note on 'Josephs coat.' " *George Herbert Journal* 1 (Fall 1977): 57–60.

Roberts, John R., ed. *Essential Articles for the Study of George Herbert's Poetry*. Hamden, Conn.: Archon Press, 1979.

Rogers, Thomas. *The Catholic Doctrine of the Church of England: An Exposition of the Thirty-Nine Articles* (1586). The Parker Society; edited by J. J. S. Perowne. Cambridge: The University Press, 1854.

Ryley, George. *Mr Herbert's Temple & Church Militant Explained & Improved by a Discourse upon Each Poem Critical & Practical by George Ryley: A Critical Edition*. Edited by John M. Heissler. Ann Arbor: University Microfilms, 1975.

Seelig, Sharon Cadman. *The Shadow of Eternity: Belief and Structure in Herbert, Vaughan, and Traherne*. Lexington: The University Press of Kentucky, 1981.

Seymour-Smith, Martin, ed. *The English Sermon, 1550–1650.* Cheadle, Cheshire: Carcanet, 1976.

Shaw, Robert B. *The Call of God: The Theme of Vocation in the Poetry of Donne and Herbert.* Cambridge, Mass.: Cowley Publications, 1981.

Stambler, Elizabeth. "The Unity of Herbert's 'Temple.' " *Cross Currents* 10 (1960): 251–66.

Stein, Arnold. *George Herbert's Lyrics.* Baltimore: Johns Hopkins Press, 1968.

Strier, Richard. "Changing the Object: Herbert and Excess." *George Herbert Journal* 2 (Fall 1978): 24–37.

———. " 'To all Angels and Saints': Herbert's Puritan Poem." *Modern Philology* 77 (1979): 132–45.

Summers, Claude J., and Ted-Larry Pebworth. "Herbert, Vaughan and Public Concerns in Private Modes." *George Herbert Journal* 3 (Fall 1979–Spring 1980): 1–21.

———, eds. *"Too Rich to Clothe the Sunne": Essays on George Herbert.* Pittsburgh: University of Pittsburgh Press, 1980.

Summers, Joseph H. *George Herbert: His Religion and Art.* London: Chatto and Windus, 1954.

———. "From 'Josephs coat' to 'A true Hymne.' " *George Herbert Journal* 2 (Fall 1978): 1–12.

Taylor, Jeremy. *The Whole Works of the Right Rev. Jeremy Taylor, D.D.* London: Ogle, Duncan, and Richard Priestly, 1822.

Torrance, T. F. *The Doctrine of Grace in the Apostolic Fathers.* Edinburgh: Oliver and Boyd, 1948.

Tuve, Rosemond. *A Reading of George Herbert.* 1952. Reprint. Chicago: University of Chicago Press, 1969.

———. *Essays by Rosemond Tuve.* Edited by Thomas P. Roche, Jr. Princeton: Princeton University Press, 1970.

Vendler, Helen. *The Poetry of George Herbert.* Cambridge: Harvard University Press, 1975.

Walton, Izaak. *The Lives of Dr. John Donne, Sir Henry Wotton, Richard Hooker, George Herbert, and Dr. Robert Sanderson.* Boston: Crosby, Nichols, Lee, 1860.

White, Helen C. *The Metaphysical Poets: A Study in Religious Experience.* 1936. Reprint. New York: Collier Books, 1966.

Whitley, W. T., ed. *The Doctrine of Grace.* New York: Macmillan, 1932.

Williams, Norman P. *The Grace of God.* London: Longmans, Green, 1930.

Wolfe, Jane A. "George Herbert's 'Assurance.' " *College Language Association Journal* 5 (1962): 213–22.

# Index